81-1209

PN
1785   Renaissance drama.   New
R4   series.
v. 9

RENAISSANCE DRAMA

New Series IX ❧ 1978

Renaissance Drama

New Series IX

Renaissance Drama in the Theater

Edited by Leonard Barkan

Northwestern University Press

EVANSTON 1978

THE ILLUSTRATION on the front cover is entitled *The Wits*.
Permission of the Folger Shakespeare Library.

Publication of this volume was made possible by a grant from the College of Arts
and Sciences, Northwestern University.

Editorial Note

R ENAISSANCE DRAMA, an annual publication, provides a forum for scholars in various parts of the globe: wherever the drama of the Renaissance is studied. Coverage, so far as subject matter is concerned, is not restricted to any single national theater. The chronological limits of the Renaissance are interpreted liberally, and space is available for essays on precursors, as well as on the use of Renaissance themes by later writers. Editorial policy favors articles of some scope. Essays that are exploratory in nature, that are concerned with critical or scholarly methodology, that raise new questions or embody fresh approaches to perennial problems are particularly appropriate for a publication that originated from the proceedings of the Modern Language Association Conference on Research Opportunities in Renaissance Drama.

The time has come, and perhaps already gone, in which literary critics need to be reminded that plays are written primarily for the stage. Indeed after the decades of the New Criticism, during which even such a man of the theater as G. Wilson Knight could publish studies of Shakespeare which turned the plays into narratives of imagery, a reaction has set in. In recent years it seems as though all studies of Renaissance drama—including many emanating from this journal—have felt the need to sell themselves as "theatrical."

The problem is that theater, so various and yet so evanescent, is much harder to talk about than texts. Of course theater history in the traditional sense, more a species of history than of literary study, has a clear path: the collection of names, dates, places, and recorded descriptions of productions. Without a century of great work in this field, the further study of texts in the theater would be impossible. But as soon as one diverges from the straight and narrow of theater history, there is no single clear pathway. The aim of this volume, then, is to demonstrate a variety of pathways. But the destination in all cases is fundamentally the same: to consider the theatrical dimension, whether in theory or practice, not as an end in itself but as a key to a better understanding of the dramatic text.

Every essay in the volume will (we hope) give the lie to the notion that literary and theatrical criticism are separate studies. Bruce Smith's study in early theatrical history opens a window onto the origins of Elizabethan tragedy, whereas at the other end of the chronological scale the essays of Brian Parker and G. K. Hunter explore the nature of significant dramatic texts through the varieties of modern performance practice. Ejner Jensen takes a glimpse at several different periods of theater history to see Jacobean drama in the light of the history of taste. Alan Dessen and Robert Graves put their research concerning practical questions of Renaissance staging in the service of literary analysis. Two essays on Jonson (Patrick Williams, Frances Teague) consider theatrical values within the texts. Marjorie Garber considers the *idea* of theater in Shakespearean tragedy, and Maurice Charney bridges the remarkably wide gap between the qualities of performance and the establishment of an accurate text for *Hamlet*.

The Editor gratefully acknowledges his debt to the members of the Editorial Committee, and similar warm thanks are due to the editorial assistant, Brenda Rosen, and to our administrative assistant, Marjorie Weiner. The efficient and expert help of the assistant editor, Janice Feldstein, has been absolutely indispensable.

Volume X (New Series) of *Renaissance Drama* is concerned with "The Theory and Practice of Comedy," and it will include essays on *Bartholomew Fair, The Alchemist, A New Way to Pay Old Debts*, Barnardo Accolti's *Virginia*, the comic techniques of Shakespeare and Jonson, and a comparison of Marlowe's Abigail with Shakespeare's Jessica.

The topic of Volume XI is Tragedy, and the guest editor is Douglas

Cole. Manuscripts, for which the deadline is 1 February 1979, should be sent to the editor at Department of English, Northwestern University, Evanston, Illinois 60201. Prospective contributors are requested to follow the recommendations of the *MLA Style Sheet* (revised edition) in preparing manuscripts.

Contents

ix

RENAISSANCE DRAMA

New Series IX ❦ 1978

Toward the Rediscovery of Tragedy: Productions of Seneca's Plays on the English Renaissance Stage

BRUCE R. SMITH

WHEN STUDENTS of Pomponius Laetus's academy mounted a five-foot-high platform in a square in Rome one day in the mid 1480s and proceeded to act out Seneca's *Hippolytus*, it was the first time that a play called tragedy had been publicly performed in well over a thousand years. Very likely it was the first time that Seneca's stoical recasting of Euripides had *ever* been performed. Of the first fact Pomponius Laetus and his collaborators were proudly aware. Remembering the event in print a year or so later, Sulpicius Verulanus pointed out that Rome had not seen enactment of a tragedy for centuries (*"iam multis saeculis"*); in the present age (*"hoc aevo"*) he and Pomponius Laetus were the first to inspire their youthful charges by teaching them to act and sing tragic drama. The humanist educators were aware that their audiences needed some preparation for an event so epoch-making.

What effect Pomponius's boys had on the unsuspecting Romans who chanced into the square that day in the 1480s we do not know, but two repeat performances were called for, one before Pope Innocent VIII in the Castel Sant'Angelo and another before an audience of cardinals and spectators crowded into the courtyard of Cardinal Raphaele Riario's palace.

3

For the second performance before the pope Sulpicius provided a prologue that tells us as much about the audience's unformed expectations as it does about the producers' intentions. Sulpicius's prologue is at pains not only to define what tragedy is but to justify it to the audience, to tell them not only what they are about to see but what they ought to feel about it as well. Today, explains the speaker of the prologue, it is a "tragedy" that will be performed—a kind of play that recounts the misfortunes of heroes: "Something new will appear before you, a grave and pitiable happening that will cause every on-looker to leave the playing-place instructed and cautioned."[1] In these words we may hear not so much a pedant's pronouncements as a producer's anxiety that the audience will not know quite what to make of the play they are about to see. How would Phaedra's incestuous lust appear to an audience whose idea of serious drama was *sacra rappresentazione*? What sense would they make of Hippolytus's unyielding chastity and horrible death?

In Sulpicius's contrast between "the present age" and all the centuries innocent of tragedy there is an unmistakable sense of a new beginning, an awareness of "middle ages" that separate the classical past from the historical present. Across that expanse of almost fifteen centuries there had been, for all the social, political, and philosophical changes that marked the end of the Roman Empire, certain continuities in dramatic activity. Allardyce Nicoll has assembled evidence of a professional but mostly subliterary tradition of entertainers who brought mime and farce to castle, town, and even monastic hall throughout the Middle Ages and who could trace their lineage directly to the civic theaters of the late Roman Empire, where mime and pantomime had supplanted the comedies of Plautus and Terence. But the tragedies of Livius, Naevius, Ennius, Pacuvius, and Accius, last heard of in the first century A.D., had not been part of that

1. My quotation from Sulpicius's prologue is translated from Wilhelm Creiznach, *Geschichte des neueren Dramas* (Halle, 1901), II, 370–371, who offers a full account of Pomponius's dramatic activities. Cf. also II, 1–7. Sulpicius's own mention of the production of *Hippolytus* occurs in his letter to Cardinal Raphaele Riario prefaced to Vitruvius, *De Architectura* (Rome, 1486), rptd. in Beriah Botfield, ed., *Prefaces to the First Editions of the Greek and Roman Classics and of the Sacred Scriptures* (London, 1861), pp. 177–179. William Beare, *The Roman Stage* (London, 1950), pp. 225–226, calls attention to the famous occasions when Nero (A.D. 37–68) "sang" Orestes, Oedipus, and Hercules in *cantica* depicting tragic scenes and takes such recitations to indicate that regular tragedy was no longer familiar on the stage.

continuous tradition. Indeed, the plays of these stage tragedians have survived only as names and fragments; the survival of Seneca's meditations in dramatic form seems a historical accident due more to their philosophical and moral interest than to their success as scripts for the stage. Most twentieth-century scholars would agree that if they were performed at all in Seneca's lifetime, it was in recitations before private gatherings, not in public theaters.[2] The evidence of history is clear: in the form of mime and farce dramatic comedy survived throughout the Middle Ages; tragedy, if it ever really flourished at all on the Roman stage, was dead by the first century A.D.

The new era, the modern rebirth of tragedy announced in Sulpicius's prologue, is with us still—so much so, in fact, that it takes a calculated leap of imagination to picture the literary universe without tragedy as one of its blazing glories. But that is a leap we must make if we are to understand Renaissance attempts to recover Greek and Roman drama not just as texts for academic study but as scripts for the stage. It is useful to be reminded that the phenomenon we call by the Greek coinage "goat-song" is not, like the sacred or the funny, a universal concept that suggests itself to all men regardless of their language or cultural heritage—a fact that may help explain the vast body of philosophical investigation and critical dispute from Plato and Aristotle onward as to just what tragedy is.[3]

When Sulpicius attempted a definition for his fifteenth-century spectators, he approached the question from two directions. One was traditional; the other, new. Tragedy is, in the first place, he says, a particular kind of narrative, a story recounting the misfortunes of a hero. This was the definition that the encyclopedists of late antiquity had bequeathed to the European Middle Ages.[4] But tragedy is also, Sulpicius assumes, a theatrical event. "Grave," "pitiable," "instructed," "cautioned"—the affective words in Sulpicius's definition describe, however crudely, a collec-

---

2. Beare, *The Roman Stage*, pp. 226–228. On the survival of mime and farce in the Middle Ages cf. Allardyce Nicoll, *Masks, Mimes, and Miracles* (London, 1931), pp. 135–213, and Benjamin Hunningher, *The Origin of the Theater* (New York, 1961), pp. 63–84.

3. Walter Kaufmann, *Tragedy and Philosophy* (New York, 1968), p. 310.

4. For a full discussion of how ideas about tragedy were transmitted from antiquity into the Middle Ages cf. John W. Cunliffe, *Early English Classical Tragedies* (Oxford, 1912), pp. ix–xiv.

tive way of responding to events the audience actually sees. The old medieval definition of tragedy as a certain kind of story, of course, survived Pomponius's revival of tragedy in the theater—indeed, it is with us still in the popular sense of "tragedy" as any unfortunate catastrophe—but in the sixteenth century tragedy came increasingly to mean a *dramatic* experience. In England at least, that particular dramatic experience assumed the dominance that once had belonged to saints' plays, morality plays, and the great Corpus Christi cycles.

Classical tragedy as a dramatic experience is the subject of this essay. How would an audience for whom serious drama was sacred drama react to the human suffering that confronted them so graphically in Greek and Roman tragedy? How would they relate what they saw and heard there to more familiar dramatic experiences? What would they have to play up, what would they have to play down to turn two-thousand-year-old playscripts in alien languages into comprehensible and meaningful dramatic events? To answer such questions we must examine not just what critics and commentators may have said about the plays as objects for study but what we can discover about the plays in production. And to see classical tragedy through the eyes of Renaissance audiences we must look first not at Sophocles or Aeschylus or Euripides but at Seneca. It is no happenstance that Seneca's *Hippolytus* was Pomponius's choice for the first modern production of classical tragedy known to us.

There are at least six productions of Greek and Roman tragedies in sixteenth-century England that are more than names and dates. Of these six, three are productions of plays by Seneca: Alexander Nowell's draft of a prologue for Seneca's *Hippolytus* at Westminster School about 1546 is preserved in manuscript; Alexander Neville's English translation of Seneca's *Oedipus*, printed in 1563 and reissued in Thomas Newton's *Seneca His Tenne Tragedies* in 1581, is said by its author to have been written for "tragicall and Pompous showe upon Stage" and was perhaps produced during Neville's student years at Trinity College, Cambridge; and William Gager's Latin prologue, epilogue, and two additional scenes for a production of Seneca's *Hippolytus* at Christ Church, Oxford, in 1592 are included as appendixes to two of Gager's neo-Latin tragedies, printed later the same year.[5] A close look at these three productions of Seneca tells us a

5. The other three productions are Sophocles' *Ajax*, King's College, Cambridge, 1564; Euripides' *Phoenician Women* in George Gascoigne and Francis Kinwelmershe's English

great deal about how sixteenth-century Englishmen experienced tragedy in performance. For Englishmen, no less than for Continental audiences, Seneca was *the* great tragic playwright, the model against which the Greek tragedians were judged.

Whatever criterion we use—the date of the *editio princeps*, the number of translations, the number of vernacular imitations, success in production—Seneca's pre-eminence remains unchallenged. Seneca's tragedies were first printed by Andrea Gallus at Ferrara at just about the time Pomponius Laetus's students were acting *Hippolytus* in Rome—fully thirty years before the Aldine editions of Sophocles and Euripides appeared in 1502 and 1503, respectively. By that time four plays by Euripides—*Medea, Hippolytus, Alcestis*, and *Andromache*—had already appeared in print, probably about 1498 and probably from the press of Alopa at Florence—a measure of how much more impressive these incident-packed plays with striking female antagonists seemed to Renaissance taste than the more neatly plotted plays of Sophocles and Aeschylus.[6]

Seneca's ascendancy over the Greeks is clearly indicated, too, in the number and range of translations into vernacular languages. R. R. Bolgar has catalogued nineteen translations of six different plays by Euripides before 1600, six of them of *Hecuba* and four of *Iphigenia in Aulis*. Again, it is remarkable that the chief figure in each play is female. In the same period there were eighteen translations of plays by Sophocles, concentrated almost exclusively on three plays, *Antigone, Oedipus Rex*, and *Electra*. By 1600, there had been not even one translation of a play by Aeschylus into Italian, French, English, German, or Spanish. Of Seneca, by contrast, there had been no fewer than thirty-seven translations by 1600—twice as many as for all the Greek tragedians combined—and those thirty-seven were chosen fairly evenly from among all Seneca's plays.[7]

version *Jocasta*, Grey's Inn, 1566–1567; and Sophocles' *Antigone* in Thomas Watson's Latin translation, St. John's College, Cambridge, c. 1583. I am at work on a book-length study of productions of classical comedies and tragedies that will include full discussion of these other three productions of classical tragedy.

6. Joseph W. Moss, *A Manual of Classical Bibliography*, 2d ed. (London, 1837), I, 6–7, 414–416; II, 575–576, 595–596.

7. R. R. Bolgar, *The Classical Heritage and its Beneficiaries* (Cambridge, 1954), provides a complete catalog of translations of the classics into vernacular languages. Cf. Appendix II, pp. 512–515, 524–525, 534–537.

As the inspiration for new "classical" tragedies in the vernacular, too, Seneca far outdistanced the Greeks. Sophocles may have had academic snob appeal; Seneca pleased audiences. Giangiorgio Trissino's *Sophonisba*, the product of scrupulous imitation of Sophocles and painstaking study of Aristotle's *Poetics*, earned its author academic praise when it was written in 1515, but it had to wait half a century, until 1562, twelve years after Trissino's death, before it was first performed. In the meantime Giambattista Cinthio Giraldi, author of the novella from which Shakespeare took the plot of *Othello*, had set a more viable precedent for Italian neoclassical tragedy with his Senecan *Orbecche*, an immediate success when it was acted at Ferrara in 1541. In a defense of his play a few years later Cinthio makes no bones about it: Seneca is in every way superior to Sophocles, and the proof is on the stage.[8]

Cinthio's bold assertion and the statistics that back it up need some qualification, however. The three English productions of Seneca's tragedies show us that Seneca as a text for study was not at all the same thing as Seneca as a script for performance. In all three cases we can observe subtle and not so subtle changes that make his plays accord with already familiar ways of putting plays onstage and already familiar ways of defining man's place in the universe.

I

North of the Alps classical tragedy must have seemed even more exotic than it did to Pomponius's Romans—and, to Protestant sensibilities, even more suspect. The prologue for the earliest known production of classical tragedy in England shows even more circumspection than Sulpicius's prologue. By remarkable coincidence, that earliest English production was a mounting of Seneca's *Hippolytus*. In his draft of a prologue for the play, presumably intended for a performance at Westminster School while he was headmaster there between 1543 and 1555, Alexander Nowell hails Seneca as the foremost among the Latin tragic poets and his *Hippolytus* as foremost among Seneca's tragedies. The performers, therefore, need not fear showing the play to the distinguished spectators, especially since Seneca's story plays upon a story to be found in the sacred Scriptures, the

8. P. R. Horne, *The Tragedies of Giambattista Cinthio Giraldi* (Oxford, 1962), pp. 23–47.

account in Genesis of Joseph and Potiphar's wife.[9] Nowell curries favor by referring the perhaps suspect genre of tragedy to something the audience already knows—and reminds us how loosely defined "tragedy" was in the early sixteenth century. In England as in Italy comedy may still have been a vital dramatic tradition; tragedy was something that had to be explained and justified.

The very fact that Alexander Nowell should write a prologue for Seneca's *Hippolytus* is testimony to how much more accessible and more familiar Roman comedy was to Renaissance audiences than Greek or Roman tragedy. No tragedy by Seneca or the Greeks begins with a prologue: that is a standard feature of the comedies of Plautus and Terence. Without any solid information about how classical tragedy had been staged it was only natural that Pomponius, Nowell, and other humanists should turn to comedy and to the short but magisterial treatise *De Comoedia* by St. Jerome's tutor Donatus. Packed into the grammarian's account, written five centuries after Terence's death, was enough information, misinformation, and pseudo-information to merit the treatise's printing in virtually every fifteenth- and sixteenth-century edition of Roman comedy.[10] For tragedy there was no such document. Seneca's plays, after all, had probably never been produced at all, and Aristotle's *Poetics*, though available in print in Giorgio Valla's Latin translation from 1498 on, has surprisingly little to say about practical matters of staging beyond the fact that choruses were sung.

The pert performer that Plautus and Terence send out before the play itself begins serves several purposes: he begs favor with the audience; he disentangles and then tangles up again the plot, in which complexity is half the fun; above all, he warms the audience up and sets the tone of the comedy to follow. Plautus's prologues, in particular, manage to communicate a facetious urbanity. Faced with audiences they knew were skeptical about a new—and pagan—dramatic kind, Pomponius and Nowell were keenly aware of the need for doing for tragedy what Plautus's and Terence's prologues do for comedy. They simply adopted the strategy

9. Nowell's draft is transcribed from Bodlein MS. Brasenose College 31, fols. 25 ff., in G. K. Hunter, "Seneca and the Elizabethans: A Case-Study in 'Influence,'" *Sh S*, xx (1967), 25, n. 10.

10. *Aeli Donati quod fertur Commentum Terentii*, ed. P. Wessner (Leipzig, 1902–1908). For a brief account of Donatus's ideas cf. Madeleine Doran, *Endeavors of Art: A Study of Form in Elizabethan Drama* (Madison, Wis., 1964), pp. 105–111.

of comic prologues to serve a new end. Like Sulpicius's prologue, Nowell's prologue before Seneca's *Hippolytus* candidly asks the audience's favor by appealing to the moral utility of the performance, then goes on to define the tragedy's subject, setting up all the while the attitude of rapt earnestness with which the audience is to watch the play. In effect, the prologue assumes the role that the third-person narrator would have played in oral recitation of a narrative poem—a reminder that the medieval idea of classical drama as pantomime to a poet's declamation had only recently been called into question.

The medieval failure to distinguish tragedy as a dramatic kind is usually said to reflect the medieval misunderstanding of how playscripts had been performed at Rome. The poet himself read all the parts from a pulpit, so the encyclopedists said, while actors below him mimed the action. It is only too easy for a twentieth-century critic to make light of what appears to be a ludicrous misunderstanding. Inaccurate as it may be for the playscripts of Plautus, Terence, Ennius, and Pacuvius, the arrangement described by the encyclopedists does explain how Roman pantomimes were performed. A chorus sang the poet's words while actors— often a single bravura performer—mimed or "danced" all the parts, using a succession of masks.[11] Pantomime, we recall, very likely survived into the Middle Ages, long after regular comedy and tragedy had been forgotten. It may be not so much the crucial misreading of passages in Livy and Valerius Maximus that prompted medieval scholars to confuse the narrative and dramatic modes when they talked about tragedy as the long vitality of mime and pantomime, not to mention the common practice of a poet's reading his verses aloud to a noble audience.[12] It would have been easy for a narrating poet to "dramatize" his characters' speeches. The famous illustration in the Corpus Christi College manuscript of Chaucer reading to an audience from a pulpit should remind us how natural it was for Chaucer to style *Troilus and Criseyde* a "tragedy" without any impropriety.[13] With his ingratiating manner and deferential tone the speaker of Nowell's prologue even suggests Chaucer's familiar persona.

11. Beare, *The Roman Stage*, p. 226.

12. It was Creiznach who first suggested the misreading of passages in Livy (VII.ii) and Valerius Maximus (II.iv) as the source of confusion. Cf. Cunliffe, *Early English Classical Tragedies*, pp. xiv–xix. On the narrator as performer cf. Ruth Crosby, "Oral Delivery in the Middle Ages," *Speculum*, xi (1936), 88–110.

13. Corpus Christi College, Cambridge, MS. 61.

In addition to apologizing for the play, defining its subject, and setting its tone, Nowell's spokesman serves the subtler function of establishing a give-and-take relationship among actors and audience. Spectators of morality plays and cycle plays would have expected as much: they were used to having players address them directly. Seneca's personages, by contrast, seem sublimely oblivious to any sort of relationship with any sort of audience. Even when other characters are apparently standing by, Seneca's speakers seem less concerned with talking *to* someone than talking *at* them. Nowell's prologue bridges the gap. His spokesman sets up that easy rapport between actors and audience that distinguishes medieval theater but is missing altogether from Seneca's text. (In this respect as in others Roman comedies fitted in much better than Roman tragedies with native theatrical traditions in the Renaissance.) Speeches that read like meditative lyrics in Seneca's text would have become dramatic direct addresses when declaimed by actors whose usual stock in trade was morality plays.

We have no way of knowing for certain, but it is likely that the physical arrangements of Nowell's stage reinforced this intimacy between actors and audience. Pomponius, Nowell, and other academic producers of classical drama could turn to the fifth book of Vitruvius's *De Architectura* (first printed, 1486) and discover some astonishingly detailed, mathematically exact information on the structure of the great civic theaters of Rome; but what they found there about the stage itself might seem, superficially at least, to accord with staging arrangements they already knew. Vitruvius's great interest is in the structure of the theater itself, in sight lines and acoustics, not in practical matters of staging. Such details as he gives about the stage could be accommodated to medieval conventions. The *scaenae frons* he describes (in the center double doors like those of a royal palace, framed left and right by doors to "guest chambers") implies a fixed sense of fictional space altogether different from the fluid sense of space assumed in most medieval playscripts, but these doors leading to different places might seem not so different from the doors of medieval "mansions" grouped about an open playing space. The raised platform of the Roman stage implies a physical and psychological relation between players and audience more distant than in the medieval arrangement of spectators grouped about an open space, but when that platform was thrust into the midst of only a few hundred spectators assembled in the great hall of a college, audience and players could enjoy the same

intimacy they were used to when there was no fixed stage. Richard Southern's survey of English playscripts from the 1540s and 1550s would lead
us to expect that Nowell's production of *Hippolytus* was played out in front
of the permanent carved screen at the lower end of Westminster School's
great hall. The openings in the screen might have figured as exits into
"manions" peculiar to Hippolytus and Phaedra. With or without a platform stage built up against the screen, the audience would likely have
surrounded the players on three sides.[14] The result, physically and
psychologically, would have been little different from the performance of a
morality play. The other two English productions that we know about
were likewise staged in the great halls of colleges.

Sulpicius defined the nature of the dramatic subject at hand by describ-
ing the shape of the plot; Nowell prefers to compare *Hippolytus* to a subject
the audience already knows well. Seneca's story of Hippolytus and
Phaedra, says Nowell, "plays upon" ("*alludit*") the story in Genesis of
Joseph and Potiphar's wife—and at no great distance, either ("*non procul*").
Genesis 37–43 recounts how Joseph, sold into slavery by his jealous
brothers, has managed to rise to a place of responsibility in his master
Potiphar's house when Potiphar's wife turns a lustful eye upon him and
offers him her bed. Joseph refuses.

Beholde, my master knoweth not what is in the house, and all that he hath, that
hath he put under my hande. And there is no man so greate in the house as I, and
he hath kepte nothinge fro me, excepte the: for thou art his wife. How shulde I
then do so great evell, and synne agaynst God?[15]

14. Richard Southern, *The Staging of Plays Before Shakespeare* (London, 1973), pp.
349–396. Vitruvius's description of the *scaenae frons* would also have seemed adaptable to
Renaissance hall screens: "The *scaena* itself displays the following scheme. In the center are
double doors decorated like those of a royal palace. At the right and left are the doors of the
guest chambers. Beyond are the spaces provided for the decoration—places that the Greeks
call *periaktoi*, because in these places are triangular pieces of machinery which revolve, each
having three decorated faces." There were separate faces appropriate to tragedy, comedy,
and satyr plays. The tragic scenes, Vitruvius notes, were "delineated with columns,
pediments, statues, and other objects suited to kings." Cf. Vitruvius, *Ten Books of Architec-
ture*, trans. M. H. Morgan (New York, 1960), Bk. 5, chap. 6, secs. 8–9, p. 150.

15. *The Coverdale Bible 1535*, introd. S. L. Greenslade (Folkestone, 1975), fol. 17ᵛ
(Genesis 39:8–9 in later translations). The Geneva Bible (1560) provides this marginal
note: "The feare of God preserved him against her continual temtations" (*The Geneva Bible*,
introd. L. E. Berry [Madison, Wis., 1969], fol. 18ᵛ).

Potiphar's wife takes her revenge: to her husband she accuses Joseph of making the very offer he has refused, and Joseph lands in prison.

Nowell's eye was sharp: the parallel with Hippolytus and Phaedra *is* striking—almost striking enough to persuade even a twentieth-century skeptic that Renaissance apologists were right about the pagans groping toward Judeo-Christian truth. At least the two stories seem to belong to the same narrative motif or mythical core. The Genesis account ends rather more inspirationally than the pagan myth, however. Far from meeting Hippolytus's horrible death, Joseph cleverly manages with Jehovah's help to turn this temporary setback into yet another triumph, and by explaining the Pharaoh's dreams he ends up as the ruler's right-hand man. To a humanist educator's point of view such an ending, with its ultimate reward for virtue, made for an even better "tragedy" than Seneca's *Hippolytus*. One of the first results of serious study of Latin tragedy was a widespread attempt to Christianize classical tragedy—or, rather, to classicize Christian drama—by applying Seneca's florid diction, five-act structure, and sententious choruses to biblical subjects. Leicester Bradner's checklist of extant neo-Latin plays from all over Renaissance Europe reveals that Joseph, so exemplary in turning every trial into stunning success, emerged during the course of the sixteenth and early seventeenth centuries as the single most popular subject for dramatization.[16] The Christian Hippolytus, Joseph dressed up in the trappings of Seneca, was the "tragic" counterpart to the Prodigal Son, dressed down in the trappings of Terence.

The impulse to pass judgment on the hero, to present him as a positive example to be embraced or a negative instance to be eschewed, is to be explained in part by the particular context in which classical drama was first produced in England. In England as in Italy Seneca and the Greek tragedians made their comeback to the stage under academic patronage. Dons and schoolmasters saw performances of classical drama as useful academic exercises. When William Gager, don at Christ Church, Oxford, and writer of neo-Latin plays himself, attempted to defend college plays from Puritan attack late in the sixteenth century, he simply echoed what

16. Leicester Bradner, "The Latin Drama of the Renaissance (1340–1640), *Studies in the Renaissance*, IV (1957), 31–70. On the Christian Terence tradition cf. Frederick S. Boas, *University Drama in the Tudor Age* (Oxford, 1914), pp. 19 ff.

humanists had been saying since the fifteenth century. Ancient professional actors, Gager will concede,

came upon the stage . . . of a lewd, vast, dissolute, wicked, impudent, prodi-
gall, monstrous humor, whereof no dowte ensued greate corruption of manners
in them selves, to say nothinge heere of the behowlders. We contrarywise doe it
to recreate owre selves, owre House, and the better parte of the *Universitye*, with
some learned Poeme or other; to practyse owre owne style eyther in prose or
verse; to be well acquantyed with *Seneca* or *Plautus*; honestly to embolden owre
pathe; to trye their voyces and confirme their memoryes; to frame their speeche,
to conforme them to convenient action; to trye what mettell is in evrye one, and
of what disposition thay are of; wherby never any one amongst us, that I knowe
was made the worse, many have byn muche the better; as I dare reporte me to all
the *Universitye*.[17]

It was easy to foist onto Seneca's heroes the admirable traits that the actors
themselves were attempting to cultivate in performing the play.

About the rest of Westminster School's production of Seneca's *Hippolytus* we have no record, but Nowell's prologue prepares the audience to
view Phaedra, not as Seneca's wretch overwhelmed by a lust she recognizes
as evil yet cannot control, but as a calculating temptress; Hippolytus
emerges, not as Seneca's austere, fanatical misogynist, but as a martyr to
integrity, trust, and the fear of God. In effect, *Hippolytus* becomes a
secular saint's play. Nowell's prologue tosses off the comparison casually
and confidently enough, but to see Hippolytus and Joseph and Phaedra as
Potiphar's wife in fact requires an audience's eyes to be focused on moral
contexts larger than the play itself provides, not to mention some rather
selective hearing of Seneca's lines. That adjustment in the audience's
perspective is just what Nowell's prologue sets out to manage. For all the
similarities to Genesis in incidents of the plot, for all the stoic sentiments
declaimed by Hippolytus and the Chorus, the grim universe of Seneca's
play is, morally speaking, worlds away from the justly ordered universe
assumed by Christian humanists. In two recent essays G. K. Hunter has
pointed out just how much Seneca's Renaissance admirers had to overlook
to make him accord with their moral prejudices and stylistic tastes. To
audiences who relished multiplicity of incident, vindication of God's
justice, and copious verbal display Seneca was really quite alien in his

17. Quoted in Boas, *ibid*, pp. 235–236.

sharp focus on single heroes, in his portrayal of unrepentant violence in plays like *Medea* and unrelieved misery in plays like *Thyestes*, and in the strong-lined compressed utterances that are as characteristic of his style as his more famous hyperbole.[18]

All told, the sense of Seneca's *Hippolytus* communicated by Nowell's prologue seems firmly grounded in medieval dramatic traditions. In the mid-1540s, we must recall, the Corpus Christi cycles were still enjoying annual performances, despite the aging Henry VIII's attempts to control dramatic activity and suppress parish plays.[19] These were the years when Roger Ascham was translating Sophocles' *Philoctetes* and George Buchanan was turning Euripides' *Alcestis* and *Medea* into Latin, but more representative of what audiences were seeing at mid-century are John Bale's Protestant resurrection play (c. 1545), Nicholas Grimald's biblical play *Archipropheta* (c. 1547), and the polemical moral plays *Impatient Poverty* (c. 1547), *Lusty Juventus* (c. 1550), and *Nice Wanton* (c. 1550). These were the dramatic experiences Nowell's audience knew already, and in his prologue Nowell draws on those experiences to help the audience find their perspective on Seneca's tragedy.

From saints' plays, morality plays, and the great cycle plays Nowell's audiences inherited a number of expectations. They brought to Seneca's tragedy, in the first place, the same simple appreciation for a good story brought to dramatic life that biblical drama satisfied. Saints' plays and biblical plays gave them, in the second place, an established repertory of character roles that were broadly conceived but eminently actable, and they used those roles to come to terms with Seneca's distant Romans. It was natural enough to view Seneca's protagonists in terms of stage roles that were already familiar and already prized. No play on Joseph and Potiphar's wife survives in English, but there were any number of models an actor could look to for playing the calculating temptress or the virtuous young man. Phaedra could be played as a kind of unredeemed Mary Magdalen; Hippolytus, as a martyred Abel. From Nowell's prologue it is clear that extant roles had much to do not only with how actors played Seneca's parts but with how audiences watched them. From polemical

18. Hunter, "Seneca and the Elizabethans," pp. 17–26; and "Seneca and Elizabethan Tragedy," in C.D.N. Costa, ed., *Seneca* (London and Boston, 1974), pp. 166–204.

19. Harold C. Gardiner, *Mysteries' End* (New Haven, Conn., 1946), pp. 46–57.

plays like *Impatient Poverty* and *Nice Wanton* Nowell's audience were pre-
disposed to view Seneca's protagonists as moral agents whose actions were
to be applauded or condemned. Their fates offered lessons to be learned.
From the Corpus Christi plays, finally, an academic audience of the 1540s
would have known how to view the dramatic events in front of them as
part of a larger whole—even when that larger whole was only implicitly
present. Each of the events dramatized in the cycle plays was chosen not
simply for its own inherent dramatic possibilities but for its foreshadow-
ing the central story of Christ's birth, death, resurrection, and offer of
salvation.[20] Nowell could count on this double perspective, this focus
simultaneously on immediate events and universal Christian truth, to
make the passion, violence, horror, and apparent injustice of Seneca's text
morally acceptable.

II

Not everyone in the sixteenth century had this talent for accommodat-
ing literal facts with figurative truths. "Squeymish Areopagites," Thomas
Newton brands them in his collected edition of *Seneca His Tenne Tragedies*
(1581) in English translation. When they hear a speech "literally tending
(at the first sight) sometime to the prayse of Ambition, sometyme to the
mayntenaunce of cruelty, now and then to the approbation of incontinen-
cie," such shortsighted critics, says Newton, fail to consider the speaker or
the dramatic context.

For it may not at any hand be thought and deemed the direct meaning of Seneca
himselfe, whose whole wrytinges (penned with a peerelesse sublimity and lof-
tinesse of Style,) are so farre from countenauncing vice, that I doubt whether
there bee amonge all the Catalogue of Heathen wryters, that with more gravity of
Philosophicall sentences, more waightynes of sappy words, or greater authority of
sound matter beateth down sinne, loose lyfe, dissolute dealinge, and unbrydled
sensuality: or that more sensibly, pithily, and bytingly layeth doune the guedon
of filthy lust, cloaked dissimulation and odious treachery: which is the dryft,
whereunto he leveleth the whole yssue of ech one of his Tragedies.[21]

A great deal depends, clearly enough, on an audience's point of view. The
English translators whose work Newton assembles were all careful not to
leave such a crucial matter to chance.

20. V. A. Kolve, *The Play Called Corpus Christi* (Stanford, Calif., 1966), pp. 57–100.
21. Thomas Newton, *Seneca His Tenne Tragedies*, introd. T. S. Eliot (London, 1927),
pp. 4–5.

Most of the translations in *Seneca His Tenne Tragedies* had originally been printed in separate editions during the twenty years prior to 1581. The earliest of these, the versions of *Troas, Thyestes*, and *Hercules Furens* by Jasper Heywood, son of John Heywood the epigrammatist and playwright, had appeared during the very years when specific tragic titles first occur in the account books of Trinity College, Cambridge. Jasper Heywood himself had been a student at Oxford in the years just before his first translation, the *Troas*, appeared in 1559. T. S. Eliot, among others, has supposed that the translations by Heywood and others in Newton's anthology were intended for acting, but in only one case do we have any direct evidence.[22]

Alexander Neville was a nineteen-year-old student at Trinity College, Cambridge, when his translation of *Oedipus* was printed in 1563. By that time Trinity had a well-established tradition of productions of classical tragedy at Christmas. From the 1540s, '50s, and '60s statutes for several Oxford and Cambridge colleges specify not just *ludi* for the Christmas revels but *comicae* and *tragoediae*. The wording of these statutes suggests, nonetheless, that classical plays had to fit in with all the spectacle, speechmaking, and music that were traditional in college celebrations of Christmas. Henry VIII's statutes for St. John's College, Cambridge (1545), for example, call for *"dialogos aut festiva aut litteraria spectacula,"* showing us that audiences expected not just straight plays but visual splendor and sententious speechmaking.[23]

This is the context we must hold in mind when we open the Junior Bursar's account books of Trinity College, Cambridge, for 1551–1552 and discover just before an expenditure of 7 pence "to Mr Rudde for his playe menechmus" the much larger expenditure of 8 shillings 6 pence "to Mr Malham for his playe troas." Rudde and Malham were, presumably, dons resident in the college; the Trinity statutes of 1560 specifically require the nine lecturers in the college to get up the Christmas plays. This relatively expensive production of what was probably Seneca's *Troades* is the first in a series of classical titles noted in the Trinity accounts over the next few

---

22. *Ibid*, pp. xlviii–xlix.

23. Boas, *University Drama in the Tudor Age*, p. 8. H. B. Charlton, *The Senecan Tradition in Renaissance Tragedy* (Manchester, 1946), p. 154, specifies that Neville's college was Trinity and provides the interesting detail that he went on to study at one of the inns of court and became the friend of George Gascoigne. Gascoigne and Francis Kinwelmershe's version of Euripides' *Phoenician Women* was acted at Grey's Inn in 1566.

years. An "Oedipus" and a "Hecuba" follow in 1559, a "Medea" and another "Troas" in 1560–1561. Unfortunately the accounts tell us nothing about these productions beyond the fact that they cost considerably more to put on than most other plays, certainly more than classical comedies.[24] We do not even know, indeed, whose "Oedipus" or "Hecuba" or "Medea" was produced: each could have been either Seneca's or Euripides' in Latin translation.

The tradition of acting classical and neoclassical tragedies must have been older than the chance survival of these entries would indicate. In *The Scholemaster* (1570), for instance, Roger Ascham looks back over his Cambridge days in the years around 1540 and singles out for special mention the *"excellent Tragedie of Absalon"* by Thomas Watson, Fellow of St. John's College from 1535 and for some years dean of the college. "M. Cheke, he, and I," Ascham remembers, "for that part of trew Imitation, had many pleasant talkes togither, in comparing the preceptes of *Aristotle* and *Horce de Arte Poetica* with the examples of *Euripides*, *Sophocles*, and *Seneca"*—which would indicate an interest not only in critical theories of tragedy but in applying those theories to Christian subjects at a date at least ten years before the earliest Trinity records.[25] Ascham himself essayed a translation of *Philoctetes* and set his pupil the future Queen Elizabeth to work translating Seneca. Neoclassical tragedies like Watson's *Absalon* would thus appear to be among the *"dialogos aut festiva aut litteraria spectacula"* called for in the new statutes for St. John's about five years after Ascham, Cheke, and Watson had their conversations there.

When Alexander Neville's *Oedipus* appeared in print in 1563, actual performances of classical tragedy were, then, well-established traditions at Cambridge, in Trinity College particularly. In his preface young Neville seems to be more than just politely apologetic when he says that his

24. G. C. Moore Smith, "The Academic Drama at Cambridge: Extracts from College Records," *Malone Society Collections*, vol. II, pt. 2 (Oxford, 1923), p. 155. "Oedipus" in 1559–1560 cost one pound 13 shillings 4 pence and "hecuba" 19 shillings, whereas "Mostellaria" the same year cost only 6 shillings (p. 160). "Troas" in 1560–1561 cost two pounds 12 shillings 8 pence and "Medea" one pound 13 shillings 7 pence. Other payments recording in 1560–1561 may relate to these two plays: 6 pence was paid for "viij ringes for the chariate in a Tragedye," and 13 shillings 4 pence was given "to the Trumpetor in the stage tyme" (pp. 161–162). The five pounds expended that season for "Amphytrio" is decidedly unusual.

25. Boas, *University Drama in the Tudor Age*, p. 62.

translation of *Oedipus* was intended to be acted on the stage, not read in print:

Albeit when first I undertoke the translation of this present Tragoedy, I minded nothing lesse, than that at any tyme thus rudely transformed it shoulde come into the Printers hands. For I to none other ende removed him, from his naturall and lofty style, to our corrupt and base, or as some men (but untruly) affyrme it, most barbarous Language: but onely to satisfy the instant requests of a few my familiar frends, who thought to have put it to the very same use, that Seneca himselfe in his Invention pretended: Which was by the tragicall and Pompous showe upon Stage, to admonish all men of their fickle Estates, to declare the unconstant head of wavering Fortune, her sodayne interchaunged and soone altered Face: and lyvely to expresse the just revenge and fearefull punishments of horrible Crimes, wherewith the wretched worlde in these our myserable dayes pyteously swarm-eth.[26]

So caught up is he in the ethical ends of tragedy that Neville fails to see the etiological incongruities in these remarks: the universe of tragedy, he suggests, can be a place either of arbitrary shifts of fortune or of ineluctable moral laws that follow on human responsibility. Either way, it the moral end of tragedy that counts, and either way that end remains the same: to make men aware of the awesome outside forces that attend on their actions.

By allying "tragicall" and "Pompous" Neville shows that he thinks of tragedy not as a kind of plot only but as a theatrical experience. Though studiously literal for the most part, his translation includes changes and additions that are designed to enhance the play onstage—and to leave no room for "squeymish Areopagites" to misconstrue what they see and hear. It was his moral purpose, Neville explains, that "caused me not to be precise in following the Author, word for word: but sometymes by addition, sometimes by subtraction, to use the aptest Phrases in geving the Sense that I could invent" (p. 188). Neville's alterations are of two kinds.

In the first place, he never scruples over amplifying a speech when he can thunder on the audience's ears and emblazon on their minds moral points that Seneca himself may have touched too briefly. Such additions tell us a great deal about how Renaissance audiences listened to tragedy in performance. From the speeches they heard declaimed onstage they ex-

---

26. *Seneca His Tenne Tragedies*, pp. 187–188. Further page references will be indicated in the text.

pected not just revelations of character and emotion but moral wisdom, formulated with epigrammatic precision and, we may suppose, uttered with appropriate emphasis. What must have been heard in the theater is visually apparent on the printed page in many sixteenth-century editions of classical and neoclassical tragedy: running quotation marks in the left-hand margin serve to set off memorable *sententiae* from the rest of the text. In the printed editions of their Englishing of Euripides' *Phoenician Women* George Gascoigne and Francis Kinwelmershe even provide marginal glosses beside such speeches. Near the beginning of the play Antigone's tutor hears the approaching rabble attending on Polyneices and advises his pupil to go back inside to "your maiden chamber." Nine lines of what is casual advice—perhaps even comic solicitude—in Euripides become 21 lines of moral exhortation in Kinwelmershe, distinguished from the rest of the text with quotation marks and labeled in the margin "A glasse for yong women." [27]

Resolute stoics that they are, Seneca's characters have plenty of such *sententiae* to speak in the Latin text; it remained for translators like Neville to expand them and give them the full rhetorical force they seemed to deserve. In his very first speech, for example, Oedipus utters one of the most quoted *sententiae* in all Seneca's tragedies:

> What king is happy on his throne? False joy,
> How many ills thy smiling face conceals! [28]

These two terse, epigrammatic lines in Latin become four diffuse, hyperbolic lines in Neville's English:

> Doth any man in Princely throne rejoyce? O brittle Joy,
> How many ills? how fayre a Face? and yet how much annoy
> In thee doth lurke, and hidden lies? what heapes of endles strife?
> They judge amisse, that deeme the Prince to have the happy life.
>
> (p. 192)

---

27. *Jocasta*, rptd. in Cunliffe, *Early English Classical Tragedies*, p. 83.

28. Seneca, *Four Tragedies and Octavia*, trans. E. F. Watling (Harmondsworth and Baltimore, 1966), p. 209. Further translations of Seneca not assigned to Neville are from Watling's version and are indicated in the text by line numbers of the Latin original. The Latin text I have consulted is that edited by F. J. Miller in *Seneca's Tragedies*, Vol. I, Loeb Library (London and New York, 1917).

Used as we are to Shakespeare's heroes, who reflect in soliloquy, not preach, we are apt to write off such effusions as Oedipus's as anti-dramatic. What to us seem cerebral intrusions that threaten both dramatic illusion and emotional continuity were for Neville and his contemporaries vital elements in a theatrical experience in which "Pompous" and "tragicall" were correlatives. Speeches like Oedipus's could pose no threat to dramatic illusion when there was no dramatic illusion—at least as later audiences came to expect. In Seneca's meditative Latin Oedipus draws his thoughts together in a single reflective moment; in Neville's morality play English he addresses the audience directly in a prepared lecture.

Audiences heard such speeches not with their minds only but with their hearts. In his definition of the *sententia* as a dramatic element Cinthio makes it clear that moral apothegms like Oedipus's were among the most powerful devices a dramatist could command. A *sententia*, explains Cinthio, is

an expression in accordance with the usage of the time, taken from everyday life and from the common opinion of men, which describes with great efficacy and with suitable variety some feature of human life that either has been, or is, or must be. They are very common in tragedies, being unbelievably effective [*credenza attisime*] as a means of presenting actions, passions, and manners, the terrible and the pathetic, to the eyes of the spectators.[29]

Far from being aural "footnotes" that a listener's mind would note in passing, *sententiae* carried an emotional charge that put them at the very heart of tragedy in performance.

Neville's second strategy in producing an actable script is to alter Seneca's choruses. In this respect his hand is a good deal freer than in his amplifications of characters' speeches. Seneca's first chorus, for example, is a rehearsal of the miseries of Thebes in the midst of the plague. Part of the horror of Seneca's vision is the utter indifference of the "insatiable gods" to the human suffering that grips the city. Presiding over Neville's Thebes, however, is a wrathful but approachable God, and the Chorus's invocation, with their plea for mercy and their self-righteous call for destruction on the heads of God's enemies, sounds more like a Psalm than the chorus of a classical tragedy. The whole of their prayer has no counterpart in Seneca's text:

29. Quoted and translated in Horne, *Tragedies of Giraldi*, p. 30.

O fowle and fearefull Fate (alas) what causeth all this wo?
O God whence springs this Pestylence that us tormenteth so?
No age, no shape, no forme is sparde, but all confounded lye.
Thus happiest now the man I count, whose chaunce was first to dye.
For hee hath shund a thousand ills, which wretched Eyes have seene:
And mischiefes great that us doe presse from him are taken cleane.
O God withhold thy fury great, thy Plagues from us remove.
Ceasse of afflicted Soules to scourge, who thee both serve and love.
Powre downe on them diseases fowle, that them deserved have.
A Guerdon just for sinne (Oh God) this this of thee wee crave,
And onely this. We aske no more, the cause and all is thyne,
A thing not usde of Gods it is, from pity to declyne.

                                              (pp. 196–197)

"Pity"? Neville has not considered the gods of Seneca's plays too closely.
From his acting script Neville omits altogether Seneca's second chorus
with its praise of Bacchus as Thebes's patron deity and its recital of famous
exploits of Theban heroes in times past.

The most significant change of all occurs in the third chorus. Following
the example of Sophocles' Theban elders, who at first do not want to
believe Teiresias's prophecies any more than Oedipus himself, Seneca's
Chorus argue that Oedipus is *not* the cause of Thebes' sufferings:

> Not yours, not yours the fault that brought such peril to us.
> Not for that do the Fates bear hard on the house of Labdacus.
> We are assailed by the ancient anger of the gods.
>
>   (ll. 709–712)

Neville's Chorus, on the other hand, never get so involved in the action
that they lose their philosophical detachment, and, unlike Seneca's
Chorus, they throw the emphasis not on "the ancient anger of the gods"
but on Oedipus as a mirror for magistrates:

> Thus hee that Princes lives, and base Estate together wayes,
> Shall finde the one a very hell, a perfect infelicity:
> The other eke a heaven right, exempted quight from mysery.
> Let Oedipus example bee of this unto you all,
> A Mirrour meete, A Patern playne, of Princes carefull thrall.
> Who late in perfect Joy as seem'de, and everlasting blis,
> Triumphantly his life out led, a Myser now hee is.
>
>   (p. 216)

For Seneca's fourth chorus, a celebration of the *via media*, Neville substitutes a lament over Fortune's power. The sentiments there are sounded again at the end of the play. In the Chorus's final dialogue with Oedipus "fate" in Seneca becomes in Neville the "tumbling fatal course of fortunes wheele" (p. 226).

The license Neville assumed in adapting Seneca's choruses came on good authority. During his stay in England in 1505–1506 Erasmus worked on Latin translations of Euripides' *Hecuba* and *Iphigenia in Aulis*— testimony to both his accomplishment in classical letters and his educational fervor, since the Greek texts of Euripides' complete plays were only just then being printed in Italy. Despite the difficulty of the still exotic Greek language, not to mention the corrupt readings of his copy texts, Erasmus produced two accurate but above all educationally useful translations that were printed at Paris on his way from England to Italy. In the whole task of translating, Erasmus writes in the letter dedicating *Iphigenia* to William Warham, Archbishop of Canterbury, he has balanced literal strictness against "failure to do justice to the theme," and in the case of Euripides' choruses that end has meant very free adaptation of the originals:

In one respect I have dared in both plays to depart from my author's practice: I have to some extent reduced the metrical diversity and licence of the choric parts, hoping that scholars would take my difficulties into account and pardon me for this; after all, Horace did not strive to reproduce the great freedom in prosody and variety in metres shown by the lyric poets, nor Seneca those of the tragedians, although each of them was merely imitating the Greeks, not translating them as well. But even if I had time among my more important studies to translate a number of other tragedies, not only should I not repent of this boldness, but I should not be reluctant to alter the style and topics of the choruses; and I should prefer either to treat of some commonplace or to deviate into some agreeable digression, rather than to waste effort upon what Horace calls "melodious trifles." For it seems to me that nowhere did the ancients write more foolishly than in choruses of this sort, where, through excessive striving for novelty of utterance, they destroyed clarity of expression, and in the hunt for marvellous verbal effects their sense of reality suffered.[30]

In adapting the choruses of Seneca's *Oedipus* young Alexander Neville was simply following the example of one of the most influential educators of the century.

---

30. *The Correspondence of Erasmus*, trans. R.A.B. Mynors and D.F.S. Thomson, *Collected Works of Erasmus*, (Toronto, 1975), II, 132–135.

Compared with Euripides' choruses, which often strike twentieth-century readers as highly ironic flights of lyric fancy in the midst of adversity and suffering, Seneca's choruses speak a language much more likely to be understood by Renaissance audiences. It was not only their more familiar Latin meters that made them comprehensible but their equally familiar, unambiguous ideas. None of Sophocles' dramatic subtlety marred Seneca's choruses, none of Euripides' illusive irony, certainly none of Aeschylus's bewildering imagery. It was Seneca's bent for moral reflection, perhaps even more than the violence and passion that loom large in his characters' consciousness if not in action onstage, that overcame his disappointing obsession with individual heroes and his sometimes suspect management of rewards and punishments, and made his tragedies far more popular in Italy and in England than the plays of Aeschylus, Sophocles, and Euripides. All that was needed to bring Seneca's choruses philosophically into line were a few tactful omissions, a few discreet substitutions, and some harmless amplifications of his best sentiments.

Three things are to be observed in Neville's alterations of Seneca's text. By leaving out the Chorus's recital of the exploits of Theban heroes and the city's devotion to Bacchus, Neville seems intent, in the first place, on playing down the historicity of the play. He glosses over those touches that would distance the events of the play from a sixteenth-century audience as something that happened in another time and another place. Rather, Neville prefers to give the impression that what the audience witnesses is a demonstration of universal truth, a pattern of events that could happen just as easily in the 1560s as in ancient Greece. Nothing could be further from our twentieth-century view of tragedy as something possible in past, more glorious ages but not in our own. In the second place, Neville thoroughly medievalizes Seneca's sense of fate: inscrutable fate in the Roman stoic becomes thoroughly scrutable Fortune in the Christian humanist. In Seneca's Latin fate is the inexorable principle that rules all the universe; in Neville's English Fortune is the principle that governs *this* world but not, by implication at least, the next. Beyond the shifts of Fortune are changeless Christian verities. Both in individual speeches and particularly in the choruses we can observe, finally, how Neville seizes every opportunity of playing up the play's *sentence*, particularly its political *sentence*. The result is a heightening of the play's immediacy both physically and philosophically. By turning Seneca's reflective asides into full-scale homilies Neville puts actors and audience into the direct contact they enjoyed in morality plays; by altering Seneca's choruses Neville makes the play's educational program—its "theme," as Erasmus would have it—unmistakably explicit. Neville's interest in Oedipus as a mirror for magistrates is strong enough to alter not only the audience's view of the hero but the hero's view of himself. Neville's universe may be a sublunary realm of chance events ruled over by Fortune, but that does not prevent him from presenting Oedipus, with a lapse of ethical logic, as a thoroughly responsible, thoroughly culpable hero.

Seneca's Oedipus voices a sense of fatedness and impending doom from the beginning of the play and at the end of the play seems to take almost masochistic delight in having blindly committed even more crimes than he first imagined. He cries out to Apollo:

> Now hear me,
> Guardian and god of truth, Fate's messenger!
> One death, my father's, did the fates demand;
> But now I have slain twice; I am more guilty
> Than I had feared to be; my crimes have brought
> My mother to her death. Phoebus, you lied!
> I have done more than was set down for me
> By evil destiny . . .
>
> . . . .
>
> Go, friends, and bring relief to those laid low.
> When I go from you, I shall take away
> All the infections of mortality
> That have consumed this land. Come, deadly Fates,
> Come, all grim spectres of Disease, black Plague,
> Corruption and intolerable Pain!
> Come with me! I could want no better guides.
>
> (ll. 1042–1046, 1057–1061)

For all his willing acceptance of misery, Seneca's Oedipus still presents himself as a victim of destiny, and the Chorus bears him out. In his acting script of 1563 Neville turns this final speech of twenty lines into a veritable litany of fifty lines in which Oedipus scourges himself as a sinful creature deserving whatever torments may yet come to him:

Thou God, thou teller out of Fates. On thee on thee, I call
My Father onely I did owe, unto the Destinies all.
Now twise a Paracide, a worse than I did feare to bee:
My mother I have slayne, (Alas) the fault is all in mee.
O Oedipus accursed wretch, lament thine owne Calamity,
Lament thy state, thy griefe lament, thou Caitife borne to misery.

.   .   .   .

Wilt thou not dye? deserving Death: thou cause of all the griefe,
And Plagues, and dreadfull mischiefs all that Thebane City prease.

.   .   .   .

O cursed head: O wicked wight, whom all men deadly hate.
O Beast, what meanst thou still to live in this unhappy state?
The Skies doe blush and are ashamed, at these thy mischiefes great:

.   .   .   .

So maist thou yet in tract of time due paynes and vengeaunce have
For thy mischevous lyfe. Thus, thus, the Gods themselves decree.
Thus, thus, thy Fates: thus the skyes appoint it for to bee.
Then headlong hence, with a mischiefe hence, thou caitife vyle away.
Away, away, thou monstrous Beast. Goe, Run.

(pp. 229–230)

For this recasting of Seneca's hero Neville has his eye on the choosing protagonist of morality-play tradition, and in his direct-address harangues Oedipus confronts the audience not as Seneca's sublimely isolated sufferer, marked out by fate for a destiny all his own, but as chastened Mankind who willfully has worked his own destruction: "the fault is all in mee."

III

When we read Nowell's prologue for *Hippolytus* and Neville's translation of *Oedipus*, it is the moral revision of Seneca that seems most prominent. When those scripts were brought to the stage, more immediate concerns than etiology engaged the audience's attention—or so eye-witness accounts would lead us to believe. Backed into a corner by hostile critics, William Gager, as we have seen, could marshal splendid arguments about the moral utility of tragedy; to judge by a spectator's account of his neo-Latin tragedy *Dido*, Gager was even more adept at marshaling splendid stage effects. In the *Chronicles of England* Raphael Holinshed recounts the grand welcome given to Albertus Alasco, Prince Palatine of Siradia in Poland, when he visited Christ Church, Oxford, in 1583. To impress their Continental guest the university put together a company of actors drawn mostly from Christ Church and St. John's and mounted two neo-Latin plays by Gager. One was a classical comedy *Rivales* that surrounded Plautus's braggart soldier and alluring bawd with what seem to have been native English country bumpkins and drunken sailors, all singing and dancing; the other was a classical tragedy *Dido* that surrounded the fate-crossed lovers of Virgil's narrative with native English hunters and some truly extraordinary stage effects:

On the second daie, his first dinner was made him at Alsoules college, where (besides dutifull receiving of him) he was solmenelie satisfied with scholerlie exercises and courtlie fare. This night and the night insuing, after sumptuous suppers in his lodging, he personaly was present with his traine in the hall, first at the plaieng of a pleasant comedie intituled Rivales; then at the setting out of a verie statelie tragedie named Dido, wherein the queenes banket (with Eneas narration of the destruction of Troie) was livelie described in a marchpaine patterne, there was also a goodlie sight of hunters with full crie of a kennell of hounds, Mercurie and Iris descending and ascending from and to an high place, the tempest wherein it hailed small confects, rained rosewater and snew an artificiall kind of snow, all strange, marvellous, and abundant.[31]

This "Raine of rosewater, and haile of sugar confects, etc." was memorable enough to merit a marginal note in Holinshed's folio. Here was a spectacle that not only *looked* good enough to eat. Onstage at least, the distance from ancient Carthage to Tudor England seems short indeed. The sugar-confect snow that drives Gager's Dido and Aeneas into their lovers' tryst in the cave belongs to the same staging tradition as the roses that the Virtues use as weapons in that most extravagant of morality plays *The Castle of Perserverance* (c. 1405–1425). "Statelie," "strange," "marvellous," "abundant"—these are the key words that help to see the catastrophic encounter of Dido and Aeneas through Renaissance eyes.

It was not in sight only that productions of tragedy thrilled the senses. When he printed an authorized edition of his pirated tragedy *Roxana* in 1632, William Alabaster carefully specified how the Latin text should be

---

31. Raphael Holinshed, *Chronicles of England* (London, 1808), IV, 508. Cf. also the account of the occasion in Boas, *University Drama in the Tudor Age*, pp. 181–182.

declaimed. Presumably Alabaster has his eye on the first performance of
his tragedy at Trinity College, Cambridge, about 1592 when he directs
actors to speak the lines "with a foaming sound, just as poets are accustomed in their tragedies, since things read in a bombastic voice [*"cum
ampulla oris"*] are somehow made even more sublime [*"in grandius
quodammodo excoluntur"*]."[32] *Granditas* is the range of style and feeling that
Alabaster aims at, and his directions show us that speeches as well as
spectacle were means to that end. We can see how Neville could find
"Pompous" and "tragicall" synonymous. The effect of tragedy was to be
above all *impressive*.

Grand-scale spectacle, flamboyant rhetoric, moral *sentence*—these three
expectations explain Gager's "improvements" to Seneca's *Hippolytus* when
Christ Church mounted the play at Shrovetide 1592. The occasion represented as much a triumph for Gager as the same play did for Pomponius
Laetus in Rome a century earlier. First Gager's new Latin play on the
return of Ulysses was performed in Christ Church hall on Sunday, 6
February; his *Rivales* was revived on Monday, 7 February; then on Tues-
day, 8 February, the last day of the festive season that had started before
Christmas, Seneca's *Hippolytus* was acted with a prologue, epilogue, and
two additional scenes by Gager.[33] But Gager's real triumph came after the
playing of *Hippolytus*: Gager brought onstage a puffed-up critic Momus
and then an "Epilogus Responsivus," who deflated Momus's objections
one by one. The old arguments against drama that had confronted Pomponius Laetus, Alexander Nowell, and Thomas Newton were still around,
and Gager had his moment of triumph on the stage. But Momus had the
last word. Dr. John Rainolds, holder of Sir Francis Walsingham's lecture-
ship for the confutation of papal doctrines, saw himself caricatured in
Momus and turned out a series of vituperative letters attacking drama in
general and Gager's productions in particular. Rainolds's letters found
their way into print. Gager's replies, significantly, did not. Gager's points
of defense, quoted earlier, help us see how the motives behind productions

32. Quoted in J. W. Binns, "Seneca and Neo-Latin Tragedy in England," in Costa,
ed., *Seneca*, p. 210. I offer a closer translation of the relevant phrases than Binns provides.

33. J. W. Binns, "William Gager's Additions to Seneca's *Hippolytus*," *Studies in the
Renaissance, XVII* (1970), 153–191, sets out the occasion in detail and reprints Gager's
additions with English translations on facing pages. My quotations are from Binns's
translation.

of classical tragedy had not changed at all in a hundred years. Nor had production devices. Adding extra scenes to a Seneca tragedy—"patches" sewn onto the play, as Gager himself puts it—might at first seem an act of hubris to match those of the chastened heroes of Seneca's plays. Knowing what we do about other productions of classical and neoclassical tragedies in England, we are in a position, however, to understand why Seneca's text would seem incomplete.

Gager's additions are of three kinds. In the first place, like Nowell introducing the same play nearly fifty years before, Gager supplies a prologue in the manner of Roman comedy. In this case, however, it is not just the strategy of the comic prologue that Gager has adopted but its flippant tone as well. "Another stage presented the story of chaste Penelope," the prologue starts out, recalling the production of *Ulysses Redux* two days before.

Lest women thereby become overweeningly proud, today's play will tell of chaste Hippolytus, so that men may obtain an equal reputation for chastity.

Here the situation is reversed. The youth is stern, he scorns to play the soft suitor. Phaedra takes the place of Penelope, a shameful woman the place of a chaste one. Here the woman solicits the man, the step-mother her step-son. Who would believe this crime? Let Crete boast of Minos, of the finest wine, of the marvelous skill of Daedalus, of being the native land of Jupiter and of a hundred cities. Whilst Crete bears Phaedra, I thank our own Island for being so far away from the dread land which gave rise to such a sin.

Therefore let no one explain such a shameful act to the women; let their disgrace be concealed.

But if some woman perchance plucks at the coat of a young man, and desires too eagerly to know what is happening here, let him ingeniously invent something new, or shamelessly make it clear that it is a fictitious story. Let the women be spared, let them not know their own disgrace.

Is there a roguish edge to all these remarks about male chastity and sparing the unsuspecting ladies? It may sound like all-male intramural humor, but Rainolds's letters make it clear that women were present at the performance: actors impersonating women in the play sat among the ladies in the audience—or so Rainolds claims—and were not detected until they stood up to act. The Prologue's shift to the narrative background of the play in the next dozen lines sounds serious enough, but his final two lines may well be as ironic as the beginning:

I entreat you give your attention to the troop of actors—at least as much as is given in the popular theatre.

Gager's second strategy is to heighten the spectacle of Seneca's play onstage. Like Mercury and Iris "descending and ascending from and to an high place" in *Dido*, like the hunting scene and snowstorm, Gager's new scene to open *Hippolytus* provides opportunity for marvelous stage effects. No sooner has the Prologue departed than Cupid and the fury Megaera rise from the Underworld, fast on the coattails of Tantalus's ghost in the first scene of Seneca's *Thyestes*. In the Underworld, it seems, Theseus and Pirithous have been attempting to abduct Proserpine, and Megaera has come to work revenge. She will make Phaedra fall in love with her own stepson. Cupid is horrified. This incestuous passion, he protests, will give love a bad name. The whole of Seneca's play, then, is set up as a kind of contest between the two deities, between the forces of Love and Revenge. This cosmic "over-plot" in which gods come onstage to pull the strings of human actors below had already been shown to advantage in plays like *The Rare Triumphs of Love and Fortune*, acted at court by Lord Derby's men in 1582–1583, and possibly in Gager's own *Dido* the same year.[34]

Finally, Gager has heightened the philosophical issues implicit in Seneca's text. Like Nowell's parallel with Joseph and Potiphar's wife, like Neville's amplifications of sententious speeches in Seneca's *Oedipus*, Gager's new beginning for Act II brings the issues of the play out into the open just as they would be stated in a morality play. Gager's Hippolytus has to be almost superhumanly resolute to ward off his tempters. Not just the Nurse and Phaedra attempt to persuade him to passion but two new

---

34. To settle a dispute as to which has the greater power over men Jupiter directs that Venus and Fortune shall take turns demonstrating their sway. Act by act, first one and then the other stage-manages the main plot of the play, a Roman comedy of frustrated lovers, estranged sons, and nobility unwittingly going about in honest poverty. Finally Mercury calls a draw, and all ends happily. Cf. *The Rare Triumphs of Love and Fortune*, Malone Society (London, 1930). This is probably the "Historie of Love and Fortune" for which the Earl of Derby's men were paid for performing before Elizabeth on 30 December 1582. Cf. Albert Feuillerat, ed., *Documents Relating to the Office of the Revels in the Time of Queen Elizabeth* (Louvain, 1908), p. 349. Mercury and Iris may well have served a similar allegorical function in Gager's *Dido*. In the *Aeneid*, IV, Mercury is sent by Jupiter to tell Aeneas to give up his entanglement with Dido and get on with his mission of founding a new nation; Iris is sent to release Dido's soul from her body when she has immolated herself in despair. Aeneas's dilemma might easily have been presented as Love versus Fortune, or Private Passion versus Public Duty.

characters as well: a lecherous Pandarus and a chaste wood-nymph Nais. As with the temptation of Mankind in morality plays, Gager seems determined to make Hippolytus's temptation as *tempting* as possible. Gager apparently succeeded. Rainolds was especially horrified by Nais, "a new *Nymph* . . . bringing fewell enough to heate and melt a heart of yse or snow"—and this response at secondhand, too. Rainolds had not even accepted Gager's invitation to attend the performance. Gager defends Nais as a foil to Phaedra:

> . . . the devyse was, partly to sett owte the constant chastetye or rather virginytye of *Hippolytus*, whoe neyther with honest love made to hym in the woods, nor with unhonest attempts in the cyttye could be overcumme; partly to expresse the affection of honest, lawfull, certuous marriage meaninge love; for no other did she profer, and therfor me thinkes she is not, unharde, to be reproched with the brode name bawderye, wherof there is no one syllable in worde or sense to be founde in all her speches.[35]

In a real morality play the tempters would have urged arguments that we in the audience could see through at once. Pandarus and Nais, however, are given arguments out of Phaedra's letter to Hippolytus in Ovid's *Heroides*—arguments rather more luscious than lascivious. Nais's love seems, in fact, so ingenuous that Gager manages to confuse the moral issue rather than clarify it. Nais's love, says Gager, is meant as a positive contrast to Phaedra's. In refusing Nais's chaste love as well as Phaedra's lecherous love Hippolytus is made to appear disagreeably stubborn. He ends up in the position of a blocking figure in a romantic comedy, a sour Malvolio incapable of feeling anything. Considering the Prologue's coy remarks about male virginity, Gager's audience might well have responded to Nais' blandishments with amusement. Hence Rainolds' objections. In any event, the spurned Nais adds her curses to Megaera's:

> But go on making sport of girls through your pride, O hard, cruel man, lead your savage triumph. Let every girl seek you, and none bear you away. Nemesis will requite this conduct, and let her requite it, I pray. Let her regard the haughty pride of this barbarous man—take vengeance, goddess. May he perish by the worst of deaths. May Hippolytus atone for hating and despising my love. May an avenger of this disgraceful repulse appear in a short time, and may she bring the furies of a woman in love, who has been scorned.

35. Quoted in Binns, "Gager's Additions," p. 161.

Phaedra, of course, figures as this avenger. The Nurse appears at once to
plead Phaedra's case even more directly than Pandarus has, this time in
speeches by Seneca. As far as Nais is concerned, Hippolytus well deserves
the punishment of Nemesis. Again, Gager rather confuses things morally.
The dying Hippolytus must figure as both the innocent passive victim of
Seneca and the culpable, hardhearted lady-killer of Gager's additions.
Gager appears not to have made up his mind which view of the hero the
audience should take, and the momentary battle lines of the debate scenes
are never carried to their logical conclusions.

Why does Gager never sense the discrepancy? There are perhaps several
reasons. One is his obvious aesthetic delight in debate for its own sake.
What his characters' elegant disputations solve or do not solve seems
almost beside the point. The dramatic vehicle best designed to satisfy such
love for debate is the morality play, and Gager has simply added to
Seneca's text two scenes of temptation and argumentation inspired by the
polemical plays that he and his academic audience already affected. The
only difficulty is that Seneca's ethical assumptions and Gager's polemical
program work at cross-purposes. Another reason for Gager's obliviousness
to ethical niceties is his passion for variety. Judged against the protean
personages who crowd into most morality plays—even when the roles
could be doubled by only three or four players—Seneca's solitary and
unchanging heroes must have seemed austere indeed. All told, Gager does
not give the impression of being a highbrow classicist. His country
bumpkins and drunken sailors crashing into a Roman comedy, his hunters
and hounds and sugar-confect snow in *Dido*, his facetious prologue and
demandes d'amour in *Hippolytus* all bespeak a man with theatrical flare who
feels the Renaissance lust for variety and knows how to satisfy it with a
measure of artistic integrity. They also bespeak a very tentative notion of
tragedy that can accommodate drollery and amorous rhetoric along with
suffering and catastrophe.

IV

When Seneca's tragic heroes came out of retirement after more than a
thousand years and mounted stages in Renaissance England's schools and
colleges, they confronted audiences who had a fresh curiosity about the
drama of antiquity but who also enjoyed flourishing dramatic traditions of

their own. "Tragedy" was not one of those traditions. For Roman actors and Renaissance audiences to understand one another some mutual adjustments were necessary. In at least three respects—in the physical surroundings they played in, in the language they spoke, and in the philosophical ideas they communicated—Seneca's tragic heroes found themselves in situations far removed from the civic theaters of ancient Rome. With almost no solid information on the Roman theater at hand, it was only natural that academic producers in England should draw on native dramatic traditions to turn Seneca's texts into actable scripts.

The physical circumstances in which Seneca's heroes were brought to dramatic life in England had little to do with the theaters of ancient Rome. Roman theaters were stupendously large affairs, and the vast distances that separated spectators and players prompted Vitruvius to give most of his attention to sight lines and acoustics; the great halls of Westminster School, Trinity College Cambridge, and Christ Church Oxford were, by contrast, relatively small rooms, and the relation between audience and actors suggested by English playscripts of the period, and by what we know about how other plays were mounted indoors, was close and intimate. So far as we know, the physical arrangements for performing Seneca's tragedies were no different from the physical arrangements for performing morality plays and other indoor entertainments. Certainly the spectacular stage effects that accompanied Gager's *Hippolytus* were established features of morality plays like *The Castle of Perseverance*, as well as an essential part of the seasonal revels in which classical comedy and classical tragedy were performed in Renaissance England.

The physical intimacy among spectators and players apparently influenced how the players spoke their lines. Looking to the example of Roman comedy and to the native custom of a poet's declaiming his narrative verses before an assembled audience, Nowell, Neville, and Gager all provide prologues for Seneca's texts. The speaker they send out before the play proper serves a number of functions: he defends the new dramatic kind the audience is about to see, he offers at least some definition of what "tragedy" is, he sets the dominant tone of the events to follow, he establishes the give-and-take relationship that audiences were used to from medieval drama in general and morality plays in particular. The cacaphonous variety of tones struck in Gager's production of *Hippolytus*—now facetious, now horrifying, now amorous, now pitiable—shows us how important it was that some bounds of definition be set and that one dominant tone be sounded above the others. William Alabaster's acting directions for his tragedy *Roxana* give that dominant tone a name: *granditas*. The reach toward sublimity involved not only marvelous stage effects but bombastic delivery of lines.

Performance of classical tragedy demanded *granditas*, in part at least, because of its high seriousness. Nowell, Neville, and Gager are unanimous in expecting their audiences to find performance of Seneca's plays morally instructive. They achieved that end in several ways. Easiest of all was to instruct the speaker of the prologue to make the lessons of the play explicit, as Nowell does in his prologue for *Hippolytus*. Whether Nowell found that ploy effective enough by itself we do not know, but Neville and Gager were impelled to make substitutions and additions to the texts themselves. Neville's method is the less radical: following the example of Erasmus in his translations of Euripides, Neville alters Seneca's choruses to heighten and clarify the moral issues implicit in the action. This impulse to play up the philosophical program of the play appears, too, in Neville's handling of Seneca's *sententiae*. The maxims that Seneca's heroes formulate in one or two epigrammatic lines become in Neville's translation homilies of a dozen lines or more. In Oedipus's case the effect of these speeches is to turn Seneca's unwitting victim into the self-determined, morally responsible protagonist of a morality play. Gager carries this design a step further: by adding to Seneca's text two scenes of temptation and debate he essentially restructures Seneca's fatalistic *Hippolytus* into a play of choices, decisions, and consequences like *Mankind*. The implication is unmistakable: for finding their perspective on the catastrophes that Seneca depicts in such lurid, compelling colors English Renaissance spectators used dramatic frames that were already at hand. It was the medieval tradition of saints' plays and morality plays, not the writings of Aristotle or Horace or Vitruvius, that taught them how to speak Seneca's lines, how to bring his texts to life with spectacle, how to make sense of the evil and anguish that dominate his vision.

It would be reductively simple, however, to suggest that in the confrontation of ancients and moderns all the reposturing had to be done by Seneca's protagonists. There was new thinking and new feeling to be done on the part of English Renaissance audiences as well. When Nowell, Neville, and Gager brought together Seneca's texts and English dramatic traditions, they set up an encounter of actors and audience that neither Roman theater nor medieval theater could accommodate alone. Humanist educators may have devised all sorts of ways to stage Seneca's texts as if they were morality plays, but the fact remains that they were *not* morality plays. The actors who performed classical tragedies as an educational exercise and the audiences who watched them as seasonal recreation were set free to explore reaches of human experience beyond the boundaries defined by saints' plays, morality plays, and the Corpus Christi cycles. In range of motives, in depth of character, in intensity of emotion, above all in the sheer rhetorical force of language, classical tragedy opened up new dramatic territory in which Renaissance audiences had to find their bearings. Existing dramatic conventions could guide them only so far. In the morality plays of William Wager, in the diverse experiments of Christopher Marlowe, and in the history plays of William Shakespeare we can feel an ever tighter tension between observed experience and the dramatic devices available for bringing that experience to the stage. The heroes of classical tragedy posed one of the most potent challenges to existing dramatic conventions.

The three productions we have surveyed make it clear that academic audiences in England had arrived at that crucial poise of responses that seems essential to tragedy, a balance between a visceral emotional response to the sufferings of an individual hero, immediately before us, and a cerebral sense of the larger issues his suffering touches. Guided by the morality-play tradition, the Englishmen who watched productions of Seneca in schools and colleges preferred those larger issues a great deal more immediate, a great deal more clearly stated, and a great deal simpler than we do. At first, the Renaissance apologists' confident insistence that tragedy demonstrates moral truth may seem wrongheaded to us, who prize above all a sense of awesome mystery in the destruction of the tragic hero. But we must remember that Renaissance audiences countered this detached "philosophical" response with what seems to have been an immediate, unembarrassed pity for undeserved suffering. Indeed, they seem much less self-conscious in this regard than we, who, at least on paper, seem anxious to write off dramatic suffering as melodrama and pity as sentimentality unless they are tempered by a conflict of philosophical and moral issues.

English Renaissance audiences may have felt, then, a *poise* of responses, but it is equally certain that they had not yet arrived at the *tension* between responses that figures for us as the central fact of tragedy in the theater. It was Hegel who first articulated the criteria that twentieth-century critics have used to deny tragic stature to merely "pathetic" plays like Arthur Miller's *Death of a Salesman*. There are two kinds of sympathy, Hegel insists:

> The first is just the ordinary sensibility—in other words, a sympathy with the misfortunes and sufferings of another, and one which is experienced as something finite and negative. Your countrified cousin is ready enough with compassion of this order. The man of nobility and greatness, however, has no wish to be smothered with this sort of pity. For just to the extent that it is merely the nugatory aspect, the negative of misfortune which is asserted, a real depreciation of misfortune is implied. True sympathy, on the contrary, is an accordant feeling with the ethical claim at the same time associated with the sufferer—that is, with what is necessarily implied in his condition as affirmative and substantive.[36]

True tragic pity, in Hegel's view, is a synthesis of our compassion for the hero as an individual with our awareness of the universal, morally justified principle that hero has embraced. The greatest Greek tragedies, Hegel proposes, show us the clash of two such heroes, the irreconcilable conflict of two such universal rights. Even in tragedies with a single hero we can see the justice of Hegel's observation: we sympathize not only with the hero and what he stands for but also, paradoxically, with the force that destroys him.

Such a tension between responses, such a double perspective, is utterly beyond the vision and feeling of Nowell, Neville, Gager, and their audiences. Their view of the protagonist is starkly simple. He must be one of two things: either the culpable choice-maker of morality-play tradition or the virtuous innocent victim of saints'-play tradition. This impulse to clear away ethical complexities is apparent in the diametrically opposite ways Nowell and Gager view Seneca's Hippolytus. Looking to the saints'-play tradition, Nowell presents him as a Joseph figure, a martyr to humanist ideals; looking to the morality-play tradition, Gager casts him as a Mankind figure who chooses wrongly. In Neville's hands Seneca's Oedipus likewise becomes a guilt-ridden tyrant.

36. Friedrich Hegel, *The Philosophy of Fine Art* (collected and published posthumously, 1835), trans. F.P.B. Osmaston (1920), excerpts rptd. in Robert W. Corrigan, ed., *Tragedy: Vision and Form* (San Francisco, 1965), p. 431.

Sulpicius, Nowell, Neville, and Gager may seem an unlikely group to act the country cousin, but they clearly are thinking of Hegel's "ordinary sensibility" whenever they speak of "pity." For figures like Neville's Oedipus or Gager's Hippolytus there can be no "accordant feeling with the ethical claim at the same time associated with the sufferer" for one simple reason: such figures *have* no ethical claim. Martyr or malefactor? The humanist impulse to pass moral judgment on the tragic protagonist makes for an emotional response to tragic drama that is intense enough but far simpler than critics after Hegel have described. For a less certain perspective on the tragic hero, and for the complicated emotions that perspective inspires, we must look to English playwrights who saw in their protagonists not an educational program, but men.

The Logic of Elizabethan Stage Violence: Some Alarms and Excursions for Modern Critics, Editors, and Directors

ALAN C. DESSEN

E LIZABETHAN DRAMATIC TEXTS supply many violent moments—duels, armed combats of many varieties, pitched battles, murders, even maimings. But evidence about the original staging of such violence is usually very limited, with little more textual support than directions like *"They fight"* or *"Kills him"* or *"Alarm."* Nonetheless, scholars have agreed on how duels and other violent scenes would have been staged at the Globe or Fortune or Rose. Particular emphasis has been placed upon the knowledgeability of the Elizabethan audience, for, it is often argued, the dramatists could introduce duels "with the confidence that they would be enacted by master fencers during a period when tournaments and barriers were still being held, when professional swordsmen were frequently mutilated and occasionally killed in their public matches, and when the gallants who sat on the stage spent a goodly portion of their time having the buttons of their doublets hit by the famous Rocco Bonetti or learning the new tactics of the equally famous Saviolo." [1] Theater historians thereby assume great skill on the part of the actors and verisimilitude

---

1. Thornton S. Graves, "The Stage Sword and Dagger," *SAQ*, XX (1921), 206.

in the presentation "in order to make the fencing scenes in their plays realistic enough to satisfy a critical audience well versed in the use of swords."[2]

To support such claims scholars offer some suggestive bits of evidence. For a sense of "realism" in stage combat they point to John Bereblock's description of the fight between Palemon and Arcite in a play performed before Queen Elizabeth at Oxford in 1566: "at the third onset, when not only the movements of their bodies and the parrying of their swords, but even their wounds and blood are visible to everybody, Palemon sinks to the ground and lies prostrate before his victorious cousin."[3] Often noted is the fact that the author of *The Rich Cabinet* (1616) includes "skill of weapon" among the "many excellent qualities" of the player.[4] To convey a sense of the efficacy of the stage duel the historian can cite Thomas Palmer's verses prefaced to the 1647 Folio of Beaumont and Fletcher's works:

> How didst thou sway the theatre! make us feel
> The players' wounds were true, and their swords, steel!
> Nay, stranger yet, how often did I know
> When the spectators ran to save the blow?
>
> (F 2 verso)

In his analysis of Benvolio's account of Mercutio's fight with Tybalt, Horace S. Craig calls attention to Shakespeare's expertise in swordplay: "the description is plainly that of a rapier-and-dagger fight; the left hand, holding the dagger or wearing a mailed gauntlet, parries the attack and the right hand thrusts with the rapier."[5] Nor is the evidence limited to

---

2. Robert E. Morsberger, *Swordplay and the Elizabethan and Jacobean Stage*, Salzburg Studies in English Literature (Salzburg, 1974), p. 5.

3. W. Y. Durand, "*Palaemon and Arcyte, Progne, Marcus Geminus* and the Theatre in Which They Were Acted, as Described by John Bereblock (1566)," *PMLA*, XX (1905), 511. Since Bereblock has his eye upon Livy as well as the staged event (he is imitating a passage from Bk. I, chap. 25), one may question the value of this description as an eyewitness account.

4. W. C. Hazlitt, ed., *The English Drama and Stage Under the Tudor and Stuart Princes 1543–1664* (London, 1869), p. 230.

5. "Dueling Scenes and Terms in Shakespeare's Plays," *University of California Publications in English*, IX (1940), 14. Citations from Shakespeare are from G. Blakemore Evans, ed., *The Riverside Shakespeare* (Boston, 1974).

stage combat, for, outside the theater, scholars can point to tournaments, barriers, and other public displays of martial skills, especially before royal audiences. Edward VI himself provides an account of an elaborate naval show at Deptford in 1550 which involved a fortress on a boat in the Thames, various galleys and pinnaces, and a series of assaults and coun-terassaults.[6] Less spectacular but still quite elaborate was the Hock-Tuesday play performed for the queen at Kenilworth in 1575 by the men of Coventry, a re-enactment of the victory of the English under Ethelred over the Danes.[7]

Still, evidence about the effects possible on the Elizabethan stage is quite limited. The shows put on for Edward and Elizabeth were one-occasion affairs, intended for a special audience, with relatively few lim-itations upon time, space, personnel, special effects, and expense. In contrast, a performance at the Globe would have meant a bare platform stage (where every property had to be carried on and off), a limited number of players, and a repertory system which involved five or six plays per week and presumably little rehearsal time. Such limitations did not preclude the staging of duels and battles (as witnessed by a play like *1 Henry VI*), events that clearly appealed to contemporary audiences. Thus, the Prologue to *The Two Merry Milkmaids* (1619) asks the viewer to forgo his usual pleasures ("To expect no noyse of Guns, Trumpets, nor Drum, / Nor Sword and Targuet") but to appreciate a "reform'd" stage "free / From the lowd Clamors it was wont to bee, / Turmoyl'd with Battailes."[8] Similarly, James Shirley, in his Prologue to *The Doubtful Heir* (1638), a play intended for the Blackfriars but presented at the Globe, tells his "grave understanders" that "what you most delight in" will not be found in his play, for "here's no target-fighting / Upon the stage, all work for cutlers barr'd."[9] But the representation of armies and battles on the

6. John Gough Nichols, ed., *Literary Remains of King Edward the Sixth* (London, 1857), II, 279.

7. F. J. Furnivall, ed., *Robert Laneham's Letter: Describing a Part of the Entertainment Unto Queen Elizabeth at the Castle of Kenilworth in 1575*, New Shakespere Society, Series 6, #14 (London and New York, 1907), pp. 26–27, 31–32.

8. Ed. John S. Farmer, Tudor Facsimile Texts (1914), A 4ᵛ. Dates attached to plays are drawn from Alfred Harbage, *Annals of English Drama 975–1700*, rev. S. Schoenbaum (London, 1964).

9. William Gifford and Alexander Dyce, eds., *The Dramatic Works and Poems of James Shirley* (London, 1833), IV, 279.

Elizabethan stage posed various problems, a fact noted gleefully by critics of the popular drama. Thus, in well-known comments, Sir Philip Sidney mocked "two Armies . . . represented with foure swords and bucklers," [10] while Ben Jonson sneered at "th'ill customs of the age" which included players who "with three rusty swords, / And help of some few foot and half-foot words, / Fight over York and Lancaster's long jars, / And in the tiring-house bring wounds to scars." [11]

Shakespeare, too, recognized the problems in presenting stage battles. Before Act IV of *Henry V* the Chorus laments:

> And so our scene must to the battle fly;
> Where—O for pity!—we shall much disgrace
> With four or five most vile and ragged foils
> (Right ill dispos'd, in brawl ridiculous)
> The name of Agincourt. Yet sit and see,
> Minding true things by what their mock'ries be.
>
> (ll. 48–53)

As Alfred Harbage points out, this modest disclaimer should not be taken too literally, for the Lord Chamberlain's Men "would have available a score of quite good foils, and actors who knew how to use them." Still, the danger of the "brawl ridiculous" must be considered in any attempt to bring armies and elaborate combat onto Shakespeare's stage. The Elizabethan solution was quite practical. In Harbage's terms: "The audience did not see the battles so much as hear them. What it saw was displays of skill by two or occasionally four combatants on that small sector of the battlefield symbolized by the stage." In addition, the players made adept use of *Alarms* or offstage sound effects ("a gong insistently clanging, trumpets blaring recognizable military signals, then steel clashing, ordnance firing") and *Excursions* ("individual pursuits and combats onstage"). [12] Consider a stage direction from *The Famous History of Captain Thomas Stukeley*: "Alarum is sounded, diuers excurtions, Stukly persues, shane Oneale, and Neale Mackener, And after a good pretty fight his Lieftenannt and Auntient rescue Stuklie, and chace the Ireshe out. Then

---

10. "An Apologie for Poetrie," *Elizabethan Critical Essays*, ed. G. Gregory Smith (Oxford, 1904), I, 197.

11. *Every Man in His Humour*, ed. J. W. Lever, Regents Renaissance Drama edition, (Lincoln, Nebr., 1971), p. 5.

12. *Theatre for Shakespeare* (Toronto, 1955), pp. 51–53.

an excurtion berwixt Herbert and O Hanlon, and so a retreat sounded." [13] Through such theatrical synecdoche, the whole of a battle is to be inferred through the parts displayed—an approach to mass combat well suited to a large platform stage and limited personnel.

Such a selective approach to stage violence need not be limited solely to battle scenes. For example, note how Thomas Heywood chose to dramatize the death of Nessus the centaur in Act I of *The Brazen Age*. Hercules, alone on stage, describes for the audience Nessus's progress across the river with Dejanira on his back ("Well plunged bold Centaure . . . .") but then must rage impotently as he witnesses the attempted rape and hears his bride cry for help (four times). Finally, Hercules announces: "I'le send till I can come, this poisonous shaft / Shall speake my fury and extract thy bloud, / Till I my selfe can crosse this raging floud." The stage direction then reads: *"Hercules shoots, and goes in: Enter Nessus with an arrow through him, and Deianeira."* Moments later, "after long strugling with *Euenus* streames," Hercules reappears "to make an end of what my shaft begunne." [14] To depict on the Elizabethan stage a figure on one side of a river shooting a figure on the other side, Heywood has resorted to alternating scenes, reported action, offstage sounds, and, most important, the presentation of the initiation and the resolution of the central event (*"Hercules shoots . . . Enter Nessus with an arrow through him"*) rather than the full sequence (the flight of the arrow and the striking of its target). Again, in the terms of Shakespeare's spokesman in *Henry V*, the audience is being asked to use its "imaginary forces" to "piece out our imperfections with your thoughts" (Prologue) or "eche out our perform-ance with your mind" (Chorus to Act III).

Since most Elizabethan dramatists were less venturesome than Heywood (the playwright least restrained by the limits of his stage), [15] fight scenes of various kinds normally follow (or appear to follow) more

13. Ed. Judith C. Levinson and G. R. Proudfoot for the Malone Society (Oxford, 1975), ll. 1170–1175.

14. *The Dramatic Works of Thomas Heywood* (London, 1874), III, 178–182.

15. For examples of Heywood's staging of difficult scenes, see the combats in Hell at the end of *The Silver Age*, the fight between Hercules and Achelous in *The Brazen Age*, the battle between Hector and Ajax in *1 The Iron Age*, the Trojan horse sequence in *2 The Iron Age*, the sea battle in *Fortune by Land and Sea*, and Horatius at the bridge in *The Rape of Lucrece*.

conventional lines. Consequently, scholars usually call attention to two basic forms of Elizabethan stage violence: the "realistic" duel or combat (Tybalt versus Mercutio), presented before a knowledgeable audience in a manner resembling as much as possible an equivalent duel outside the theater; and the "realistic" but selective stage battle, created by "four or five most vile and ragged foils," alarms, and excursions. Neither type of theatrical combat places an inordinate strain upon the tastes or assumptions of a modern viewer, while both are suited to the facilities and personnel available to the original production. Even the shooting of Nessus shows Heywood selecting those parts of an event that can be presented as "believable" in an Elizabethan theater.

But the important question remains: need we stop here? Is "realism" or "verisimilitude" or "truth to life" the only yardstick to be applied to Elizabethan stage combats? After all, the battles performed for royal audiences were not limited to naval combats at Deptford or armed encounters at Kenilworth. Thus, in 1581 the queen and the French ambassadors watched an assault upon a fortress by a group of attackers supported by cannons mounted upon a rolling platform. But the fortress was the Fortress of Perfect Beauty, while the attackers were led by the Four Foster Children of Desire (one of whom was Sir Philip Sidney). Most revealing, after the long speeches and compliments to the queen, "the two canons were shot off, the one with sweet powder, and the other with sweet water, verie odoriferous and pleasant, and the noise of the shooting was verie excellent consent of melodie within the Mount. And after that was store of pretie scaling-ladders, and the footmen threw floures and such fansies against the wals, with all such devises as might seeme fit shot for Desire."[16] Clearly, the deployment of this battle flowed not from the logic of the battlefield but from the logic of what constitutes "fit shot for Desire." To the modern eye the example may appear quaint, but the principle— the presence of an alternative kind of logic for scenes of violence—could be fundamental.

Such an alternative logic was readily available in the English dramatic tradition, especially in the morality plays. An excellent example can be found in one of the earliest extant English plays, *The Castle of Perse-*

16. John Nichols, ed., *The Progresses and Public Processions of Queen Elizabeth* (London, 1823), II, 319.

verance,[17] when Superbia, Invidia, and Ira storm the castle only to be
beaten back by Meekness, Charity, and Patience. The only stage direction
(*Tunc pugnabunt diu*) is unrevealing; as Richard Southern points out, "the
Sins are armed with slings, lances, shot and bows . . . , and the Virtues,
it seems, pelt them with the symbolic roses."[18] After his defeat, each Sin
complains for a stanza about how he was "al betyn blak and blo" (l. 2219)
or gained a broken head (l. 2211) or was undone, all because of the "fayre
rosys" or "flourys swete" or "a rose pat on rode was rent" (ll. 2211, 2213,
2220). The Sins have raged and threatened with conventional weapons but
have been bested by the qualities of their opposing Virtues epitomized by
the roses associated with the Passion. But the crucial theatrical question,
so easily missed or misconstrued (as in Southern's use of "pelt"), is: how
are the roses to be delivered in this stage combat? Although verisimilitude
obviously has little relevance to this allegorical play, our habits of thought
automatically translate a rose as a weapon into a projectile; we readily
assume that the Virtues *hurl* the flowers at the Sins, thinking either of the
thorns (never mentioned in the dialogue) or the force of the throw (so that
Meekness, Charity, and Patience become fast-balling baseball pitchers).
But, quite the contrary, the beauty and spiritual meaning of the scene
may lie in the *contrast* between the raging Sins and the calm Virtues who
respond to violence and insults by delicately dropping roses (or rose petals)
or perhaps by throwing the flowers heavenward to have them descend
upon their enemies. Consider the theatrical effect if the colorful flowers
float down gently yet wreak havoc upon the assaulters. The illogic in our
"realistic" terms would then create the logic or force of the scene—the
power and the beauty of man's spiritual or virtuous nature.

Although lacking the pageantry and scope of *The Castle of Perseverance*,
moralities from Queen Elizabeth's reign also provide evidence for an allegorical or symbolic logic behind stage violence. In most of these plays
the most notable figure is the Vice who carries a memorable prop, a
dagger of lath, which he uses to belabor freely his vice-lieutenants and his
victims. This dagger play can thereby serve both as a source of laughter
and "good theater" and as part of a larger pattern in which the comic
violence of the Vice (or some other figure) is answered by an alternative

17. Text used is Mark Eccles, ed., *The Macro Plays*, EETS #262 (Oxford, 1969).
18. *The Medieval Theatre in the Round* (London, 1957), p. 198.

spiritual force wielding a sword. In Ulpian Fulwell's *Like Will to Like* (1568) the Vice (Nichol Newfangle) with his wooden dagger is contrasted to Severity, a figure of justice who carries a sword as his major prop. In W. Wager's *Enough is as Good as a Feast* (1560)[19] the Vice (Covetous) also uses a great deal of verbal and physical intimidation; one stage direction tells us: *"He fighteth with them both with his dagger"* (l. 440). Near the end of the play Worldly Man, who has been corrupted by the Vice and has consistently misused his worldly possessions, ignores the warning of the prophet and goes to sleep onstage. At this point, *"Enter* God's Plague *and stand behind him awhile before he speak"* (l. 1222 s.d.); the long speech concludes:

> I am the plague of God properly called
> Which cometh on the wicked suddenly;
> I go through all towns and cities strongly walled,
> Striking to death, and that without all mercy.
> Here thou wicked, covetous person I do strike . . .
>
> (ll. 1243–1247)

Worldly Man later describes his dream: "And methought before me the Plague of God did stand / Ready to strike me with a sword in his hand" (ll. 1301–1302). The bulk of this play has been concerned with the power of the Vice in this world, a power often represented by his dagger, but the final movement displays the justice awaiting worldly men in the next world, a justice represented by the sword of God's Plague.

Interplay between true and false weapons need not be limited to the Vice's dagger of lath. Thus, in Wager's *The Longer Thou Livest the More Fool Thou Art* (1559) Moros's foolishness is continually displayed by his inept use of the sword and dagger given him by Wrath. The foolish protagonist announces that "to be fighting now is all my desire" (l. 837), makes impossible claims about what he will do to his virtuous advisers, fights alone until out of breath, but then collapses when Discipline re-enters (*"Let* Moros *let fall his sword and hide him"*—l. 948 s.d.). In a later scene first his dagger (l. 1629) and then his sword (l. 1653) are stuck and cannot be pulled forth. In the final stage of his career, Moros enters *"furiously with a grey beard"* (l. 1742 s.d.) and again fights alone on stage (l. 1752 s.d.), at

---

19. Text used for *Enough* and *The Longer Thou Livest* is the Regents Renaissance Drama edition, ed. R. Mark Benbow (Lincoln, Nebr., 1967).

which point the dramatist brings on God's Judgment *"with a terrible visure"* (l. 1758 s.d.) and with a sword. Moros calls upon his followers to "bring your clubs, bills, bows and staves" to support him (l. 1773), but God's Judgment underscores the efficacy of the higher power he represents:

> I represent God's severe judgment,
> Which dallieth not where to strike he doth purpose.
> Hither am I sent to the punishment
> Of this impious fool, here called Moros
> Who hath said there is no God in his heart. . . .
> For as much as vengeance to God doth belong
> And he will the same recompense,
> That he is a God of power, mighty and strong,
> The fools shall know by experience.
> With this sword of vengeance I strike thee.
>   *Strike* Moros *and let him fall down*
>   (ll. 1763–1767; 1787–1791)

Here at the climax of the play a false or limited weapon, which (like the Vice's dagger of lath) has hitherto been a source of laughter, is juxtaposed with a truly potent weapon wielded by a figure who represents a higher power ignored by the foolish protagonist. The various references to the dangers of sharp "edge-tools" in the hands of a fool or madman (ll. 842–845; 1947–1950) further develop this distinction between weapons that are abused and that higher "sword of vengeance" that awaits erring humanity.

The most interesting use of the dagger and sword is to be found in George Wapull's *The Tide Tarrieth No Man* (1576).[20] Throughout the play Courage, the Vice, indulges in the usual threats and physical action; at one point Wapull directs: *"Out quickly with his dagger"* (l. 200 s.d.). In contrast to Courage's ascendancy during the first two-thirds of this morality is the plight of Christianity, who should be exhibiting the well-known Pauline armor but instead is "deformed" in appearance: *"Christianity must enter with a sword, with a title of pollicy, but on the other syde of the tytle, must be written gods word, also a Shield, wheron must be written riches, but on the other syde of the Shield must be Fayth"* (l. 1439 s.d.). Although moments later Faithful Few turns the titles so that Faith and God's Word take their

20. Ed. Ernst Ruhl, *SJ*, XLIII (1907), 1–52.

proper place, Christianity is soon forced to resume the burden of Riches and Policy owing to the continued depravity of Greediness and the Vice. The restoration of the true sword and shield must wait until the final scene. Again Faithful Few is onstage, this time with Authority, who bears "this sword of Gods power" (l. 1837). When Correction tries to arrest the Vice, Courage *"draweth his dagger and fyghteth"* (l. 1821 s.d.), once more attempting to assert his power. But the Vice's dagger, which earlier had dominated the action, now fails, physically and allegorically, when juxtaposed with the sword of God's authority and the correction that accompanies it. With Courage offstage and under arrest, Christianity's sword and shield can be restored to their pristine state in the final action of the play.

The morality dramatists could thereby use two sets of weapons—one of which is associated with the temporary, worldly power of the Vice, the other with the higher powers invoked at the end of the action—to call attention to the two phases of their plays. Scenes involving the dagger of lath or Moros's sword can be meaningful and amusing in their own right yet still function as a part of a larger pattern basic to the play as a whole. To cite another example, the author of *The Trial of Treasure* (1567)[21] provides three scenes that span the play wherein: the hero, Just, "bridles" the Vice, Inclination; the other protagonist, Lust, unbridles the Vice who subsequently leads Lust to his destruction; and, in the final scene, Just rebridles Inclination to win Lady Trust. The dramatist leaves us in no doubt about the point of this sequence: "Thus should every man, that will be called Just, / Bridle and subdue his beastly inclination, / That he in the end may obtain perfect trust, / The messenger of God to give sight to salvation" (p. 279). Again, individual moments take on added meaning as part of a larger pattern, here quite obvious.

Far less obvious is how such scenes would have been staged. Although the reader can visualize with little difficulty the Vice's use of his dagger, how would God's Plague or God's Justice deliver a blow against a foolish sinner? With a savage chop? a graceful, sweeping movement? or, in contrast to the Vice's comic energy, a mere touch with the sword? The only external evidence I can offer comes from an account of a lost play, *The Cradle of Security*, where R. Willis describes the arrival of "two old men"

21. W. Carew Hazlitt, ed., *A Select Collection of Old English Plays Originally Published by Robert Dodsley in the Year 1744*, 4th ed. (London, 1874–1876), III, 257–301.

representing "the end of the world, and the last judgement" who bear a sword and a mace: "the foremost old man with his Mace stroke a fearfull blow upon the Cradle; whereat all the Courtiers with the three Ladies and the vizard all vanished; and the desolate Prince starting up bare faced, and finding himselfe thus sent for to judgement, made a lamentable complaint of his miserable case . . . " However delivered, this "fearfull blow" had an enormous impact upon at least one viewer, for Willis, some sixty or seventy years later, states: "This sight tooke such impression in me, that when I came towards mans estate, it was as fresh in my memory, as if I had seen it newly acted." [22] But neither this account nor various stage directions nor information from dumb shows in plays like *Gorboduc* and *Jocasta* can confirm how verisimilar or how stylized would have been the original staging.

Consideration of some of the stage violence in plays before the age of Shakespeare therefore leaves us with questions rather than answers. Of what value, then, are such moments from relatively obscure plays to the critic or director not particularly interested in theatrical history? After all, the plays of Shakespeare contain no cannons firing sweet powder and sweet water, no Virtues dropping roses upon Sins, no figures of heavenly judgment wielding irresistible swords or maces. I certainly am not arguing for an allegorical dimension for every stage duel in the age of Shakespeare, nor am I challenging all the conclusions of modern scholars. But I *am* questioning the modern tendency to discuss such scenes solely in terms of "realism." When the overt allegory of the morality play became less fashionable, can we safely assume that the stagecraft and symbolic potential in such moments disappeared as well? Can we be confident that a blow in a nonallegorical Elizabethan play would be delivered with the speed, force, and timing of a similar blow in the street outside the theater? Need a moment of stage violence at the Globe exist as an end in itself, adhering to a logic derived from an equivalent moment in "real life," or could it be linked to a symbolic or patterned logic relevant to the world of the play? Although examples from the morality plays cannot "prove" anything about scenes from *Romeo and Juliet, King Lear*, and *Cymbeline*, this evidence should at least make us cautious about what we take for granted in the later, better plays.

22. *Mount Tabor, or Private Exercises of a Penitent Sinner* (London, 1639), pp. 111–113.

To provide even tentative answers to such questions requires an investigation of a variety of scenes from the age of Shakespeare. First, let me return to the plays of Heywood, a dramatist often praised for his "realism." In Part I of *If You Know Not Me You Know Nobody* (1604),[23] Princess Elizabeth, afraid for her life, falls asleep on stage. Heywood then provides a dumb show: "Enter *Winchester, Constable, Barwick*, and *Fryars*: at the other dore 2. *Angels*: the *Fryar* steps to her, offering to kill her: the *Angels* driues them back. *Exeunt*. The *Angel* opens the Bible, and puts it in her hand as she sleepes, *Exeunt Angels, she wakes*" (ll. 1049–1053). The book, it turns out, is open to the passage: "*Whoso putteth his trust in the Lord, / Shall not be confounded*" (ll. 1064–1065). The scene surely needs no explication. Note, however, the interesting parallel to a scene in Heywood's best-known play, *A Woman Killed With Kindness* (1603),[24] a tragedy that lacks angels and dumb shows. After Frankford has discovered his wife in bed with Wendoll, Heywood directs the seducer to run "*over the stage in a night gown*" with the husband "*after him with his sword drawn; the Maid in her smock stays his hand and clasps hold on him. He pauses awhile*" (xiii.67.s.d.). After the pause, Frankford states: "I thank thee, maid; thou like the angel's hand / Hast stay'd me from a bloody sacrifice" (ll. 68–69). This supernumerary maid has no assigned place in Frankford's fictional household (unlike the other servants who *are* developed as "characters"). Rather, Heywood is again using a moment of threatened but prevented violence, this time with no obvious supernatural force, to call attention to the role of Heaven or mercy/reason in a decision at the heart of his play. Surely, neither the angel nor the maid should wrestle vigorously with the would-be violent figure, but, as in *The Castle of Perseverance*, the full effect is linked to the contrasting style and spirit of the alternative force. Rather than being a liability, this lack of "realism" creates a special emphasis, a theatrical *italics*, that singles out such a moment for the viewer.

For another heavenly intervention consider the climax of *The Atheist's Tragedy* (1609)[25] where the villain, D'Amville, whose schemes have brought Charlemont and Castabella to the brink of public execution, chooses to take upon himself the role of headsman. Tourneur's stage direction reads: "*As he raises up the axe strikes out his own brains, staggers off*

23. Ed. Madeleine Doran for the Malone Society (Oxford, 1935).
24. Ed. R. W. Van Fossen, Revels Plays editions (London, 1961).
25. Ed. Irving Ribner, Revels Plays editions (Cambridge, Mass., 1964).

the scaffold" (V.ii.241.s.d.). The speeches that follow leave no doubt about the significance of the violent event just witnessed. Thus, the atheist D'Amville can observe: "There is a power / Above her [Nature] that hath overthrown the pride / Of all my projects and posterity" and "yond' power that struck me knew / The judgment I deserv'd, and gave it" (ll. 258–260, 265–266). A judge then comments about "the power of that eternal providence / Which overthrew his projects in their pride," and Charlemont replies: "Only to Heav'n I attribute the work" (ll. 271–275). Obviously, this scene defies any expectations linked to "realism"; after all, how is a modern actor in the tradition of Ibsen and Stanislavski to play a character who "strikes out his own brains" and then lives on for almost thirty lines, delivering two major speeches? But as in Heywood (or *The Castle of Perseverance*) the absence of "realism" can be an asset rather than a liability. Indeed, the startling misdirection of the blow which unexpectedly brings justice to the apparently successful villain is the key to the final effect of this tragedy, a striking rebuttal to the claims and assumptions of this atheist who has relied solely upon his reason or "brains." A less spectacular conclusion might be more "believable" to us but would drastically change the play, for Tourneur, like Heywood, has used theatrical italics to underscore the presence of a power above nature and beyond human reasoning.[26]

Less obvious to the reader but equivalent in effect are several scenes from Shakespeare's *1 Henry VI*. The links between Joan of Arc and the forces of Hell are spelled out late in the play when the fiends forsake her, ignoring her pleas for help against the English forces (V.iii), but earlier scenes could also provide a sense of the larger powers behind Joan's achievements. Particularly revealing is the confrontation between Joan and Talbot, the symbol of English chivalry. Thus, at the beginning of I.v. Talbot pursues the Dauphin across the stage, but Joan then enters, driving the English soldiers in front of her. The scene proceeds as follows:

TALBOT
Where is my strength, my valor, and my force?
Our English troops retire, I cannot stay them;
A woman clad in armor chaseth them.
Enter Pucelle.

26. Such scenes are regularly to be found in plays that depict conversions to Christianity or martyrdom (e.g., *A Shoemaker a Gentleman*, *The Two Noble Ladies*).

Here, here she comes. I'll have a bout with thee;
Devil or devil's dam, I'll conjure thee.
Blood will I draw on thee—thou art a witch—
And straightway give thy soul to him thou serv'st.

PUCELLE

Come, come, 'tis only I that must disgrace thee.
    Here they fight.

TALBOT

Heavens, can you suffer hell so to prevail?
My breast I'll burst with straining of my courage,
And from my shoulders crack my arms asunder,
But I will chastise this high-minded strumpet.
    They fight again.

PUCELLE

Talbot, farewell, thy hour is not yet come.
I must go victual Orleance forthwith.
    A short alarum: then enter the town with soldiers.
O'ertake me if thou canst, I scorn thy strength.

                                            (I.v.1–15)

Alone on stage, confused, ashamed, Talbot tells us: "My thoughts are
whirled like a potter's wheel, / I know not where I am, nor what I do. / A
witch by fear, not force, like Hannibal, / Drives back our troops and
conquers as she lists" (ll. 19–22).

This confrontation posed severe problems for director Will Huddleston
and actor Eric Miller in the Ashland, Oregon, production of 1975. How
does one choreograph a stage fight before a modern audience between a
chivalric superhero and a slip of a girl (with actress Randi Douglas scarcely
able to wield the large sword assigned her, thereby increasing the danger
of injury)? Without question, the point of the scene lies in the surprising
failure of the strength, valor, and force of the formidable hero and the
equally surprising success of his apparently inferior opponent (who actually has larger powers behind her and can therefore scorn his strength).
Such surprise or illogic is necessary for the scene to work. In the Ashland
production, Joan made a few magical signs in the air before the combat;
Miller, as Talbot, then fought at half speed, moving as if wading in
molasses. Although I can offer no historical evidence, I would prefer to

have Pucelle, a slight figure in armor who does not resemble a soldier in stature or expertise, wield a sword that need only touch her opponent or his weapon to achieve potent results. For me, such a strident violation of our sense of "realism" would make far better theatrical sense of Talbot's failure and Joan's unexpected strength than would a Pucelle who could match Talbot move for move in battlefield tactics. The logic of both this scene and the play as a whole could be heightened if a mere touch from Joan's sword would have the effect of a sledge-hammer blow.

Such a solution runs counter to the working assumptions of most critics, editors, and directors. Thus, in his useful, practical study, Arthur Wise argues that "the purpose of an authentic weapon is to kill" but "the purpose of a theatrical weapon is to *appear* to do so." For the last scene of *Hamlet* Wise would use a theatrical rather than an authentic weapon to deal the various death-inducing wounds: "It is stretching the imagination of both audience and actor too far to expect them to believe that this can be done. It is not in the nature of that featherweight practice weapon, the modern fencing foil, to inflict two such wounds. An audience—and an actor—must be shown a weapon which, within the theatrical terms of reference, can be believed capable of performing what it is supposed to perform."[27] No roses here.

But can Wise's arguments and assumptions account for the many weapons and combats found in Elizabethan plays? Consider two scenes in which a worthy English yeoman, armed only with a cudgel or staff, defeats two or three supposedly superior opponents armed with swords. First, in the final scene of *The Blind Beggar of Bednal Green* (1600) the good and evil figures choose their weapons for a trial by combat before the king. All the figures choose swords of different varieties except for Tom Strowd, the folk hero of the play (given special billing on the title page), who rejects such "bars of Iron" and chooses instead "an ashen Gibbet" or "a good Cudgell" to fight the two figures who have abused him throughout the play. Tom then defeats his two tormentors and is singled out by the king as "a lusty fellow" ("we have too few such Subjects in our Land").[28] Similarly, the hero of *George a Greene* (1590)[29] traps the three traitors (the

27. *Weapons in the Theatre* (New York, 1968), pp. 18–19.

28. Ed. John S. Farmer, Tudor Facsimile Texts (1914), I 4ᵛ–K 1ʳ. The title page advertises "the merry humor of *Tom Strowd* the *Norfolk* Yeoman."

29. Ed. F. W. Clarke and W. W. Greg for the Malone Society (Oxford, 1911).

Earl of Kendall, Lord Bonfield, and Sir Gilbert Armstrong) by posing as a
fortuneteller, and, after calling for his staff, challenges all three to combat: *"Here they fight, George kils sir Gilbert, and takes the other two prisoners"*
(ll. 741–742). The vanquished figures announce that they would rather
bide the king's doom "then here be murthered by a seruile grome" (l. 747).
A neutral spokesman provides the moralization: "Now, my Lord of
Kendal, where be al your threats? / Euen as the cause, so is the combat
fallen, / Else one could neuer have conquerd three" (ll. 753–755).
George's victory against the odds thereby becomes both a comment upon
the justice of his cause and a display of native English prowess, as
suggested in part through the weapon used.[30] The cudgel or staff as used
by Tom Strowd or George a Greene can convey qualities or values that
supersede the logic advanced by Wise.[31]

Unfortunately, many scenes that might derive added meaning from the
use of a cudgel do not specify the weapon to be used. The best Shakespearean example is Edgar's fight with Oswald in *King Lear*. Oswald, who
sees the blind, helpless Gloucester only as "a proclaim'd prize," announces
that "the sword is out / That must destroy thee" (IV.vi.226, 229–230),
but Edgar, disguised as a peasant and using a stock stage accent, inter-
poses, taking Gloucester's arm (ll. 231–235). The only evidence about
Edgar's weapon is found in his threat: "Nay, come not near th' old man;
keep out, che vor' ye, or Ice try whither your costard or my ballow be the
harder" (ll. 239–242). Edgar has reasserted the bond with his father,

---

30. Similar associations are to be found in *The Shoemakers' Holiday*, where the shoemakers oppose their clubs or cudgels to the swords of Hammon's group; in *Locrine*, where the
old warrior Corineus bests Hubba and Segar, two giant Scythians, with his club; and in
Henry V, V.i, where Fluellen cudgels Pistol.

31. The apotheosis of this weapon is achieved in the exploits on- and especially offstage
of the celebrated Dick Pike. According to the *DNB*, the English adventurer Richard Pike
or Peake was captured at Cadiz in 1625 and later questioned by the Spanish. Given an
opportunity to display his prowess, he bested a Spanish champion with rapier and poniard.
"Thereupon, armed with a quarter-staff, which he described as his national weapon, he
gave battle to three Spaniards armed with rapiers and poniards. He killed one of his foes
and disarmed the other two." Honored and freed by the Spaniards, Pike returned to
England in 1626 and in July published his account of his victory (*Three to One*); his exploits
were soon brought on stage in *Dick of Devonshire*. Throughout both pamphlet and play, the
quarterstaff is referred to as "mine own countrey weapon" or "my old trusty friend." Pike's
exploits, we should remember, occurred over three decades after *George a Greene*, a chronol-
ogy that raises some interesting speculations about life imitating art.

summarized visually by the joined arms indicated in the text, and defeats a minor villain with a "ballow" or cudgel, a weapon not of the court but from the world of unaccommodated man. Perhaps we should also take a cue from Edgar's reference to Oswald's "costard" or head and his final threat—"Chill pick your teeth, zir" (l. 244), both of which may indicate a blow to the head as the culmination of this fight. Oswald is certainly not a D'Amville figure of intellect and false reasoning who sees the truth only when his brains are dashed out, but a blow to the head of a minor schemer, delivered with a simple yet powerful weapon by a figure just emerging from his Poor Tom role, could have larger ramifications for the world of *King Lear* where ultimately an Edgar can defeat an Edmund.[32]

Discussion need not be limited to combats in which cudgels are pitted against swords. Thus, as with Tom Strowd and George a Greene, victories against apparent odds can be theatrically spectacular and can display the justice of a cause. For example, in the climactic scene of *The Trial of Chivalry* (1601)[33] two of the heroes who epitomize the chivalric values of the play (Ferdinand and Pembroke) take on two armies, while the third hero (Philip) disposes of the arch villain (Roderick) in single combat: "*Alarum, they fight: enter to Pembrooke Nauar, Bowyer & Souldiers: to Ferdinand, Fraunce, Flaunders & Souldiers: they fight and keepe them backe: Rodricke would scape, still kept in the midst, and kild by Philip*" (I 3ʳ). One observer later states: "Behold these two, which thousands could not daunt" (I 4ᵛ). True chivalry has triumphed over villainy and misunderstanding, with both the triumph and the inherent value of such chivalric qualities italicized by the disparity in numbers. A more developed example is to be found in *Cymbeline* where four figures (Posthumus, Belarius, Guiderius, and Arviragus) stand off the Roman army and rally the faltering British forces to victory. Since Shakespeare devotes much of V.iii to a description of this battle, it is not clear how much was actually

---

32. For valuable contexts for this and other cudgel scenes, see A. L. Soens, "Cudgels and Rapiers: The Staging of the Edgar-Oswald Fight in Lear," *Shak S*, V (1969), 149–158. According to Soens, "Shakespeare makes Edgar into a popular champion by arming him with the plebeian cudgel, and pitting his English techniques against the aristocratic rapier and the Italian technique of Oswald" (p. 150). Soens also observes that Shakespeare's fights "are as much a part of his dramatic vocabulary as is his poetry, and we should no more disregard fencing technique than we should disregard blank verse" (p. 153).

33. Ed. John S. Farmer, Tudor Facsimile Texts (1912).

displayed on stage. The two stage directions from V.ii read: *"The battle continues, the Britains fly,* Cymbeline *is taken: then enter, to his rescue,* Belarius, Guiderius, *and* Arviragus,*"* and, three lines later: *"Enter* Posthumus *and seconds the Britains. They rescue Cymbeline and exeunt.*" The fleeing Britains, as represented by the lord of V.iii, undoubtedly seem to be well appointed, even soldierly, but the restoration and regeneration of Cymbeline's England require the virtues and qualities of the old man, the "two striplings," and the "fourth man, in a silly habit" (V.iii.19, 86) who, as later is said of Posthumus, "promis'd nought / But beggary and poor looks" but provided "precious deeds" (V.v.9–10). As in *The Trial of Chivalry,* the greater the disparity in numbers in this combat, the more emphatic the theatrical point and effect.

Also important for the combats cited so far is the element of surprise, especially when an apparently weaker or less impressive combatant performs in an unexpectedly forceful way. Earlier in *Cymbeline* Shakespeare had provided two such moments. Thinking Imogen dead at his command, Posthumus takes off his Italian weeds upon his return to England and dresses as "a Britain peasant" to let "men know / More valor in me than my habits show" and to display "The fashion: less without and more within" (V.i.24, 29–30, 33). Following the British army *"like a poor soldier,"* Posthumus *"vanquisheth and disarmeth Jachimo"* (V.ii.o.s.d.); the latter concludes that "the heaviness and guilt within my bosom / Takes off my manhood"; otherwise, how "could this carl, / A very drudge of nature's, have subdu'd me / In my profession?" (ll. 1–2, 4–6). Posthumus's weapon is not specified (although a cudgel would be appropriate); as with Edgar's defeat of Oswald, the triumph of a figure visually equated with peasantry or baseness over a more impressive-looking figure equated with cunning and the court is a prelude to some semblance of reordering in the kingdom. Earlier, in an even more obvious symbolic confrontation, the villainous Cloten, dressed resplendently in Posthumus's garments, had been defeated by a Guiderius scorned by Cloten as a "rustic mountaineer" (IV.ii.100). In a play that acts out the hollowness of a court epitomized by false assumptions about clothing and manners, the answers are provided by figures who show "less without and more within." In production, these stage combats underscore this major theme.

Of equal interest are scenes in which a figure's moral stature is called into question by his inability to defeat a supposedly inferior opponent (as with Jachimo's humiliating loss to the "poor soldier"). Thus, in *Philaster* (1609)[34] the hero, who has debased himself through his unjust suspicions of Arethusa and Bellario, has drawn his sword and wounded Arethusa (IV.v.85.s.d.) when interrupted by a "country fellow" who accuses the prince of being "a craven" for assaulting a woman (l. 86). The country fellow is armed with a sword, not a cudgel (he brags that "I made my father's old fox fly about his ears"—ll. 129–130); nonetheless, the contrast between the two combatants in bearing and costume should be striking. Philaster himself concludes: "I am hurt, / The gods take part against me, could this boor / Have held me thus else?" (ll. 102–104). Here an apparently unequal fight produces a surprising result that in turn serves as a clear comment upon the degradation of the hero. Philaster's false use of his sword against Arethusa (and later against the sleeping Bellario in IV.vi) suggests a corruption of manhood and moral stature that can then be spelled out in his failure to best an apparently inferior opponent.

A far more suggestive example of the impugning of a hero through stage combat is to be found in the last scene of *Othello*. Earlier in the tragedy, Othello had twice stifled real or threatened violence by his stature or mere presence (I.ii, II.iii), but in Act V he appears briefly to cheer on a murder in the dark and then departs to kill his innocent wife. After murdering Desdemona (with his hands, not a weapon), Othello is demonstrably no longer the man he once was. Near the end of the temptation sequence, the hero had bid farewell to "the plumed troops and the big wars," to "the neighing steed and the shrill trump, / The spirit-stirring drum, th' ear-piercing fife, / The royal banner, and all quality, / Pride, pomp, and circumstance of glorious war" and had concluded: "Farewell! Othello's occupation's gone" (III.iii.347–357). The effect of Iago's poison is then acted out in the ocular proof scene (IV.i), the brothel scene (IV.ii), and the hero's appearance in V.i. Lodovico, for one, calls attention to the change:

> Is this the noble Moor whom our full Senate
> Call all in all sufficient? Is this the nature
> Whom passion could not shake? whose solid virtue
> The shot of accident nor dart of chance
> Could neither graze nor pierce?
>
> (IV.i.264–268)

34. Ed. Andrew Gurr, Revels Plays editions (London, 1969).

To underscore this changed condition, Shakespeare then provides some striking stage business after the murder. In his soliloquy over the sleeping Desdemona the Moor had praised her "balmy breath, that dost almost persuade / Justice to break her sword" (V.ii.16–17); later, Emilia, cursing the murderer of her mistress, states: "I care not for thy sword, I'll make thee known, / Though I lost twenty lives" (ll. 165–166). After Emilia's revelations, Othello tries to use his sword against Iago (who has no difficulty fatally wounding his wife) only to lose that weapon to Montano ("take you this weapon / Which I have here recover'd from the Moor"— ll. 239–240); Othello concludes: "I am not valiant neither, / But every puny whipster gets my sword" (ll. 243–244). The guilt-ridden hero then finds "another weapon in this chamber" (l. 252) which he praises at length in a speech that compares his heroic past to his tainted present:

> Behold, I have a weapon;
> A better never did itself sustain
> Upon a soldier's thigh. I have seen the day
> That with this little arm, and this good sword,
> I have made my way through more impediments
> Than twenty times your stop. But (O vain boast!)
> Who can control his fate? 'tis not so now.
> Be not afraid though you do see me weapon'd;
> Here is my journey's end, here is my butt
> And very sea-mark of my utmost sail.
> Do you go back dismay'd? 'Tis a lost fear;
> Man but a rush against Othello's breast,
> And he retires.
>
> (ll. 259–271)

In a second assault upon Iago (which wounds but does not kill his nemesis), the Moor then loses this second weapon as well ("wrench his sword from him" says Lodovico—l. 288), and thereby must kill himself with a weapon snatched from someone else or, more likely, a knife secreted on his person (the weapon of an assassin, not a warrior). Since so much of importance is happening during this climactic scene, the reader can easily lose sight of the striking theatrical progression wherein Othello, who once might have triumphed over "more impediments / Than twenty times your stop," now twice loses his weapon to lesser men (including Montano, one of the figures controlled by the Moor in II.iii). In imagistic or symbolic terms, Othello at this point has lost his occupation, destroyed the better part of himself, the light within, the daily beauty in his life, thereby making his sword, formerly the expression of his stature and strength, subject to "every puny whipster." Like the weapons of Courage or Moros, Othello's swords fail him in a bad cause, while his startling weakness (like Philaster's) serves as a climactic display of his descent.[35]

I can offer no evidence for how an Elizabethan actor would have played the surprising failure of an Othello or Philaster (or Macbeth after the final revelation from Macduff) as combatant. The effect for the viewer need not be as extreme as the shower of roses in *The Castle of Perseverance* or D'Amville's self-inflicted death, but if the scenes are to achieve their full impact, the staging should heighten the surprise and apparent illogic rather than conceal it. Remember, both Philaster and Othello (like Talbot and Jachimo) verbally call attention to their weakness and disappointment, thereby underscoring the effect. Similarly, when a small group of figures holds off an entire army or when a less impressive figure bests opponents superior in costume and bearing, the full effect can only be realized by emphasizing rather than softening the shock or surprise. In his advice to the players, Hamlet argues that the antics of the clown should not over-shadow "some necessary question of the play" (III.ii.42–43). Any attempt to make moments based upon the logic of surprise compatible with our sense of "realism" may also bury necessary questions that would be heightened if the staging were guided by a different logic.

This logic of surprise, however, is only one alternative to our prevailing logic of "realism." Thus, as with the twin Heywood scenes or D'Amville's fate, violent moments also lend themselves readily to symbolic effects. Consider, for example, the blinding of Gloucester in *King Lear*. One critic has argued that this scene "is painfully realistic; its cruelty has all the immediate horror of everyday life. . . . By showing us directly this

---

35. Other Shakespearean passages provide glosses on such symbolic weakness. Thus, in *The Merry Wives of Windsor* Falstaff explains his acceptance of the fairies: "I was three or four times in the thought they were not fairies, and yet the guiltiness of my mind, the sudden surprise of my powers, drove the grossness of the foppery into a receiv'd belief, in despite of the teeth of all rhyme and reason, that they were fairies" (V.v.121–126). In *The Tempest*, Prospero easily disarms Ferdinand, describing the latter (inaccurately) as one "who mak'st a show but dar'st not strike, thy conscience / Is so possess'd with guilt" (I.ii.471–472). See also the speeches of Arbaces and Mardonius in Beaumont and Fletcher's *A King and No King*, ed. Robert K. Turner, Jr. (Lincoln, Nebr., 1963), III.iii.88–92, IV.ii.220–226.

scene of almost unbearable cruelty, Shakespeare is insisting that the evil at the heart of the play is real and unmetaphoric" with Regan and Cornwall acting out "the farthest limit of human depravity."[36] To act out on stage this depravity, most actors and directors resort instinctively to hands (or nails), seeking a direct physical extension of this human animality. But the text directs otherwise, at least for Gloucester's first eye; thus, Cornwall instructs his servants: "Fellows, hold the chair, / Upon these eyes of thine I'll set my foot" (III.vii.67–68). Since Shakespeare does not make clear how a foot is to put out an eye (through a spur? the tip of a boot?), the action implicit in this passage seems physically awkward and "unrealistic" to the modern actor. But if we use a different logic, the stage picture that follows from Shakespeare's signal can be particularly rich in significance. If Gloucester, bound to a chair, is lowered to the stage floor so that his head is under Cornwall's foot, the audience will then witness a powerful symbolic tableau that epitomizes not only injustice and oppression but, given the associations with the head (as in D'Amville's dashing out his brains), also acts out the failure of reason and "cause" to deal with the world of the storm. This visual image is linked to other moments in the play (e.g., Tom "throwing his head" in the previous scene or Lear beating upon his head in I.iv.271–272) and, as with the blindness/sight motif, can generate meanings and associations that inform the entire tragedy. If the logic of the blinding is understood as symbolic rather than physiological, the result again can be a kind of theatrical italics that transcends verisimilitude to yield a larger, richer effect.

To confront this scene is to face several traps awaiting the modern critic, editor, or director. Most obvious is the danger of misreading or ignoring the signals in the text ("upon these eyes of thine I'll set my foot"), thereby blurring the original poetic or visual language in favor of more convenient modern assumptions. Equally dangerous, especially when dealing with any rich Shakespearean play, is the isolation of one such moment from the flow of the entire play so that a scene is viewed as an end in itself rather than as a significant part of an informing pattern. Critics, actors, and directors rarely make such a mistake about problems of "character," because, as heirs of the novel and Ibsen, we have been con-

36. Maurice Charney, "The Persuasiveness of Violence in Elizabethan Plays," *RenD*, N.S. II (1969), 62–63.

ditioned to expect discrete speeches and actions, even of minor figures, to be "consistent" with a central psychological core that can be inferred and analyzed. But the director or fight master who designs stage combats for modern productions often is not particularly concerned with such consistency but rather views duels, battles, and violence in general as ends in themselves that adhere to no larger logic than that which generates the most suspense or titillation for an audience. Thus, in a production of *King Lear* at Stratford, Ontario in 1972, the blinding scene was drawn out interminably while Cornwall stripped down to a leather tunic and then chose his gouging tool from a large rack of gleaming instruments that had been wheeled onto the stage. In the Ashland, Oregon, production of 1976, both Edgar and Oswald in IV.vi suddenly became savvy streetfighters, employing tactics and expertise quite inconsistent with their "characters" as displayed elsewhere in the play. But, we should remember, even the "primitive" morality plays contain progressions of scenes that use the Vice's dagger and the sword of heavenly justice to establish a larger pattern. To treat any Elizabethan scene as a discrete, separable event is to flirt with the danger of missing a logic based upon patterned action that at times can supersede our sense of verisimilitude or psychological realism.

To explore such a patterned presentation of violence let me return to *King Lear*. Most critics and directors would agree that the final confrontation between Edmund and Edgar is an important part of the climax of this tragedy, but less obvious are the relevant moments that lead up to and prepare us for this climactic combat, especially the carefully orchestrated activities of four figures: Edgar, Edmund, Kent, and Oswald. Kent, already banished for his outspoken loyalty, has in disguise endeared himself again to Lear by tripping up Oswald in front of the king; meanwhile, Edmund's manipulative skills have been amply demonstrated, especially in II.i, where he uses a mock combat and a self-inflicted wound to set up the ocular proof necessary to have Edgar outlawed and disinherited. An important new sequence then begins with II.ii when Kent confronts Oswald not before a supportive Lear but in the domain of Cornwall and Regan. Despite a series of insults and threats, Kent is unable to get Oswald to draw his sword, and, by the end of the scene, only succeeds in getting himself stocked by Cornwall and Regan; the only physical combat, moreover, is between Kent and Edmund and takes place in front of the ranking figures. Thus, in response to Oswald's cries for help, the Quarto reads: *"Enter Edmund with his rapier drawne, Gloster the Duke and Dutchesse"*; while the Folio directs: *"Enter Bastard, Cornewall, Regan, Gloster, Seruants."* Both editions agree that Edmund enters with the larger group and therefore has his bout with Kent before an audience that includes his father, Regan, and Cornwall.

I belabor this point because the editors of several widely used modern texts (the Variorum, the New Arden, the New Cambridge, the Folger, and the Riverside) would have it otherwise. Here is the passage as printed in the Riverside edition:

OSWALD

Help ho! murther, murther!
Enter Bastard [Edmund, *with his rapier drawn*].

EDMUND

How now, what's the matter? Part!

KENT

With you, goodman boy, and you please!
Come, I'll flesh ye, come on, young master.
[*Enter*] Cornwall, Regan, Gloucester, Servants.

GLOUCESTER

Weapons? arms? What's the matter here?

CORNWALL

Keep peace, upon your lives!
He dies that strikes again. What is the matter?

(II.ii.43–49)

The note in the New Cambridge edition (p. 180) justifies this change by arguing that "Edmund would not take it upon himself to speak peremptorily to the brawlers if his seniors were present"; the logic of propriety or decorum is used to "improve" a moment in the text that makes the editors uncomfortable. To the modern eye, moreover, Edmund's role here may appear gratuitous, a piece of dramatic filler. After all, why should a bastard son, recently wounded, be the one to intervene against Kent, especially if, as the Folio indicates, Cornwall's servants are onstage? Perhaps most puzzling is the question of timing. If Edmund enters as part of a larger group, even if his rapier is already drawn, why does it take so long for Gloucester and especially Cornwall to react and stop the combat? To the modern editor or director, then, the scene makes far more literal and theatrical sense if the entrance of the larger group is delayed.

But such a change, based upon modern reasoning, can distort or bury the logic of the original text which may have been based upon quite different assumptions. By this point, Kent has been carefully defined for us, with his speeches during the remainder of this scene, especially his comments on the "holy cords," clarifying his values even further. In the world epitomized by the new rulers, Cornwall and Regan, this worthy representative of an older order is unable to defeat an Oswald who will not fight or an Edmund who will. If we accept the original stage directions, Kent's failure to defeat either or both of these opponents is acted out in front of the figures who represent the new regime; his subsequent placement in the stocks then becomes an apt comment upon the helplessness and vulnerability of the qualities he embodies in the present world of the play. Meanwhile, Edgar (whom we saw in the previous scene with a sword drawn unsuccessfully against Edmund) has also become an outcast deprived of his identity, a juxtaposition that should be quite clear when Edgar, taking on his Poor Tom disguise, delivers his soliloquy (II.iii) while Kent is (or should be) visible, asleep in the stocks. The modern director usually resorts to lighting to black out and thereby draw attention away from Kent during Edgar's speech, but in the original production at the Globe, by natural light on a bare stage, the parallel straits of the two figures would have been obvious and emphatic. Kent's bout with Edmund, then, serves as an important symbolic comment upon what is working and what is failing in the world of Act II and, as such, can only take on its full meaning when staged before an audience that includes Cornwall and Regan, regardless of any modern logic to the contrary.

The full implications of this moment, moreover, extend beyond the boundaries of Act II, especially when one recognizes the strong link forged in II.ii and II.iii between Kent and Edgar. Throughout the remainder of the tragedy Kent is a relatively helpless figure who can comfort his master but do little to reshape the world of the play. Rather, it is Edgar, after his descent to the Poor Tom level, who contributes most to whatever positive side is to be found in the resolution. A major part of that contribution comes when he defeats those same two figures Kent had fought but failed to best in II.ii. As noted earlier, the triumph of Edgar's ballow over Oswald's sword involves two scales of values as well as two weapons (and leads to the discovery of the letters that will help to undo Edmund). Then, in contrast to the abortive mock combat of II.i, Edgar's victory over his brother (who has been told by Albany to "trust to thy single virtue"—V.iii.103) does yield positive results, even though it does not save Cordelia. Like the bout between Kent and Edmund, moreover, this climactic fight takes place in front of the ranking figures in the play (Albany and Goneril rather than Cornwall and Regan), with the presence of Albany, which made the challenge possible in the first place, marking a significant change from Act II. The blocking of both combatants and onlookers should therefore echo the earlier scene; conversely, part of the logic behind the stage direction in II.ii that bothers some editors lies in the anticipation of this climactic moment. Kent's bouts with two opponents, followed closely by the juxtaposition of Kent in the stocks with Edgar in flight, should set in motion a larger pattern that can only be fulfilled when Edgar in the last two acts bests these same two figures and what they stand for. The logic of the earlier and the full meaning of the later scene cannot be understood in isolation but can only be fully appreciated as part of a larger design that supersedes social proprieties and stage realism.

For another example of the pitfalls in viewing scenes in isolation consider Marlowe's *Edward II*.[37] After the king and Gaveston have been reunited, the Bishop of Coventry, who had played a major role in exiling the favorite, comes on stage promising to incense Parliament again. Enraged, Edward directs Gaveston to "throw off his golden mitre, rend his stole, / And in the channel christen him anew," while Kent pleads with the king ("lay not violent hands on him") and Gaveston talks of revenge (I.i.186–191). Before our eyes, an elaborately attired symbol of the religion that gives the king his legitimacy is being mocked, stripped, degraded, and "christened" with filthy water by two figures who take sardonic pleasure in the act. But this early scene, like Kent's bouts in II.ii, should take on added meaning later in the action. Thus, near the end of the play Edward himself, rather than the Bishop of Coventry, is degraded by two figures, Matrevis and Gurney; when the king asks for water, he too is offered "channel water" and seemingly threatened, so that he responds: "Traitors away, what, will you murther me, / Or choke your sovereign with puddle water?" (V.iii.27–30) Edward's struggles are ineffectual, for the stage direction reads: *"They wash him with puddle water, and shave his beard away."* This moment has obvious symbolic value, especially as an inversion of the anointing of a king, an act

37. Ed. W. Moelwyn Merchant, New Mermaid edition (New York, 1968).

of unkinging linked to what Edward has done to himself and to his office. But if the staging also echoes the analogous treatment of the bishop, a more specific link may be forged between Edward's degradation of a figure who should have been a support to his crown and the king's similar degradation here. To add to the potential parallel, Kent, who had stood by helplessly in the earlier scene, also appears here only to be arrested and taken away to his fateful final meeting with Mortimer. If the critic or director perceives these two moments of violence and degradation as related rather than discrete, he may then recognize a symbolic cause-and-effect whereby the earlier action against the bishop condoned by Edward II has led to his helplessness here at the hands of two tormentors who act out a role visually analogous to that of the king and Gaveston in Act I. Such a link could heighten for the viewer Edward's own contribution to his present degradation, a responsibility he himself is not prepared to admit. But such an effect can only be realized through a logic that transcends the individual scene.[38]

Similar patterns that build upon moments of stage violence can be seen in two plays that span Shakespeare's career, *1 Henry VI* and *Coriolanus*, both of which display the vulnerability of a military hero who lacks the support of other elements in his society. In the earlier history play, many scenes act out divisions in England, especially the feuding between Gloucester and Winchester and between York and Somerset; the latter quarrel, moreover, is clearly linked to the demise of Talbot, the epitome of English heroic virtue. But Shakespeare also explores the limitations placed upon Talbot through a sequence of scenes analogous to the patterned violence in *King Lear*. As noted earlier, Talbot by himself was unable to defeat Joan in I.v., with the result that Orleans was temporarily lost. But a major English victory at Orleans soon follows in II.i when Talbot, this time supported by Bedford and Burgundy, scales the walls and takes the town in one of Shakespeare's most spectacular battle scenes. In his New Arden edition, Andrew Cairncross observes that Burgundy "is here introduced, unnecessarily, to prepare for his later part in the action" (p. 36). Quite the contrary, Burgundy's appearance *is* "necessary" to set up a revealing sequence or larger pattern. As established in the dialogue (II.i.28–34) the three figures ascend their scaling ladders simultaneously (Talbot presumably in the center, the other

---

38. For a more extensive discussion of such linking analogues, see Alan C. Dessen, *Elizabethan Drama and the Viewer's Eye* (Chapel Hill, N.C., 1977), pp. 50–70.

two at their respective "corners") so that, in a very distinctive scene for the eye, the viewer witnesses the victory as a combined effort of three heroes acting together. Shortly thereafter the Countess of Auvergne is told that Talbot alone "is but shadow of himself" without his soldiers and supporters, "his substance, sinews, arms, and strength" (II.iii.62–63). Starting, however, in II.iv (the Temple Garden scene), the emphasis again is upon division rather than unity, an emphasis continued in Mortimer's legacy to York (II.v) and the various arguments before the king in III.i. Note, then, what happens to the component parts of that victorious combination that had scaled the walls in unison in II.i. First, at the end of III.ii, Bedford dies in his chair while watching the retaking of Rouen; heroic to the last, this old soldier refuses to be bestowed "in some better place" but announces: "Here will I sit before the walls of Roan / And will be partner of your weal or woe" (III.ii.88, 91–92). In the next scene, Burgundy, the other major participant in the victory at Orleans, proves vulnerable to Joan's appeals and switches sides, an event displayed at length in III.ii and emphasized again in IV.i. Old age and treachery have undermined Talbot's "substance." The spectacular wall-scaling of II.i thereby functions not as an end in itself, a martial display for an audience demanding clamor and titillation, but rather as a means of setting up a winning combination of three figures, a group that by the end of III.iii has been reduced to one—and, with the death of Talbot in Act IV, to none. There *is* a necessary logic behind Burgundy's appearance in II.i and behind the scene as a whole, a logic not readily apparent to the editor, critic, or director who asks the wrong questions.

Late in his career Shakespeare uses an analogous device in I.iv of *Coriolanus* where the hero gains his name through his spectacular deeds. Much has been written about the staging of this scene, with modern assumptions often at odds with the evidence in the text. By appearing above at line 12, the two Volscian senators establish the rear tiring-house wall as the walls of Corioli, so that a stage door can represent the city gates from which issues the Volscian army at line 22. Scholars do not agree on how the ensuing battle would have been staged (particularly the disposition of Titus Lartius and the interpretation of *"the Romans are beat back to their trenches"*), but clearly, in the key moment of the scene, Caius Martius follows the Volscian soldiers *"to the gates,"* *"enter[s] the gates,"* and *"is shut in"* (s.d.s at I.iv.42, 45, 46). Less heroic (or foolhardy), the Roman soldiers hold back, telling Titus Lartius that

Martius, "following the fliers at the very heels, / With them he enters; who upon the sudden / Clapp'd to their gates. He is himself alone, / To answer all the city" (ll. 49–52). Titus's premature epitaph is interrupted by the entrance of "Martius, *bleeding, assaulted by the enemy*" (l. 61 s.d.), so that the Roman forces now "*fight, and all enter the city*" (l. 62 s.d.).

At the heart of this scene, then, is the striking stage image of Caius Martius isolated within the walls of Corioli. Shakespeare has provided the viewer with a vivid demonstration that under very special conditions, in wartime, with none of the demands of the give-and-take of politics, this overbearing hero can, for a moment, stand "himself alone, / To answer all the city." Here is the one moment when the hero lives up to his claim that he can stand alone "as if a man were author of himself, / And knew no other kin" (V.iii.36–37). But the remainder of the play emphasizes the failure of Coriolanus either to be self-sufficient or to find a place in any city. Again and again he stands by himself, whether in his appearance before the senators (II.ii.36.s.d.) or in his gown of humility or waiting for Aufidius in IV.v, or he stands in opposition to family or plebeians. In response to the decree of banishment, he can tell the Roman tribunes and mob "I banish you!" adding "there is a world elsewhere" (III.iii.123, 135); in the final scene, again confronting an entire city (the supposed "world elsewhere"), he can recall but not repeat his earlier victory ("alone I did it"—V.vi.116). His capitulation to the three women and the boy in V.iii is the most obvious but by no means the only event to be measured against the striking triumph and independence of I.iv. In a manner analogous to the victory at Orleans by Talbot, Burgundy, and Bedford, Shakespeare has provided his tragic hero with a remarkable, eye-catching accomplishment early in the play which cannot be matched again, especially in peacetime in a world of politics, rhetoric, and cynicism, where the protagonist's heroic anger can be triggered by manipulation of key words ("boy," "traitor"). The spectacular battle scenes in both *1 Henry VI* and *Coriolanus* can thereby generate symbolic possibilities and initiate larger patterns significant for the plays as a whole, but only when we ask the proper questions and sidestep misleading assumptions about "realism."

Throughout this essay I have sought to be selective rather than exhaustive, suggestive rather than conclusive, so that a great deal of terrain has been left unexplored and many possibilities not pursued. For example, to what extent would the sequence of actions in an individual stage combat (e.g., Hal versus Hotspur) have been designed to comment upon the participants or upon some larger issue? To cite one more example from the moralities, in the opening scene of *The Trial of Treasure* Lust and Just meet for the only time in the play to engage in a wrestling match. Lust appears *"to have the better at the first"* but is eventually cast down and driven off by Just. Allegorically, we have witnessed "the conflict of the just, / Which all good men ought to use and frequent"; just so, every man should strive against lust: "And though, at the first, he seem sturdy to be, / The Lord will convince him for you in the end" (pp. 266–267). Here, as with many battles in *The Faerie Queene*, both the sequence of events and the outcome have clear allegorical significance, but, lacking sufficient evidence, I find it difficult to determine the relevance of this technique to later plays that lack overt allegory and neat summaries.

To see the difficulties in reconstructing Elizabethan stage violence, consider one last Shakespearean example, the rather unhelpful Folio stage direction for the final fight in *Richard III*: *"Alarum, Enter Richard and Richmond, they fight, Richard is slaine."* Clearly, this combat serves as an exciting climax to a long play, but, given the many speeches and actions that have preceded this moment, *"they fight"* leaves open many possibilities. Let me note a few that draw upon the alternatives to "realism" cited in this essay. If the critic or director prizes the logic of patterning, the blow that kills Richard can echo unmistakably the thrust he asks for but does not receive from Lady Anne in I.ii (a link established in both the Stratford, Ontario, production of 1977 and the Ashland, Oregon, production of 1978). If the emphasis is placed upon Richmond as God's captain (see especially V.iii.108–117, 240–270), his blows could fall with more than human force upon Richard (as with my suggested staging for Joan's encounter with Talbot). If Richard eventually is killed with his own weapon (an often-used conclusion to modern stage fights), his fate could confirm Buckingham's assertion of the power of "that high All-Seer" who forces "the swords of wicked men / To turn their own points in their masters' bosoms" (V.i.20–24). If Richard dies when forsaken by Ratcliff or others in the final moments, his demise could be linked to Margaret's curse: "Thy friends suspect for traitors while thou liv'st, / And take deep traitors for thy dearest friends!" (I.iii.222–223). If the staging suggests not Richmond's strength but Richard's weakness or surprising ineptness, the fight could be the final moment in a series started by the "myself myself confound" oath (IV.iv.397–405), where Richard pawns his future success, and continued in the "coward conscience" soliloquy, with its emphasis upon guilt and revenging "myself upon myself" (V.iii.177–206). Not all of these choices are incompatible with stage "realism" nor are they all mutually exclusive, but each draws its potential meaning or force from a somewhat different logic, whether that logic is based upon patterning or surprise or symbolism or iterative imagery. From the limited evidence we cannot determine how this moment would have been staged in the original production, yet the director or critic or editor who fails to consider such options may unwittingly be diminishing an important moment in a rich play by considering only those possibilities consonant with our prevailing tastes or assumptions. Rather, as with Edgar versus Edmund or Macduff versus Macbeth, a climactic Shakespearean fight, like a climactic Shakespearean speech, may weave together various threads into a highly theatrical yet intensely meaningful moment and may leave the audience with an epitome of what has gone before, a realization in action of central motifs or images or oppositions.

In conclusion, let me emphasize how little we know about Elizabethan dramatic conventions and playhouse practice. Undisputed facts are few; external evidence is very limited (and rarely tells us what we want most to know); inferences from the plays themselves are highly vulnerable to the often unacknowledged assumptions of the investigator; yesterday's truths quickly turn up on today's dustheap (the inner stage, "another part of the forest"). Given our distance, both temporal and cultural, from Shakespeare's Globe, to "prove" the authenticity of *any* suggested staging—verisimilar, symbolic, or patterned—is difficult if not impossible. After much ado, my goals in this essay are therefore rather modest. Thus, I will have achieved the purpose behind my sustained attack if my verbal violence has produced an increased reluctance to view Elizabethan scenes solely through the spectacles of "realism" and if my combative stance has called attention to the advantages of an alternative dramatic logic that can give meaning to moments otherwise puzzling or inexplicable. To travel too far down the road to realism is to narrow the range of Elizabethan drama and to invite upon our heads a painful shower of roses or the sword of heavenly judgment.

"Vassal Actors": The Role of the Audience in Shakespearean Tragedy

MARJORIE GARBER

Make no noise, make no noise; draw the curtains.

King Lear, III.vi.82–83 [1]

WHEN, AS HE LIES MORTALLY WOUNDED, Hamlet addresses himself to "You that look pale and tremble at this chance, / That are but mutes or audience to this act" (V.ii.336–337), he addresses, as well, a crucial aspect of Shakespearean drama. "Act," as we know from the gravedigger, means not only "event," but also "performance"—the observers respond with fear and trembling both to the death of Hamlet and to the enactment of that death as part of a play. But who are these onlookers, these "mutes or audience"? Manifestly, they are both on the stage and off it, a community whose human bond transcends the limitations of the stage itself. They are an audience—which is to say, they hear; but they are also spectators, who see; and, as Hamlet tellingly points

1. Text used is *William Shakespeare: The Complete Works*, ed. Peter Alexander (London, 1951).

71

out, they are also "mutes," who cannot—or will not—speak. It is this specific and peculiar combination of elements which casts the audience of a Shakespearean play as surely in its role as Hamlet and Claudius are cast in theirs. At once active—in emotional response, in pity and terror, in sympathy or identification—and passive—in its entrapment in seats or boxes, and its inability to intervene—the audience occupies a dichotomous position which is both difficult to maintain, and essential to the workings of the play.

In considering the general situation of Shakespeare's tragic audiences, we may conveniently begin with those moments in the plays when an audience is explicitly convened upon the stage. The most clear-cut example of this is the play-within-the-play, but the category is usefully extended to include such moments as Iago's masterful misinterpretation of Cassio's behavior to Desdemona, and the final scenes of *Hamlet, Othello,* and *King Lear*. Not surprisingly, Hamlet provides the paradigm: the play-within, of course, is "The Mousetrap," and its onstage audience includes Claudius and Gertrude, Horatio and Ophelia. But as the "Mousetrap" progresses, some members of this group, at least, begin to realize what we have already learned: that the crucial play is not on the "stage" but in the "audience," in the reactions of the spectator, Claudius, who is the real Player King of the scene. As for Claudius himself, his error lies in relaxing his vigilance: in the premature and overconfident assumption that he can tell the actors from the audience, the play from "real life." The offstage audience has been conditioned, from the play's opening scene, to perceive the virtual impossibility of making such a distinction: Horatio, the Ghost, even the "dawn in russet mantle clad," all clamor for attention as actors, and are surrounded by a succession of audiences—who are, themselves, soon drawn into the action.[2] The sentries are protected by their willingness to be mere spectators; by contrast Hamlet, who has first perceived the Ghost as a dumb show, finds when he has urged it to speech that in so doing he has himself become an actor. It is not enough for him to remember, or to set down the Ghost's words in his tables like the spectator who produced the Bad Quarto; the time is out of joint and he is born to set it right.

2. For a valuable reading of the succession of entrances in this scene, see Stephen Booth, "On the Value of *Hamlet*," in Norman Rabkin, ed., *Reinterpretations of Elizabethan Drama* (Selected Papers from the English Institute), (New York, 1969), pp. 137–176.

Claudius's confidence that he is safe because he is in the audience proves his undoing: "the king rises" and speaks, calling for lights and for the breaking off of the play. Likewise Polonius, that adept of acting and eminent critic of the theater—who once played Julius Caesar and was killed in the Capitol—fails to profit from his own knowledge of playing. Twice he constitutes himself an audience, safely placed behind the arras, out of harm's way. In the first instance (III.i.), he and Claudius are "lawful espials," in Polonius's own happy phrase, unobserved observers of the mad Hamlet and Ophelia "loosed" to him in the lobby. Shortly thereafter (III.iv.), again at his own suggestion, he takes up a post behind the arras in the Queen's closet, contending that "some more audience than a mother" (III.iii.31) should overhear the conversation between Hamlet and Gertrude. "Audience" is an interesting word here, as is Polonius's initial determination to "be plac'd . . . in the ear / Of all their conference" (III.i.184–185). He hears, but cannot see, and hearing, he misconstrues Hamlet's intentions.

> QUEEN
> What wilt thou do? Thou wilt not murder me?
> Help, help, ho!
>
> POLONIUS [*Behind*]
> What, ho! help, help, help!
>
> HAMLET [*Draws*]
> How now! a rat? Dead, for a ducat, dead!
>
> (III.iv.21–23)

Hamlet does not intend to murder his mother, but rather to set up a "glass" for her in the form of the two opposed portraits. But Polonius commits the one action which "mutes or audience" cannot do: he speaks. Like Hamlet on the battlements, like Claudius at the play, he breaches theatrical decorum—and Hamlet stabs through the arras and kills him. But it is Polonius, really, who has rent the arras; lulled, like Claudius, into the false security of knowing himself to be an audience, he oversteps the bounds of dramatic convention—and in acting, meets his death.

For Gertrude, the opposite reversal takes place in this scene: she has believed herself to be an actor, participating in a painful and chastening conversation—but she is abruptly transformed into an audience upon the entrance of the Ghost:

HAMLET

Do you see nothing there?

QUEEN

Nothing at all; yet all that is I see.

HAMLET

Nor did you nothing hear?

QUEEN

No, nothing but ourselves.
(III.iv.132–133)

She is a spectator who does not see, an audience who does not hear. If we are attentive, we will, I think, feel some of the same bewilderment. How much are *we* missing, when we are sure that we see and hear all that is to be seen and heard? The Queen's certainty is an ensign which cannot be ignored; she is in error, there is more to see. But everything in *Hamlet* works in just this way to undermine our certainty. Why should we be safer than Polonius, who shares with us the secure identity of an audience, lawful espials hidden behind an arras? Why should we be safer than Claudius, who knows that he is watching a play, but fails to notice the audience which watches him? Is it not possible that we, like all of these unwitting actors, are part of the play?[3]

We have noted that such a multiplication of uncertainties is especially germane to *Hamlet*, a play which turns, in part, upon questions of epistemology. If we look further, however, we will discover that the other major tragedies are likewise deeply concerned with the definition of an audience and its role. For the audience of *Othello*, the dilemma is not one of uncertainty, as it was in *Hamlet*, but rather one of certainty. We know the truth, and Othello believes a lie. Iago, himself a playwright, first makes opportunity out of chance by appointing himself as impromptu chorus to interpret the dumb show of Cassio's leavetaking from Desdemona.

---

3. Some interesting observations on the role of the spectator in individual Shakespearean productions may be found in Robert Hapgood, "Shakespeare and the Included Spectator," in Rabkin, *Reinterpretations of Elizabethan Drama*, pp. 117–136.

OTHELLO

Was not that Cassio parted from my wife?

IAGO

Cassio, my lord? No, sure, I cannot think it,
That he would sneak away so guilty-like,
Seeing your coming.

OTHELLO

I do believe 'twas he.

(III.iii.38–41)

In a moment Desdemona will come to them with her unfortunate reference to "talking with a suitor" (l. 43), and the "truth" of Iago's play seems
proved. Later, of course, we will see him move from dumb show to spoken
action, by joking with Cassio about Bianca's easy virtue in such a way that
he seems, again, to be speaking of Desdemona. In both "plays" Othello is
forced into the position of audience, and he sees and hears exactly—and
only—what Iago wants him to see and hear. We, the offstage audience,
see better, hear better. Yet such is the convention of the drama that we do
not speak. It is probable that we have all, at some time in our lives,
longed to intervene in an ongoing fiction—to warn Oedipus where his
systematic inquiry is leading, to caution Joseph Surface that Lady Teazle is
hiding behind the screen. As children we may have applauded, eagerly, to
bring Tinker Bell back to life—for we did, then, believe in fairies. As
adults, however, we repress this impulse to intervene, and substitute an
obedient decorum which acknowledges that we know the difference between art and life. But we pay a price for this self-denial, a price which is
intrinsic to the working of tragedy. Our suffering in *Othello* is not only an
empathetic sharing of Othello's own agony; it is also a private and particular suffering of our own, wrought of the repressed desire to intervene, to
call out as Emilia does (but so much later) "He lies to th' heart" (V.ii.159)
—a desire which is checked by our prescribed roles as "mutes or audience,"
and which therefore, inevitably, turns to guilt.

To a considerable degree, this same tension between the desire to
intervene and the recognition of our passive role as spectators is brought to
the surface in *King Lear*. The blinded Gloucester is for Lear literally an
"audience," or "hearer,"—and in the heart-rending meeting of the blind

duke and the mad king on the heath we see the confrontation of one who
would not "see better" into his daughter's love, and one who accepted
"auricular assurance" of his son's supposed guilt. Lear and Gloucester, a
bad spectator and a bad audience, are each made actors in their own
tragedies. Stanley Cavell has argued provocatively that Edgar's decision
not to reveal himself to his father is an act of cruelty which "deprived
Gloucester of his eyes again," [4] and that the Dover cliff scene, in which
Gloucester leaps from no cliff to no beach, is a cruel spectacle which belies
Edgar's own explanation ("Why I do trifle thus with his despair / Is done
to cure it" [IV.vi.33–34]). Here again we have a staged and directed scene
about which the offstage audience knows the "truth"—that there is no
cliff, no beach, no sea, no fishermen, no one who gathers samphire,
"dreadful trade." In keeping silent here, while Edgar practices deceit, we
implicitly give our assent to that deceit. In another context, a football
game, perhaps, or a quiz show, we would not show such restraint—we
would urge the truth as we saw it, to those upon the stage. Here, as the
audience of tragedy, we choose the opposite course; we stand mute. We
choose, that is, Cordelia's way—love and be silent—and once again our
suffering takes on her pattern of empathy, while at the same time it
remains particularly and privately our own. Lear's fantasy that he and
Cordelia can "away to prison," where they will "take upon's the mystery
of things / As if we were God's spies" (V.iii.16–17), recalls Polonius's
"lawful espials," and reveals a similar misunderstanding of the privilege of
the audience. Lear's agony is that he cannot escape the action of the play;
ours, at this point, is that we cannot enter it.

To do so, to break the convention and tear through the arras, was fatal
to Polonius and to Claudius—and it is so again for Macbeth. Not content
to be an audience, not willing, in fact, to be a spectator, he chooses to act,
and intrudes himself heedlessly upon the spectacles of which he is, properly, only a passive observer. Confronted by the witches' prophecies,
Macbeth refuses merely to accept them; the witches are "imperfect speakers," from whom he demands more precise information. A bad audience,
he is also a bad critic, misinterpreting what he sees, and moving swiftly
and inappropriately to the most irreversible of actions: murder. When in

---

4. "The Avoidance of Love; A Reading of King Lear," in *Must We Mean What We Say?*
(New York, 1969), p. 283. The entire essay (pp. 267–353) is of considerable interest.

Act IV he again seeks out the witches, he is repeatedly instructed in audience decorum: "Hear his speech, but say thou nought"; "Listen, but speak not to 't"; "Seek to know no more" (IV.i.70, 89, 103). Again he misinterprets the omens; he is an audience but not a spectator, he listens but he does not see—for to the offstage audience the apparitions which rise before him offer clear explanations of the witches' riddling words. The armed head is his own, and not Macduff's; the bloody child indicates the existence of one not "of woman born," the crowned child with the tree in his hand offers an answer to "Who can impress the forest, bid the tree / Unfix his earth-bound root?" (ll. 95–96). But Macbeth fails to comprehend the true task of an audience, which is not only to observe, but also to interpret. The gap in knowledge between the onstage and offstage audiences is the difference, here, between death and life.

To the extent that our sympathies lie with Macbeth, despite his transgressions, we may once again feel something of the conflict that we felt with *Othello*: an impulse to intervene and correct the erring protagonist, to forestall or prevent his inevitable tragedy. Elsewhere in *Macbeth*, Shakespeare accommodates this need by providing an onstage audience which mediates between the tragic discoveries taking place in the play and the audience which observes them. The key moment here, of course, is the sleepwalking scene, V.i. The onstage audience is comprised of a doctor and a waiting gentlewoman, both attendant upon Lady Macbeth. Like the sentries in *Hamlet*, the gentlewoman has seen this disquieting apparition before; the doctor, like Horatio, is summoned to see for himself, and has watched two nights without success. What they see, when the Lady at last appears, is really no more than testimony to what we have already learned; the deed which so astounds them is already known to us. But their presence as naïve observers permits us to relive our own experience, to recapture the shock of murder and its effect upon the human mind. Doctor and gentlewoman thus serve as scale figures, quintessentially normal observers whose dramatic inconsequence is confirmed by their immediate disappearance from stage and plot. They exist only to function as an audience. They are horrified—and we are horrified anew. Yet we are also in part relieved that our horror, heretofore private, has found expression upon the stage.

In the sleepwalking scene, Shakespeare makes use of what may perhaps be called "tragic relief"—a displacement of tragic emotion from offstage to onstage audience which makes the full brunt of tragedy marginally easier to bear. A similar sharing of emotional response is made possible in *King Lear* through the character of Edgar, who increasingly comes to mediate between audience and actors—himself often an actor, but at other times a horrified and disbelieving observer.

> I would not take this from report. It is,
> And my heart breaks at it.
>
> (IV.vi.141–142)

> Poor Tom's a-cold. [*Aside.*] I cannot daub it further. . . .
> And yet I must.—Bless thy sweet eyes, they bleed.
>
> (IV.i.53, 55)

We have already noticed Edgar's belief in the healing power of fiction— "Why I do trifle thus with his despair / Is done to cure it." As an onstage audience and mediator, he frequently assumes the characteristic trait of passivity which is implicit in the audience role, and, unable to manipulate or intercede, he becomes a paradigm of suffering. His concept of "the worst," significantly, is a vicarious one—he is made worse than e'er he was, not by the role of poor Tom, but by his first sight of the blinded Gloucester. A highly complex dramatic character, Edgar serves a number of functions, but not the least of them is to represent us upon the stage, confirming the evidence of our eyes and ears, and giving expression to what we long to express. Doctor Johnson, writing of the blinding of Gloucester, said that it seemed "an act too horrid to be endured in dramatic exhibition, and such as must always compel the mind to relieve its distress by incredulity."[5] Shakespeare will not permit us that incredulity, but through Edgar he does offer us a way, however limited and mediated, to participate in a community of tragic response. The absence of such a representative and mediating figure may account for the extreme discomfort felt by many audiences of *Othello*, where until the final act no voice is raised in defense of what we know to be the truth.

In considering the dramatic effect of *Othello*, in fact, we come upon an entirely different aspect of the audience's role. We have been considering what might be described as the mode of analogy: the audience both compares and contrasts itself with audiences constituted upon the stage,

5. *Johnson on Shakespeare*, ed. Arthur Sherbo, 2 vols. (New Haven and London, 1968), II, 703.

whether they be formal ("The Mousetrap"), informal (Othello watching Cassio and Desdemona), large ("The Mousetrap" again; Coriolanus showing his wounds; Antony's funeral oration) or small (Edgar; Othello; Cleopatra's maids). But the audience of Shakespearean tragedy is involved not only by analogy, but also by confrontation—and the most significant dramaturgical vehicle for confrontation is the soliloquy. Formally speaking, the soliloquy is the play's Ancient Mariner, which stops us in our tracks and holds us with a glittering eye; like the Wedding Guest, we cannot choose but hear. Richard of Gloucester, perhaps the most masterful of Shakespeare's early soliloquists, suggests just such a deadly fascination when he announces his plans for the future at the close of *3 Henry VI*. "I'll slay more gazers than the basilisk;" he declares, "I'll play the orator as well as Nestor" (III.ii.187–188). This telling juxtaposition of images reflects the self-conscious power of Richard's language; as the basilisk turned to stone those who gazed upon it, so Richard's oratory will paralyze his listeners and hold them spellbound.

Richard's character, of course, is among other things that of a Machiavel, and for that reason his relationship to the offstage audience is of a special kind. The soliloquy is the device through which, by convention, we see into his mind and understand the real motivation behind the "childish-foolish" façade. In the later figure of Iago, however, Shakespeare alters the convention of the reliable soliloquist, with a curious and disquieting effect upon the audience. Iago's soliloquies are, like Richard's, Machiavellian discourses, direct addresses by the Vice to the audience, in accordance with the custom of the morality play—but they are also something more. Iago purports to tell us his motives: why he hates the Moor. However, as many commentators have observed, none of his suggested motives is persuasive, and they are mutually inconsistent. Does he really believe that Othello has slept with Emilia, or that Cassio has? Did he actually have the sponsorship of "three great ones of the city" for the lieutenancy? These are his claims—and they put the audience in a quandary. For if we do not believe him—and most critics do not[6]—we are compelled to acknowledge that he is practicing upon us as he practices upon Roderigo and Othello. In defiance of both contemporary stage con-

6. Stanley Edgar Hyman, *Iago: Some Approaches to His Motivation* (New York, 1970), provides a useful summary of critical approaches to Iago's credibility. See especially pp. 61–76.

vention and Shakespeare's own custom, what Iago says in soliloquy is not
an inner truth but a manipulative fiction, intended to sway our feelings
and perhaps our actions. He is a malign playwright, and we are his
audience, as well as Shakespeare's. The play offers no escape from the
burden of witness; however we may interpret his soliloquies, they force us
to realize that we are privy to information known by no one else on the
stage. *Othello*, as we have already observed, is alone among Shakespeare's
tragedies in providing no other observer, no other listener, to mediate our
emotion or give expression to it. As a result, we are placed in an uncom-
fortably confidential and intimate relationship with Iago, whether we
choose it or not.

If Iago's soliloquies confront the audience by their audacious fictionality, Hamlet's may be said to do so through their relentless search for
truth; Iago's soliloquies are virtually all role, and Hamlet's virtually all
persona. The four major soliloquies in *Hamlet* are cunningly set, one in
each of the first four acts, so that each replaces and displaces action, until
in Act V the soliloquy disappears, and Hamlet kills the king.
Language—those words, words, words—is in itself a delaying tactic, as
Hamlet himself repeatedly observes. But it is not he alone who delays.
We, the audience, delay as well. Our fascination with Hamlet's character
and the workings of his mind conflicts with our eagerness to see the deed
done, to have him kill Claudius once and for all—for when he does this,
there will be no more play. The Ghost's stern warning in the closet scene,

> this visitation
> Is but to whet thy almost blunted purpose
>
> (III.iv.110–111)

seems aptly directed at us, as well as at Hamlet. The bond forged in
soliloquy by the interaction of speaker and audience competes for primacy
with the working out of the plot. Are we, too, then, guilty creatures
sitting at a play?

In each of these instances, a disturbing suggestion continues to surface:
that the audience, itself, is at least in part at fault for what is happening
on the stage—that we are in complicity with the tragic action. Does the
convention of noninterference, the very role of audience and spectator in
which we have been cast by the playwright, place us in complicity with

the wicked Iago, in complicity with Edgar when he deceives Gloucester, whatever his motives, in complicity with Cleopatra when she sends false news of her death to Antony, and drives him to a botched suicide? We have seen what happens to apparently passive audiences on the stage: Polonius, who thinks that there is such a thing as a "lawful espial"; Lear, who sets himself up as one of "God's spies," watching the events of the world as if from some heavenly balcony; Rosencrantz and Guildenstern, who thought that they could safely spy on Hamlet; or Roderigo, who, newly bearded, believes himself safe in darkness, following Othello and Desdemona to Cyprus. Lawful espials, all, perhaps—but they all perish. They are all drawn into the tragedy of which they are helplessly a part. Their chosen roles as spectators do not protect them from the ongoing action of the play, and when they act, they die.

By contrast, it is possible for the offstage audience to consider that it escapes too lightly from the consequences of the drama. Lear, Hamlet, Othello, all suffer and die, and we rise and take our leave from the theater, sure that we—like Polonius—know where reality ends and fiction stops, sure that the actor who plays Hamlet will himself rise once the curtain falls, and play the same role tomorrow. Are we, then, voyeurs of the tragic action? Onlookers who draw satisfaction out of our differences from these suffering figures, as well as empathy from our correspondence to them? We might be—if we were really so detached as this attitude makes us appear, if we really felt that we were God's spies, lawful espials. That we do not is suggested by the particular and private suffering imposed upon us by our own predetermined inaction—that is, by the role Shakespeare has assigned to us, as surely as he assigned the parts of Hamlet, and Desdemona, and Lady Macbeth.

Shakespeare's plays do make demands upon us as an audience, and demands of the most stringent kind. They demand, for example, our admiration, our respect and affection for the gallantness of spirit which distinguishes the tragic hero from the common herd. They demand, as well, our discrimination, in measuring the difference between Edmund's deceit and Edgar's, between Claudius's murder and Hamlet's, between Hamlet's grief and Laertes'—actions and attitudes which wear the same shapes, but which are distinguished from one another within the dramatic context. Most directly, however, the plays demand our participation, and in doing so offer us a way to escape from "the worst"—from the burden of being powerless spectators who suffer guilt as a result of our own powerlessness, our essential complicity with man's inhumanity to man.

There are of course, significant moments in the major tragedies which must rank as exceptions to this rule: moments which suggest that art and life have no common points of reference, that drama is discontinuous with reality, that acting is not an action. One celebrated instance occurs when Macbeth, unable to make sense of the play in which he bears a part, offers a characteristic revision of the *topos* of "all the world's a stage":

> Life's but a walking shadow, a poor player,
> That struts and frets his hour upon the stage
> And then is heard no more; it is a tale
> Told by an idiot, full of sound and fury,
> Signifying nothing.
>
> (V.v.24–28)

In this formulation, life itself is a bad imitation of life, which finds its sole and ironic significance in lack of significance, in nihilism. But we must bear in mind that the person to whom it signifies nothing is Macbeth himself.[7] Once again he has confused his own perceptions with the evidence of the world around him and committed an error of misreading. For what signifies in *Macbeth* is finally Macbeth himself transformed into a sign:

7. A close analogy from the romances is Leontes' speech on jealousy in *The Winter's Tale*, in which, once again, the self becomes everything, and the external world appears to be "signifying nothing."

> Is whispering nothing?
> Is leaning cheek to cheek? Is meeting noses?
> Kissing with inside lip? Stopping the career
> Of laughter with a sign (a note infallible
> Of breaking honestly)? Horsing foot on foot?
> Skulking in corners? Wishing clocks more swift?
> Hours, minutes? Noon, midnight? And all eyes
> Blind with the pin and web, but theirs; theirs only,
> That would unseen be wicked? Is this nothing?
> Why, then the world and all that's in't is nothing,
> The covering sky is nothing, Bohemia nothing,
> My wife is nothing, nor nothing have these nothings,
> If this be nothing.
>
> (I.ii.284–296)

The irony here, of course, is that his suspicions, since they are groundless, *are* nothing; the short answer to all these tortured questions is "yes."

> Then yield thee, coward,
> And live to be the show and gaze o' th' time.
> We'll have thee, as our rarer monsters are,
> Painted upon a pole, and underwrit
> "Here may you see the tyrant."
> (V.viii.23–27)

As a "monster," literally a warning or marvel, he becomes "the show and gaze o' th' time," the true tale emblematized for his own age and for ours. As the painted banner is to the onstage society of Macduff's and Malcolm's Scotland, so the play is to us, and is not "heard no more," but rather heard—and played—over and over again.

Another key instance of dramatic misreading is suggested by Cleopatra in her uncannily accurate portrait of the Roman (and Elizabethan) stage. In this case, of course, the misunderstanding is Rome's and not her own.

> the quick comedians
> Extemporally will stage us, and present
> Our Alexandrian revels; Antony
> Shall be brought drunken forth, and I shall see
> Some squeaking Cleopatra boy my greatness
> I' th' posture of a whore.
> (V.ii.215–220)

Such diminution is given the lie by Shakespeare's own dramaturgical risk here, for it is in fact a boy who speaks these lines, and yet we remain persuaded of Cleopatra's greatness. Where Macbeth curses a play for signifying nothing, Cleopatra dreads a play which signifies wrongly, and immortalizes a reductive parody of truth. These are anti-plays, plays which diminish rather than aggrandize, denying meaning in dramatic patterns, and thus falsifying what they depict. And as we have already observed, the arch-anti-playwright of Shakespearean drama is Iago, whose "play" attempts to encompass and replace that of Shakespeare himself. Iago thinks he is the author of what has happened in *Othello*; he has "engendered" the plot and brought it to monstrous birth. The deaths of Othello and Desdemona, Emilia and Roderigo, and the wounding of Cassio are all his doing, as Lodovico points out at the close:

> Look on the tragic loading of this bed.
> This is thy work.
> (V.ii.365–366)

Such an acknowledgment is balm to the aspiring playwright's soul; the bodies are indeed "thy work," Iago's parodic creation. But to view the work as successfully completed at this moment is to make Iago's own mistake, and Macbeth's, and Leontes': to take the self for the larger world of which it is only a part. What Iago does not realize—and what is therefore left for the audience to learn—is that the significance of this dramatic development lies in the implicit contrast of "thy work" with "my work," a work which belongs to the state, to the society, and to Shakespeare. The play does not end with the drawing of the bed curtains, but rather with Lodovico's final words of resolve:

> Myself will straight aboard; and to the state
> This heavy act with heavy heart relate.
>
> (ll. 373–374)

To "relate" becomes, in fact, the crucial action afforded to the spectator of tragedy, both on and off the stage. He is invited to "relate" in two senses—to retell the tale, and in retelling it to reconstitute the human bond which has been severed, to re-make a community and a society by placing the hero and his downfall in the instructive context of history, and by "giv[ing] sorrow words," as Malcolm urges Macduff (*Mac.* IV.ii.209), in order to come to terms with loss. Lodovico will return to Venice and "relate" the story of Othello, which is to say, the events of the play itself. It is therefore both appropriate and necessary that the tragedies of Shakespeare should each end with an injunction to retell—to make history into story, fact into fable—in short, to replay the play, and bring it back to life. Thus Hamlet enjoins Horatio,

> If thou didst ever hold me in thy heart,
> Absent thee from felicity awhile,
> And in this harsh world draw thy breath in pain,
> To tell my story.
>
> (V.ii.339–341)

Othello enjoins the Venetians,

> When you shall these unlucky deeds relate,
> Speak of me as I am; nothing extenuate,
> Nor set down aught in malice. Then must you speak
> Of one that lov'd not wisely, but too well.
>
> (V.ii.344–347)

Nor, as we have already seen in *Othello*, is this sensibility confined to the doomed protagonist. At the close of *Romeo and Juliet* the Prince of Verona, a spectator to the tragedy, instructs his subjects (and his audience), "Go hence, to have more talk of these sad things" (V.iii.306). In similar terms Edgar, a survivor of the storm and a friend and kinsman of its victims, addresses the remaining English forces:

> The weight of this sad time we must obey;
> Speak what we feel, not what we ought to say.
> The oldest hath borne most; we that are young
> Shall never see so much, nor live so long.
>
> (*King Lear* V.iii.323–326)

Here, in accordance with the changed circumstances, explicit retelling— "Speak what we feel"—entails, as well, implicit remembering and recording. "We that are young" refers not only to those of Edgar's own generation, but to those who will follow—the newly young of each succeeding generation, audience as well as actors, who are asked to remember and to learn from the tragic past.

Moreover, even those who have caused the deaths of tragic heroes invite us, in fact command us, to remember them. Aufidius says of Coriolanus, "Yet he shall have a noble memory" (V.vi.154); Macduff says of Macbeth, "Then . . . live to be the show and gaze o' th' time" (V.viii.23–24); Octavius says of Antony and Cleopatra, "No grave upon the earth shall clip in it / A pair so famous" (V.vii.356–357). Thus, at the close of every tragedy, our attention is drawn to the necessary act of retrospection without which the tragic experience would be incomplete.

Yet in each of these cases the relationship of onstage to offstage audience is carefully measured, to suggest not only a conjunction, but also a disjunction between them. Horatio is asked to "tell my story," and he complies immediately by requesting those remaining—among whom we may properly number ourselves—to see "that these bodies / High on a stage be placed to the view" (ll. 369–370). The stage from which they are to be regarded, of course, is simultaneously playhouse and platform. But then Horatio goes on, in effect, to summarize his story to the "yet unknowing world":

> So shall you hear
> Of carnal, bloody, and unnatural acts;
> Of accidental judgements, casual slaughters;

> Of deaths put on by cunning and forc'd cause;
> And, in this upshot, purposes mistook
> Fall'n on th' inventors' heads—all this can I
> Truly deliver.
>
>   (*Hamlet*, V.ii.372–378)

He can "truly deliver" so far as he comprehends what he has seen. But do we recognize *The Tragedy of Hamlet, Prince of Denmark*, in this catalogue of catastrophes? Horatio, who cautions against considering too curiously, is himself a curious figure for the role of amanuensis; there are parts of Hamlet—and therefore of *Hamlet*—which he has never understood. Most obviously, he has not heard the soliloquies, without which the play of *Hamlet* as we know it is unimaginable. It is therefore to us as well as to Horatio that Hamlet—and Shakespeare—speak, in the command to "tell my story." We, mutes and audience, are the only ones who "truly" know it.

These final speeches of summation have sometimes been accused of a certain patness—of attempting to make all right with the world, when in fact that world has been destroyed. But this patness, when it exists, seems to me to be a part of the play's central design, and of the design it has upon its audience. Lodovico is even less qualified than Horatio to "relate" the tragedy of which he is a part. He does not arrive at Cyprus until the beginning of Act IV, and has therefore missed, not only Iago's soliloquies, but the whole story of Othello's downfall. His account, were he to give it, would begin with the striking of Desdemona, omitting the delicate psychological interplay which lies at the heart of the tragedy. Edgar, who speaks of "we that are young," counts himself among them, though he has been part of the tragedy of Gloucester and Lear. But to say that we "shall never see so much, nor live so long," is to overlook, for a moment, the radical role of the spectator, who has seen it all—and through whose eyes and ears the personae of *King Lear* continue to live long after the actors have left the stage.

The Montagues and Capulets, though united by mutual tragedy, remain blindly competitive, each pledging to rear a more appropriate monument to the other's child; the golden statues they intend to raise are mockingly lifeless counterparts of the flesh and blood children they have lost, and bear no relation to the "story of . . . woe . . . of Juliet and her Romeo" (V.iii.308–309). As for Octavius, his belated generosity is, as always, mitigated by self-interest:

No grave upon the earth shall clip in it
A pair so famous. High events as these
Strike those that make them; and their story is
No less in pity than his glory which
Brought them to be lamented.
                              (*Antony and Cleopatra*, V.ii.356–360)

The "story" of Antony and Cleopatra is "pity," a tragedy; that of Octavius is "glory," a chronicle. But the easy rhyme of "story" and "glory," which seems to balance two types of fame, in fact suggests a false analogy. The play is not evenly divided in its emphasis between the lovers and the aspiring emperor; its conclusion is not greeted by the audience impartially, with an auspicious and a dropping eye—our sympathies and commitment are reserved for the dead, though we may recognize the political sagacity of those who survive. Octavius, in fact, does not understand his play, and would almost surely have staged in Rome the "squeaking," "drunken" parody Cleopatra imagines. The limited vision of the final speaker once again emphasizes the radical disjunction between his view and that of the work of art. Only in his intuition that the play must be replayed does he anticipate the response of the offstage audience; for just as Cleopatra herself declares, "I am again for Cydnus, / To meet Mark Antony" (V.ii.227–228), so Octavius senses in her death a paradoxical sign of continuity:

                    she looks like sleep,
        As she would catch another Antony
        In her strong toil of grace.
                              (V.ii.343–345)

The dramatic character of Cleopatra inhabits a self-renewing world which will outlast any single spectator, and any single performance.

In short, Horatio might conceivably write a *Horatio*, and Octavius an *Octavius Caesar*, but neither would accord completely with the plays as we have experienced them. As participants in the tragic drama they can speak only what they know; we, who know more, have, in exchange for that privilege, forfeited our right to speak. And in Shakespeare's tragedies the abdication of speech, whether by Iago, Cordelia, Coriolanus, or Banquo's ghost, is fraught with danger; the character who refuses speech is vulnerable to the accusation that he is concurrently refusing the human bond. Manifestly, for Cordelia and Coriolanus, this is not the case: "love and be silent," and "[*holds her by the hand, silent*]" demarcate two of the most moving instances of human interaction in the Shakespearean canon. But as moving as they are, these moments are also tragic. Not to speak is to make oneself a victim, by dissociating oneself from the world of human communication. Iago does this explicitly at the close of *Othello*, but essentially he has been in this condition throughout the play, speaking never with an intent to communicate, but always to deceive. The audience, by accepting, as it must, the role of "mutes," accepts, as well, the danger and responsibility of this failed communication—and also something more. Our hearing, our seeing—that is, our identity as audience and spectators—has been our suffering, our participation in the tragic experience. This experience has been deepened, made more private and perhaps more painful, by the very passivity forced upon us. We cannot act to affect the play's outcome any more than the tragic hero can act to save himself. Such is the decorum of our stage that we cannot even cry out and expect to be heard. We are thus as surely victims of the play, as the play's protagonists are victims of its actions.

But if we are its victims, we are also its survivors and its celebrants. Old Hamlet, having told his tale of murder, exits on a line which seems addressed to the audience as well as to his son: "Adieu, adieu, adieu! Remember me" (I.v.91), and the words linger in the air after their speaker has departed the stage. Hamlet, mulling them as a text, seems likewise to speak for both audiences, for all audiences, in his reply.

> Remember thee!
> Ay, thou poor ghost, whiles memory holds a seat
> In this distracted globe.
>
> (ll. 95–97)

The triple pun on "globe"—head, world, theater—is underscored by the ambiguity of "seat." "Sitting at a play," the audience of tragedy is precisely what Hamlet says it is—the memory of the play's world, the record of its action. When Aufidius promises that Coriolanus "shall have a noble memory," it is only the audience which can keep his promise, and the nobility of this role is insisted upon:

> Let us haste to hear it,
> And call the noblest to the audience.
>
> (*Hamlet*, V.ii.378–379)

In the comedies, this recognition of reciprocity between the worlds on and off the stage is often accomplished through the use of an epilogue, a device which, like the soliloquy, allows for a direct confrontation between actor and audience. Thus Rosalind "conjures" her hearers "that the play may please," and requests them to bid her farewell with their applause. Prospero, having drowned his book, declares himself powerless, and asks for the help of our "good hands" and "gentle breath" to release him and sail him back to Milan. Puck, likewise, seeks our "hands," in friendship and applause. In each case the speaker of the epilogue acknowledges his own fictionality at the same time that he, like Puck, teases us with the dramatist's favorite conundrum, that perhaps only the fictive is true.

But in the world of Shakespearean tragedy there is no such moment suspended between "fiction" and "reality" in which the protagonist may reveal himself and the charm dissolve apace—nor, significantly, is there an explicit clarification and release, as manifested in the welcome activity of applause. Hamlet and Lear are dead, and in a more than literal sense their fame lies in our hands—and in our gentle breath. The injunction to replay the play, "to tell my story," to bear the bodies to the stage, suggests the ultimate role of the audience, no longer mute, and the ultimate reconstitution of the society disrupted by the tragic action. For each member of the tragic audience is asked to see himself as a survivor. Denied the easier mode of participation offered by comedy—a revels moment of song, dance, or solicited applause which assures the communal bond—the spectator of tragedy is at once isolated and chosen, privileged and obligated by what he has seen and heard. He is a witness, and he must testify. Troubled, paradoxically, by both his unwilling complicity and his unwilling passivity, the spectator at last becomes an actor—or, perhaps, recognizes that he has been one all along.

The Royal Shakespeare Company
Plays Henry VI

G. K. HUNTER

T HE HENRY VI PLAYS offer one of the great challenges to the Shakespeare producer, for there is no obvious method of making these
plays powerfully effective on the stage; nor is there any legendarily successful production to provide a model by which success can be judged (like
Peter Brooke's *Love's Labour's Lost* or *Titus Andronicus*). The Royal Shakespeare Company has tried twice since the war to stage these plays, once in
1963/64 and again in 1977/78, and these productions are interestingly
related to one another (and to the plays Shakespeare wrote) in the options
they have taken and the qualities they have emphasized. They may be
thought to represent the perils and successes of alternative attacks on the
trilogy, highlighting opposite qualities: to state it crudely, the 1963 production went for plot, the 1977 one for character. And each achieved its
success partly by using what is in the plays and partly by evading or
distorting the elements that Shakespeare planted there (I assume that
Shakespeare is the responsible agent throughout).

The 1963/64 production was part of the bold and ambitious plan by Sir
Peter Hall and the RSC to celebrate the quatercentenary of Shakespeare's
birth with a unique and stunning theatrical experience—a production of

all Shakespeare's history plays (leaving aside *King John* and *Henry VIII*), covering five reigns in eight, or rather (as bookbinders say) eight-in-seven plays. One must first comment on the imagination and energy required to conceive and carry through such a project. One should also note that the production was in many ways a summing up of critical attitudes propounded in the previous decades, particularly by Cambridge scholars (the moving spirits in the Stratford theater were Cambridge English graduates). Tillyard had rescued the history plays from easy assumptions about their merely anecdotal nature by insisting on their reference to ideas of order and disorder that the Tudor court was anxiously promoting in Shakespeare's age. Under the aegis of this interpretation (and related symbolist ideas about the unity of the artist's oeuvre) the eight history plays were found to offer continuity and consistency of viewpoint to the attentive reader. Each play was conceived to be more meaningful and therefore better when seen in sequence rather than in isolation.

Since this seems to be an assumption common to the two productions I am talking about, it may be well to begin by discussing this very point. Are the Henry VI plays (and so by implication the Henry IV plays) so written that the advantage lies with the spectator who has seen them all in sequence, with the same actors playing the major roles—Henry VI, Margaret, Warwick, York? Shakespeare called his plays "Part I," "Part II," "Part III," and this may seem an invitation to see them as necessarily bound together. But the model of Marlowe's *Tamburlaine* suggests that a play called "Part II" may follow one called "Part I" simply because the first self-sufficient play was a great commercial success:

> The general welcomes Tamburlaine received
> When he arrived last upon our stage
> Hath made our poet pen his second part.

The theatrical conditions of Shakespeare's age were not much like those of Wagner's *Festspielhaus*; the separate plays had to be separately intelligible to casual theatergoers, and there is good evidence that the separate parts of *Henry VI* were not conceived as fragments of a fifteen-act epic but plays in their own right. It is worth noticing that of the thirty-eight named characters in Part I only nine survive into Part II (out of forty-seven in Part II only seven [or eight] survive to Part III); what is more, those who survive are not those with the greatest presence or largest number of lines.

The principal antagonists of Part I, Talbot and Joan la Pucelle, both die. Margaret, who becomes a dominant character in Part II, appears in only one scene of Part I, and then as part of Suffolk's ambition rather than as a self-directing character. A company with limited resources would be well advised to show its principal actor of female parts as Joan in Part I and as Margaret in Part II, and recast Talbot as York. We should not assume that the conspicuous expenditure of modern theatrical companies such as the RSC was possible for Shakespeare's company. It follows that the decision to play the three Parts in sequence, with the same actors (the stars) giving depth and continuity to the depiction of the same characters in play after play, is an interpretative decision, not a merely executive one. Such a performance creates a forward trajectory and momentum which the plays do not necessarily require. Critics have concerned themselves with the question how effectively Peggy Ashcroft or Helen Mirren advances Margaret from the passive maiden of Part I to the terrifying harridan of Part III, or of *Richard III*; but this is a question which does not arise naturally from the plays themselves. Each Margaret (*Henry VI* I, II, III and *Richard III*) is in fact a different Margaret, accommodated to a different structure and operating in terms of a different range of relationships and effects. For the separate subject matters of the separate plays, no less than the major part of the cast, are clearly demarcated. Part I is centered on the loss of the French inheritance that Henry V bequeathed to the play just before it opened. This is the subject matter that gives Talbot and Joan la Pucelle their dominating hold on the play. And Part I ends not only with their deaths but with the truce that allows Charles the Dauphin to have secured *de facto* control over France, while the marriage of Henry and Margaret gives personal expression to the stasis that now operates between the two countries. Part II, on the other hand, is England-bound. The opposition is now dynastic rather than national. The first three acts set the many peers against the one (Humphrey of Gloucester), and the section ends with the deaths of the principals (Gloucester, Winchester, Sussex). Act IV is occupied by Cade and his parody Yorkist claim. Act V shows us civil war itself and ends with York replacing Lancaster as the power in England.

From one point of view this final act is a preparation or bridge to Part III, just as the arrival of Margaret at the end of Part I could be said to be a bridge carrying attention to the material of Part II. Part III is certainly concerned with the physical violences of all-out civil war. But it has its

own separate principles of shaping and development. The first two acts set
the battles of Wakefield and Towton against one another in opposed but
repetitive expressions of savagery. The remaining acts pursue individual
treacheries at a more personal level, as Warwick swings from York to
Lancaster and Clarence double turns to Henry and away again. The structure of Part III seems designed to devalue progressively the thing that is
being struggled for, and the emergent dominance of Richard Crookback
finally states the manic selfishness of power in its simplest form. Again it
is possible to see the emergence of Richard at the end of the play as a
parasceue or cliff-hanger for *Richard III*. These connections are there; but
overemphasis easily gives rise to a circular argument for the continuity of
the four plays. Knowing the existence of the historical sequence, we are
able to interpret every element which points up the sequence as part of
Shakespeare's purpose. But if we did not know of the sequence we would
have little difficulty in pointing to the integral nature of these "anticipa-
tory" or "preparatory" elements. There is no need for us to assume at the
end of Part I that Margaret has further actions to perform, without which
we do not understand her role. Likewise at the end of Part II the outbreak
of civil war completes the pattern established at the beginning, when we
see the peers unable to accept any single definition of the national good. In
Part III the final contrast between the saintly and prophetic Henry and the
active but unperceiving Richard completes the statement of pragmatic
success bought by the abolition of moral meaning. Nothing is set up here
which the following play (*Richard III*) has to deny or displace; but the
conclusion of *3 Henry VI* does not leave us dissatisfied with what we have
been shown—the death of the titular hero and the end of the Lancastrian
claim.

The claim for continuity as something demanded by the plays and
particularly effective in the theater was much stronger in the 1963/64
production than in the 1977/78 one; but even in the latter the performance of the plays in sequence and the retention of the principal actors in
one play after another make an implicit demand that the meaning be seen
to accumulate steadily over fifteen acts. But the producer of the 1977
version, Terry Hands, has done little to force the plays into this mold; and
in the theater the natural dispersal of interest continually asserts itself
against his comparatively weak pressure. Of these effects I shall have more
to say; but it may be better to begin with the direr methods by which the
earlier production countered the individual plays' centrifugal tendencies.

The method was, by and large, one of rewriting, so that the plays changed their natures. The 12,350 lines of the original tetralogy were reduced to some 6,000 lines of Shakespeare, augmented by some 1,450 new lines penned by Sir Peter Hall's coadjutor, John Barton.[1]

This extraordinary piece of surgery was greeted with general critical approval. The newspaper critics fell over one another with delight. Bernard Levin was not far ahead of the pack in his remark that this was "one of the mightiest stage projects of our time . . . a production to remember all our lives . . . great drama interpreted by men of imagination and understanding" (*Daily Mail*, 21 August 1963). *The Liverpool Post* told us that "this is undoubtedly a case of improving on Shakespeare without disturbing the essentials" (18 July 1963), and even the skeptical *Guardian* allowed that the rewriting "sharpens the plays' meaning" (25 July 1963). The reduction of the three parts of *Henry VI* to two plays (called here *Henry VI* and *Edward IV*) seems, however, to have been suggested to Mr. Hall and his collaborators by economic as well as aesthetic reasoning. The Stratford-on-Avon theatrical authorities seem, then, to have reckoned that two "unpopular" plays were the most the box office could stand in a single season.[2] Three Henry VI plays thus expressed a formula for economic disaster. It is, no doubt, the mark of the great impresario that economic necessity can be translated into aesthetic choice; and Mr. Hall and Mr. Barton seem to have convinced themselves before they convinced others that Shakespeare had left considerable room for improvement. They were able to draw on a tradition of respectable, though even by then, slightly old-fashioned scholarship, to suggest that the originals were only partly Shakespearean. For Peter Hall "so much of it is frankly padding."[3] John Barton speaks of the same easy-to-detect inconsistency, finding that much of Part III is "Elizabethan hack work, dry of imagery and vigour, and different in kind as well as quality, from the remainder."[4] It follows that there is no real loss in slicing up these primitive compilations into more commercially possible structures. In

---

1. See *The Wars of the Roses, adapted for the Royal Shakespeare Company from William Shakespeare's Henry VI, Parts I, II and III and Richard III*, by John Barton and Peter Hall (London, 1970), p. xvi (hereafter cited as *WR*).

2. *Ibid.*

3. Interview with Trussler in Charles Marowitz and Simon Trussler, *Theatre at Work* (London, 1967), p. 152.

4. *WR*, p. xxiv.

1953, Sir Barry Jackson recorded his opinion that "dire failure . . . must be the fate of any attempt, no matter how skilful, to boil down or condense the trilogy for dramatic presentation";[5] but the production of the three plays (by Douglas Seale) in Sir Barry Jackson's own Birmingham Repertory Theatre in 1953 had achieved only a *succès d'estime*. The prize of commercial success in the much larger Stratford house was by no means assured by the Birmingham precedent. On economic grounds there may well have seemed no alternative to the action taken—cut half of Shakespeare's lines and reconstitute the rest as two closely integrated plays.

It is no part of my purpose to say, even on aesthetic grounds, that the decision to condense was wrong of necessity. No normal production of Shakespeare fails to tamper with the text; and the continued vitality of Shakespeare's plays in the theater is a good for which purists must be willing to pay a certain price. These plays are to some extent like aging bodies that can only be kept alive by medical and even surgical attention. The failure of such operations might seem, however, to bear a direct relation to the ambition of the surgeon. Short-term effects may indeed be spectacular: the patient moves with galvanic energy for a year or two. Even if then he suddenly collapses, the challenge is one that the surgeon can hardly be expected to resist; and my interest as a surgical commentator is only in the nature of the particular techniques used by Barton and Hall, not in the moral problem of undertaking transplant surgery.

The surgeon begins by accepting a diagnosis of the disease he is concerned with—if I may continue with this grisly metaphor for a few lines more—and critical statements that the *Henry VI* plays suffer from a fatty-degenerative condition are not hard to find. Barton tells us, in the preface to the printed version of his text, that "the *Henry VI* plays, immensely diffuse and uneven in quality, were not viable as they stand,"[6] and Peter Hall, in the same volume, adds that what he found in other productions of these plays was "a mess of angry and undifferentiated barons thrashing about in a mass of diffuse narrative" (p. vii). Some may remember the sketch in the *Beyond the Fringe* review in which kings, uncertain whether they are Henry or Richard or Edward, order barons equally uncertain in name, York or Warwick or Pembroke, to counties that bear the same

5. Sir Barry Jackson, "On Producing *Henry VI*," *Sh S*, VI (1953), 50.
6. *WR*, p. xv.

names, producing a total confusion of subject and object. Play surgeons, however, have a disadvantage against body surgeons: their decision about the nature of the disease they will remedy depends on a definition of health which is hard to prove. Hall and Barton apparently considered the swollen and ungainly body of *Henry VI* and made a decision about what they call "the central action"; this seems to be defined by them as a continuous political narrative moving forward steadily from beginning to end and explaining what is subsequent by what precedes it and causes it. Having defined this they can then cut away the superfluous fat, tap out the unhealthy fluids, and rescue from the diffuse, stumbling, dropsical giant a trim, lithe, and with-it figure, sharp and resilient like Hall and Barton, and certainly sharing many of their current interests.

It is high time that I shut up the operating theater and returned to the real one. I wish, however, to carry away one product of the metaphor—the doubt I have expressed about the idea of "health" that has been drawn on; for I find that the ideal of dramatic excellence implied by the statements and the rewriting is one which appears nowhere else in Shakespeare. The efficiency and singleness of purpose that have been procured by the treatment are modern and not Elizabethan characteristics. Barton and Hall consider that the central issue of the *Henry VI* plays is power. Hall tells us that "the nature of power and the irony of power and the corruption of power . . . was what I was concerned with showing." [7] Now there can be little doubt that power is one of the continuous concerns of Shakespeare's *Henry VI*. But the attitude toward power which Shakespeare producers took up in the sixties from Jan Kott (who seems in turn to have learned it from Peter Brooke's 1955 *Titus Andronicus*) is much more contemporary than Shakespearean. In Kott's formulation Shakespeare revealed history as a relentless and unceasing round of murder-rule-be murdered, so that though the decades passed the pattern remained the same. This constant pattern could thus be seen to offer unity to the divergent material the history plays were so full of. The cast of a history play is thus given the very modern choice of being political or being irrelevant: their characteristics as human beings are to be focused narrowly but intensely on the will to power, and in this they are part of the play's pattern, but not otherwise. This narrowing and sharpening of focus is found everywhere in the

7. Marowitz and Trussler, *Theatre at Work*, p. 151.

Barton-Hall *Wars of the Roses*. John Bury, the designer, tells us that the box of rusted steel which enclosed much of the action was intended to tell us that "nothing yields . . . The countryside offers no escape." Surrounding all is "the great steel cage of war." [8]

Such separate and "irrelevant" episodes as that of the Countess of Auvergne (*1 Henry VI*, II.iii) might seem to blow a hole in the neat symmetries of this prison. She cannot be chained to any of its categories. In her "capture" of Talbot she might indeed seem to be making a political move, but it is a move without consequence. These politics are domestic and comic, and the human motives shown are more interesting than the political meaning. It is, of course, possible to use the word *political* to cover every situation; but if the Countess does mount Kott's "great staircase" of the will to political power, she does so with a difference. Her high-spirited and comic female parody of chivalric combat expresses free and individual choice. Her sense of her own power turns out to be comically mistaken; but the mistake is not a defeat in any of the dimensions that are important for this scene. Talbot tells her that his body, which she has captured, is no more the substance of himself than is the picture that she keeps in her gallery. His true substance is the body of armed men who enter when he *winds his horn*. But the mailed fist appears in the scene only as a preparation for magnanimity. Power is turned to charm and politics culminates in personal relations:

COUNTESS

Victorious Talbot! pardon my abuse.
I find thou art no less than fame hath bruited,
And more than may be gathered by thy shape.
Let my presumption not provoke thy wrath,
For I am sorry that with reverence
I did not entertain thee as thou art.

TALBOT

Be not dismayed, fair lady, nor misconster
The mind of Talbot as you did mistake
The outward composition of his body.
What you hath done hath not offended me;
Nor other satisfaction do I crave
But only, with your patience, that we may

8. *WR*, p. 237.

Taste of your wine and see what cates you have;
For soldiers' stomachs always serve them well.

COUNTESS

With all my heart, and think me honoured
To feast so great a warrior in my house.

(ll. 67–82)

Neither character emerges from this scene as simple exploiter or exploited. The mechanisms of politics hold back a little to allow us to participate in an alternative and unsubdued value system. This presence of unsubdued alternatives is in fact more pervasive in the *Henry VI* plays than seeing *The Wars of the Roses* might suggest. Talbot is, in his career, a central part of the political process of *1 Henry VI*; but his political role is only one of a series of roles he is seen to be playing—as father, as loyalist, as commander, as quasi-lover (as here). Each of these roles is parallel to the others, but none is felt to be shackled to the others inside historical necessity, except perhaps in the constant terms of an over-all final view. And it is, of course, the obliterating primacy of the "final view" that I am questioning. Are we faced in fact by the alternatives of either one unified, forward-moving action where each detail is dovetailed into the others to support a single, central and continuously present judgment, or are we left with a series of "vignettes from the chronicles," "scented moments with Holinshed," with no claim to over-all judgment or unity? The answer to such a question cannot be argued abstractly; it can only emerge from a perception of the plays as organized by Shakespeare (with a parallel perception of them as reorganized in Barton-Hall). Only a gesture toward such a proceeding is possible here; but I trust that it may fairly (like the Chorus in *Henry V*) "Attest in little place a million."

The first part of *Henry VI* carried us from the death of Henry V to the truce with France, and from the *de jure* accession to his marriage. The main substance of the action—the loss of the French domain—is represented in a series of overlapping trajectories: that of Joan la Pucelle, bringing power and comfort to the French, that represented by the English quarrels between Humphrey of Gloucester and Cardinal Beaufort, the trajectory of the York-Lancaster dynastic issue, and finally, but more notionally represented, the trajectory of Henry VI himself, that oxymoronic figure, Wordsworth's "royal saint." These parallel trajectories

move together, in complex harmonic motion, from stasis at the beginning, through a series of shifts and adjustments, to a respite at the end;
but no single trajectory explains why things move in one direction and not
in another. Each responds, of course, to the others: Joan's success conditions and is conditioned by the English quarrels; Winchester's factiousness
is made possible (as appears from the end of I.i) by the obsession of the lay
nobles with France.

But the separate parts are more than functions of the whole; we respond
as much to the separateness, indeed uniqueness, of each personal world as
to their relatedness or interdependence. Even as we detect connection we
should note distinctions. The play is, among other things, "about" the
bonding of fathers and sons—Henry V and Henry VI in the plays' largest
terms, Old Talbot and Young Talbot, the Gunner of Orleans and his son,
and the parallel cases of Old Mortimer and Richard Plantagenet, and
Shepherd and Joan. The question of inheritance appears in all these cases,
and in some instances this has political importance. But no simple pattern
can be drawn.

The strongest theatrical expression of the father-son relationship comes
from the Talbots and is virtually without political resonance. The moment
of our knowledge of Young Talbot is a moment only, but the values it
expresses run into the rest of the play. It is partly of course that politics is
evaluated for us by its destruction of personal relations and moral norms.
But much more resonance is set up by the positive demonstration that the
deepest levels of these lives draw on personal and familial relationships
which feed into politics but are not controlled by politics. In Kott's vision
of the Shakespearean world individuality is a bourgeois luxury that the
historical process must crush into insignificance; but in Shakespeare's
actual texts individuality is the substance out of which all history is made,
without whose contradictions and discontinuities the processes of history
are too abstracted to express values.

The decision to perform the plays as an integrated sequence has the
inevitable effect of reinforcing the forward-moving pattern at the expense
of individual moments. The trivia of individualizing detail may seem
tolerable inside a single play; but the progressive momentum of the
historical juggernaut makes these halts to examine detail seem impossible.
The Barton-Hall cutting and rewriting pushed the plays still further in
this direction, and as a result the individual lives became thin and dia-

grammatic.[9] Barton and Hall took the pursuit of power to be the thread on which the material of the plays is strung (or ought to be restrung). Seen as an unrelenting struggle to achieve political stability, the action cannot be properly halted before the coming of the heaven-sent Richmond, and the progressive movement thus seems to show us the Kottian picture of dog eating dog. The producers were not, however, content with this: they aimed to give us also an attendant analysis of the digestive processes, rendering the reign of Henry VI between the upper and lower jaws of oligarchy and autocracy. The perception of these alternatives as the real issues of the reign looks more and more curious as time passes; and it is worth noticing that the evidence for the issue derives principally from Barton's invention, not Shakespeare's. It seems fair to suppose that its centrality in the production measures the interests of these producers and of the early sixties rather than anything in the plays. In the preface to the printed version Sir Peter Hall tells us: "I became more and more fascinated by politicians, and by the corrupting seductions experienced by anyone who wields power." It would not seem too great an invasion of privacy to suppose that the position of Director of the Royal Shakespeare Company stands among the positions of power that offer invitations to corruption! But the good man in power seeks for preventatives against corruption, and in a hopeful ethic the idea of sharing power, of government through committee, will always seem to offer prophylaxis.[10] In one of his notes to Barton Peter Hall remarks that "men and countries must be open to a rational equilibrium produced by all the forces working on them."[11] In a program note of 1963 he expands: "so the selfish instincts of men must be checked—by Parliament, democracy, tradition, religion—or else the men of ambition will misgovern the rest."

Reading the Barton-Hall text or seeing the production makes it easy to note how these interests were presented as central supports to carry the burden of the Henry VI story. In visual terms the stage was set to show a

9. Compare John Russell Brown, "Three Kinds of Shakespeare," *Sh S*, XVIII (1965), 147–155, reprinted in his *Shakespeare's Plays in Performance* (London, 1966).

10. It is worth noticing that the Stratford History Cycle was itself a deliberate experiment in "collective directing," involving a distribution of responsibility through the whole team. See David Addenbrook, *The Royal Shakespeare Company* (London, 1974), pp. 128–129.

11. *WR*, pp. xix–xx.

polarization between the throne and the council table, each drawn to our attention by its mechanical efficiency—the former rushing forward like an express train, the latter rising from the floor like a cinema organ. Each was alternately made the focus of the competing politicians. It is hard, of course, to find much about these matters in Shakespeare's text. Barton was willing, however, to mend what was deficient, and a series of new interpretations of what is going on were written into the plays. I have time to deal with only a few of these, but they may serve to indicate the main methods of reinterpreation. At the end of Shakespeare's *1 Henry VI* Suffolk persuades Henry to marry Margaret, in a context which is sharply personal but politically unfocused. A Barton addition tells us that this was in fact a constitutional crux and misuse of government:

> My lord, if you mislike these articles,
> Tomorrow, then, and at the council-board,
> Let us resolve this by our general voice
>
> .   .   .   .
>
> Why then, The greater part uphold these articles,
> And Warwick, howso'er he likes them not,
> Must honour and approve the general.

(xvii)

It is allowed that the council sometimes operates justly. When Humphrey can exert the authority of the King in council the system is offered as an image of English constitutionality. Winchester makes this point to Margaret:

> Madam, what say'st thou to these gentle means
> By which our loving council doth determine
> What tendeth best unto our kingdom's good?
>
> MARGARET
>
> In faith, I wonder at it, sir.

(xix)

Margaret's scorn for the petitioners (an example of personal jealousy in Shakespeare—*2 Henry VI*, I.iii.1 ff.) becomes an expression of scorn for English constitutional methods; but she soon learns to pack the council so that it becomes an unrepresentative body. Most obviously this is used by Barton to explain the condemnation of Humphrey. The packed council is said to be incapable of functioning justly:

KING

Good uncle Exeter,
Why speak'st thou not upon the Duke's behalf?

EXETER

Because this Council is too obdurate,
Too predetermin'd to brook argument.

(xxii)

The King is represented as too weak to challenge even a packed council:

SUFFOLK

What say you now, my liege? I challenge law
And am content to abide the general voice.
(*They place their hands on the council table*)

KING

Since all approve, I must abide it, too.
Prithee, sweet lord, to yield me up to the seal. . . .

GLOUCESTER

As thou art King, now answer like a King.

KING

We do consent: and henceforth are resolv'd
The Council's will shall be our conscience.

(xxii)

The method of evading constitutional responsibility by packing the council is seen as a key instance of political corruption throughout the whole sequence of *The Wars of the Roses*. At a later point Clarence makes complaint against Edward IV:

I like it not he doth advance Lord Rivers
And other upstart kinsmen of the Queen:
Why doth he so but to disfurnish us?
This is the trick was fashion'd, as I think,
By Margaret against our royal father,
Who pack'd the Council once with minion peers
To countercheck her mighty opposites.

(xliv)

This evasion of constitutionality is shown to lead naturally to tyranny, and when the tyrant Richard III is secure he no longer needs the evasion. This was demonstrated in a visually spectacular way when Richard's leather-clad storm troopers broke up the council table with their maces. The issue that had been invented to sustain the material of *Henry VI* and *Edward IV* was allowed to shatter into something more like the authentic Shakespeare of *Richard III*.

That the brawling barons of the three parts of *Henry VI* can be confusing no one disputes.[12] But the confusion is tied in with the authentic richness of the material. Shakespeare makes these lives available to us primarily at the level of individual moments and personal emotion and only sec-ondarily at the level of political abstraction or historical overview. In his view political decisions arise out of personal history, temperament, vendetta, family loyalty; and without these tentacular roots their be-havior resembles shallow, cartoonlike "animations" rather than human actions. Thus the personal relationship of Humphrey and Elinor, to which Shakespeare devotes considerable space, does much to make credible the "goodness" as well as the vulnerability of the Lord Protector; deprived of this backing (as in Barton-Hall) his so-called goodness becomes a merely political attribute, an expression on a public face. Similarly, Joan la Pucelle's curse (*1 Henry VI*, V.iv) loses, when pieced out with sundry Shakespearean scraps forecasting the Wars of the Roses, all its particular reinforcement of the unique physical moment in the life of the witch-saint; she too shrinks to the wraithlike existence of a political tendency. Political continuity, Kottian "contemporaneity," the focus on power—these are bought at a price which may seem too high. The things that are lost might seem more Shakespearean: unemphatic parallelism of divergent moments, complex juxtapositions of the personal, the local, the particu-lar, seen together with their opposites—cause-and-effect overview or forward-pressing interpretation. By such juxtapositions Shakespeare in-vites the audience to seek explanations of what they see, but leaves the

---

12. See Barton's note to Hall, printed in *WR*, p. xix: "I think we can also cut down the personal brawling a good deal further, and should get away from baronial rhodomontade by using the council-table as much as possible." If one wished one might find a source for the technique in Kott (Hall had read Kott just before the rehearsals): "for Shakespeare, power . . . is a relentless struggle of living people who sit together at one table" (*Shake-speare our Contemporary* [Garden City, N.Y., 1964], p. 7).

web of relationship so complex that, whenever we read or whenever we contemplate staging the plays, there are always more explanations than are needed.

I have suggested above that the 1977 production by Terry Hands shares some but not all of these 1963 characteristics. The plays seem to be presented, in the main, in the texts that Shakespeare wrote, and the theatrical effect depends principally on the effective projection of Shakespeare's words by the skilled actors who perform the major roles. The whole production is untendentious and unfussy. One has also to confess, alas, that the plays that emerge from this treatment are diffuse and dull; the Barton-Hall argument against Shakespeare might seem to be sustained, however long after the letter. Before one allows this, however, one ought to look at the later production in some detail. It would seem to be a characteristic of the modern theater that the standard conventions of realism take over whenever the director fails to take sufficient measures in counteraction—and such is the case here. The actors (through whom the convention operates most powerfully and most subtly) act their hearts out in giving Stanislavski-esque "depth" to the characters: Joan la Pucelle swaggers and giggles as one supposes a maidenly soldier would have to, in real life; Elinor Cobham preens and sighs; Edmund Mortimer acts his age as well as expressing it. Emrys James, on the other hand, camps up the Duke of York with fluting exaggerations and Anton Lesser outacts Olivier acting Richard III. Between these separate effects the plays fall to the ground. Noticing that the "success" of such characterizations almost necessarily involves the failure of *Henry VI*, it begins to become clear that the characters of these plays bear a special relation to one another and to the structures and repetitions of the plays and require the utmost discretion from the whole company.

Critics have noticed that the three Frenchwomen we meet in *1 Henry VI* bear a simple relation to one another.[13] Joan's end is matched to Margaret's beginning, so that one seems to take up the role laid down by the other—the role of the treacherous and destructive Frenchwoman, of which the Countess of Auvergne offers a comic variant. The passing of role from hand to hand is not, however, confined to these ladies. In Part I again we

13. See David Bevington, "The Domineering Female in *Henry VI*," *Sh Stud*, II (1966), 51–58.

see the role of English champion and scourge of France pass from Salisbury to Talbot. The text makes this quite specific:

TALBOT

Hear, hear, how dying Salisbury doth groan!
It irks his heart he cannot be revenged.
Frenchmen, I'll be a Salisbury to you.

(I.iv.104–106)

In the same way, a little later, Talbot also takes over the role of Bedford, too sick to participate in the assault on Rouen, but able to pass on the gifts of his spirit. In 2 *Henry VI* the repeated pattern of hunter and hunted passes through several hands. The hunting of Humphrey dominates the early part of the play. In nearly every other scene of the first three acts we watch the pack of peers snapping at his heels and coming closer and closer to the kill. In III.i.191 ff., when he is stripped of his protectorship, he specifically passes on the role to Henry, who carries it into Part III.[14] But the quick transformation of hunter into hunted is to be seen several times before that. Suffolk has no sooner achieved his aim as victimizer than he becomes the victim, baited and killed by another group—the sailors who capture him. The Cade group form another pack; in the almost ritualized process of accusation and assault they dispose of their bewildered victims, the Clerk of Chartham and Lord Say, Henry's men seen as the victims of York's man as Henry is the victim of York.

The persistence of these patterns is easy to notice in the play, but they are likely to remain concealed from the modern theatergoer, for the individuals who compose the patterns are continually changing. Even in the obvious sequence of the hunting of Humphrey the rhetoric of ensnarement and abuse is perpetually passed from hand to hand. We first hear the attack from Winchester, Somerset, Buckingham (I.i.); in I.iii. the speakers are Queen, Suffolk, Buckingham, Winchester; in II.i. they are Queen, Suffolk, Winchester; while in III.i. Queen, Suffolk, Winchester, York,

14. It is presumably no accident that the final "capturing" of Henry is represented by Shakespeare as effected by professional huntsmen (or Keepers) who see the king as a substitute for their intended prey: "Ay, here's a deer whose skin's a keeper's fee: / This is the quondam king; let's seize upon him" (III.i.23–24). King Edward, on the other hand, escapes from his last captivity while engaged in hunting and quickly turns his hunt from animals to men.

and Buckingham all join in for the kill. The appearance of Winchester in all these groupings is, of course, significant; but he is not allowed to dominate the rhetoric against Humphrey. Nor is anyone else. The speeches of blame and complaint could be redistributed among the members of the group without any loss. Shakespeare does not offer us the simple massing of one group against another—goodies against baddies—but the similarities between one factious nobleman and another is probably more important than the differences. A modern actor who believes that it is his business to give maximum individualization to the character he plays will inevitably work toward differentiation, and so work against the system. And it is not only the actor; the modern reader, studious over genealogies and footnotes, desperately hopes to remember how Somerset and Buckingham fit into the historical situation. But though his book learning is designed to recapture an Elizabethan point of view, it probably only gets in the way of a truly theatrical indifference to facts not included in the play. Inside the play most characters are best known by the company they keep; and the style of acting that seems to be demanded is one which can occasionally rise to individualization, but elsewhere merges into the identity of the group.

The argument pursued here may seem one for flattening and simplifying the plays, after the manner of Barton and Hall. It certainly marches with them in the assumption that the plays need more than a simple leave-it-to-the-actors approach. But where they believed that the trilogy was "about" power I am proposing patterns somewhere below the level of ideology. We see the world founder while the pirates wrangle; but our attention is not focused on the technical means by which the shipwreck is achieved. We are rather invited to attend to the continuous copresence of loyalty and disloyalty, patriotism and betrayal, understanding and ignorance, often in the same people; but not as facts of psychology but rather as facets of the different contexts and different groupings. York as father of Rutland, or as victim of Margaret, is different from York with Warwick and Salisbury, or York against Humphrey, or the York that is represented by Cade. Only by overreading can consistency of psychology or politics be argued for; and even then the labor is in vain since the plays do not operate chiefly through the progressions that such consistency can achieve. The individual characters are not shown, in psychology or political status, to be moving from one irrevocable condition to another. The possibilities are never totally closed, and the sense of latency, waiting for the new ensemble to reveal the new power is an important part of our response. We are repeatedly reminded, for example, that effective rule is only a hairsbreadth away, even for Henry VI, as at the moments when he ennobles Talbot or banishes Suffolk or rewards Iden. Only the most unselfish ensemble playing, however, more like that of a chamber orchestra than of a modern theatrical company, can hope to use its instruments in this way, as they appear now in one group now in another, now with the top-line melody, now with the counter-tune, now as harmonic background, now as victim or victimizer, loyalist or usurper, retaining enough continuity and forward pressure to support the story and yet keeping enough in reserve to allow us the sense that the potentials are inexhaustible.

This is what the Henry VI plays seem to demand; it is hard to see how the demand can be satisfied under the conditions of the modern professional stage.

Hamlet's O-groans and
Textual Criticism

MAURICE CHARNEY

S O MUCH SCORN has been heaped on Hamlet's last words in the Folio
text—"O, o, o, o" (l. 3847)[1]—that I hesitate to reopen this painful
subject. Perhaps we should just let Hamlet die metaphorically with "The
rest is silence" and let it go at that. Mardian reports that Cleopatra died in
the very act of speaking the name Anthony:

> Then in the midd'st a tearing grone did breake
> The name of *Anthony*: it was diuided
> Betweene her heart, and lips: she rendred life
> Thy name so buried in her.
>
> (ll. 2861–2864)

That is a grand death, so grand in fact that it never takes place and serves
instead as a rhetorical model for how to die well. But "O, o, o, o"? Dover
Wilson quotes Dowden's disapproval of these "unhappy" "O's" and goes

Paper presented at the Modern Language Association, December 27, 1976, in a shorter
version. I am indebted to Paul Bertram for a number of valuable suggestions.

1. All quotations from Shakespeare's Folio text are from the Norton facsimile of the
First Folio edited by Charlton Hinman (New York, 1968). A few obviously typographical
errors have been silently corrected.

on to inveigh against "little ejaculatory words or phrases which a player in
the excitement of performance would be likely to add to his lines." "O, o,
o, o" is "preposterous" and an "enormity"; it is one of those "players'
tricks of speech" that we find "creeping into the prompt-book or into
actors' parts."[2]

It is difficult, then, to go about defending Hamlet's "O, o, o, o" in the
face of such determined opposition. Dover Wilson's views are solidly
supported by the fact that these unseemly dying groans of Hamlet have
been excluded from virtually all editions of the play since Rowe (1709),
the older editions based on Folio as well as the newer ones based on Quarto
2, which nevertheless include most of the other so-called Folio interpolations, as in Wilson's own edition of *Hamlet* in the New Cambridge Shakespeare (2d ed., 1957). Critics seem to agree almost unanimously in reject-
ing these harsh and ineloquent "O's." After "The rest is silence," the rest
is indeed silence for Hamlet—at least by common consent of critics and
editors. If Richard Burbage liked to fatten his part with a string of catchy
O-groans, we must indulge him his own histrionic eccentricities, but as
for Hamlet the dramatic character, we cannot let his already "too too
sullied flesh" be any further sullied in death.

Yet the O-groans keep coming at us from other parts of Shakespeare to
mark moments of high passion and intense sorrow. Othello's agonized
speech of self-loathing, in which he invokes all the torments of hell to
punish him for his murder of the innocent Desdemona, ends mysteriously
with a quiet (but more painful, because less rhetorical) sense of tragic loss:
"Oh *Desdemon*! dead *Desdemon*: dead. Oh, oh!" (l. 3581). In the Quarto of
1622 the line ends with three "O's," a reading favored by Sisson in his
New Readings in Shakespeare.[3] If the "O's" are already hypermetrical, it
hardly matters if there are two or three of them; in other words, the line is
not more or less correct metrically because it has fewer "O's." Othello's
"O's" survive in most editions, while Hamlet's have disappeared, although they are both analogous in dramatic and emotive function. As
hypermetrical, speech-ending "O's"—something extra—they are obviously vulnerable to cutting, especially in print, where metrics take a
highly visual and arithmetic form.

2. J. Dover Wilson, *The Manuscript of Shakespeare's Hamlet and the Problems of Its Trans-
mission* (Cambridge, Eng., 1934), I, 77–79.

3. C. J. Sisson, *New Readings in Shakespeare* (London, 1956; rpt. 1961), II, 258.

King Lear's O-groans in the Pied Bull Quarto of 1608 have also vanished from modern editions, although in context they have a brute force
very apt for the old king's final burst of energy before he dies: "O thou
wilt come no more, neuer, neuer, neuer, pray you vndo this button,
thanke you sir, O, o, o, o" (V.iii.307–308).[4] Quarto 2 (1619) has a string
of five "O's" here, whereas the Folio text has five "never's" and no "O's."
The Quarto texts suffer from what is usually diagnosed as "memorial
contamination," which, like "actor's interpolation," creates a distinct
sense of skulduggery on the part of the actors and/or shorthand tran-
scribers, who had the effrontery to speak more than was set down for them
in the only true copy of the play. There is a clear conflict between those
who conceive the play that Shakespeare wrote as a historical document
written and/or printed and those who would allow performance some
status and authenticity of its own. We may ask, naïvely, what precisely is
being contaminated and what is being coarsened by the ravages of interpolation? Not being a practicing textual critic, I am deliberately stating the
argument in a popular and nontechnical form. The exaggerated polarities
should clarify the basic issues.

The corroborating evidence seems to indicate that Burbage used
O-groans freely in performance. Was Shakespeare aware of the liberties his
leading actor was taking with the text and did he warn him to cease and
desist? This seems hardly likely, since the two were close—perhaps
daily—associates in the same theatrical enterprise. Some of Burbage's
interpolated flourishes—even the O-groans—have found their way into
the best texts of Shakespeare. One cannot help wondering if Shakespeare
himself picked up a few hints from his leading actor, or must one pos-
tulate, as Alice Walker does for *Hamlet*,[5] that the promptbook transcripts
used as printer's copy for the Folio included some of these tabooed actor's
interpolations?

In other words, the manuscript of the play that was kept in the theater
and used for performance (the "promptbook") must have been edited, as
we know later promptbooks were, to account for some of the words spoken
on stage that were different from what the author originally wrote. I don't

---

4. Quoted from the Shakespeare Quarto Facsimiles series, no. 1, ed. Sir Walter Greg
and Charlton Hinman (Oxford, 1939).

5. Alice Walker, *Textual Problems of the First Folio* (Cambridge, Eng., 1953), chap. 6.

mean that the promptbook was constantly revised after every hot flash of an ad-libbing actor, but at some point significant changes that had become established in performance must have been recorded. This whole issue of performance raises special problems for editors of plays,[6] problems that don't exist for nondramatic texts (although public readings may create analogous problems for authors such as Dickens, Twain, and Frost). How should we deal with changes introduced in performance? The purist would like to ignore them as not being part of the author's original intention, but a more adventurous critic could argue that these changes actualize or realize what is, at the start, merely a hypothetical, potential, and trial text. There is nothing sacrosanct about the script a playwright begins with, and, in the nature of things, there can be no final, perfect, fully authentic version of a dramatic manuscript. The Platonic idea of the play must have a slightly different manifestation at each performance, so that any play text we choose to print represents a subtle compromise between the written and the spoken word. One would think, as a matter of historical vitality, that editors of Shakespeare would be eager to include as many indications of contemporary performance as they could substantiate.

We know that Burbage was particularly remembered for his powerful death scenes, in which the O-groans are only one small detail. An anonymous funeral elegy on the death of Burbage on March 13, 1618, makes a metaphysical conceit out of the actor's ability to counterfeit death so convincingly:

> Oft haue I seene him, play this part in ieast,
> Soe liuly, that Spectators, and the rest
> Of his sad Crew, whilst he but seem'd to bleed,
> Amazed, thought euen then hee dyed in deed. . . .[7]

Beaumont must surely be thinking specifically of Burbage, when, in *The Knight of the Burning Pestle* (1607),[8] he has Rafe die with a high-flown

---

6. See L. A. Beaurline, "The Director, the Script, and Author's Revisions: A Critical Problem," *Papers on Dramatic Theory and Criticism*, ed. David M. Knauf (Iowa City, 1963), pp. 78–91.

7. Quoted from Edwin Nungezer, *A Dictionary of Actors* (Ithaca, N.Y., 1929), p. 74.

8. Dates of plays are given from Alfred Harbage, *Annals of English Drama 975–1700*, rev. S. Schoenbaum (London, 1964).

parody of tragic sentiments: "I die, flie, flie my soule to *Grocers* Hall. Oh, oh, oh, &c" (V. 327).[9] The final "etcetera" allows for an infinite regress of O-groans to suit the histrionic occasion.

To return to the Shakespearean context, "O" was also used to indicate a sigh. There is, in fact, no way of distinguishing between sighs and groans, except that, traditionally, a groan is a more radical, profound, and painful expression of emotion than a mere sigh. In Elizabethan physiology, sighs and groans draw blood from the heart and thereby shorten human life. Ophelia describes the lovelorn Hamlet who appears to her while she is sewing in her chamber as raising "a sigh, so pittious and profound, / That it did seeme to shatter all his bulke, / And end his being" (ll. 991–993), or Claudius speaks of "a spend thrifts sigh, / That hurts by easing" (Quarto 2, 4.7.123–124).[10]

Lady Macbeth's O-sighs in the Sleepwalking Scene are a powerful expression of guilt:

> Heere's the smell of the blood still: all the perfumes of
> Arabia will not sweeten this little hand. Oh, oh, oh.
>
> > (ll. 2142–2144)

There seems to be a rhetorical and/or histrionic assumption that the O-sighs or groans belong at the end of a speech, as if to give it a special emotional emphasis and extension beyond the five-beat line. The Doctor underscores Lady Macbeth's perturbation of mind: "What a sigh is there? The hart is sorely charg'd" (l. 2145). "Charg'd" means "overfull," as if the sighs were meant to relieve an acute congestion of the heart, and the Waiting Gentlewoman aptly comments: "I would not haue such a heart in my bosome, for the dignity of the whole body" (ll. 2146–2147). There is an almost exactly analogous passage about the physiology of sighing in the Seduction Scene of *A Woman Killed with Kindness* (1603) by Thomas Heywood:

ANNE

O Master Wendoll, O.

---

9. *The Dramatic Works in the Beaumont and Fletcher Canon*, ed. Fredson Bowers (Cambridge, Eng., 1966), I, 87. *The Knight of the Burning Pestle* is edited by Cyrus Hoy.

10. Quoted from the Shakespeare Quarto Facsimiles series, no. 4, ed. Sir Walter Greg and Charlton Hinman (Oxford, 1940).

WENDOLL
Sigh not, sweet saint,
For every sigh you breathe draws from my heart
A drop of blood.[11]

(VI. 152–154)

Presumably actors would know how to render "O" in the proper degree of
wistful sigh or pathetic groan, but never as a meaningless expletive.

"O" is an emotional word in Shakespeare and his fellow dramatists, and
the frenzied guilt of Lady Macbeth can be matched in other scenes of
distraction. In the hysterical Fly Scene of *Titus Andronicus*, Titus bursts
into piercing, declamatory "O's" at his brother's comforting explanation:

It was a blacke illfauour'd Fly,
Like to the Empresse Moore, therefore I kild him.

ANDRONICUS
O, o, o,
Then pardon me for reprehending thee,
For thou hast done a Charitable deed. . . .

(ll. 1521–1525)

Titus's "O's" offer the actor a good chance to express himself in the mad
style. They are, in practice, open, ad-lib words, more or less insignificant
and meaningless on the printed page, but full of emotional possibilities
for the actor. To literalize what we have been talking about, the "O's" can
also be used as a series of painful howls. Falstaff's reaction to the burning
taper that Parson Evans puts to his fingers is completely natural and
unpremeditated:

EVANS
Come: will this wood take fire?

FALSTAFF
Oh, oh, oh.
(*The Merry Wives of Windsor*, ll. 2572–2573)

It shouldn't surprise us that Burbage would want to exploit the gamut
of sound effects that could be produced with a string of "O's," and we

11. Thomas Heywood, *A Woman Killed with Kindness*, ed. R. W. Van Fossen, The
Revels Plays (London, 1961).

have no idea how many of his best "O's" never found their way into play manuscripts or printed texts. The "O's" are only one among many ways of conveying powerful feelings in a highly stylized form. The most casual reading of Elizabethan-Jacobean drama keeps turning up O-groans and O-sighs and O-howls for those who are seeking them. I would insist that these many examples confirm the status of "O" as an expected, regular, standardized, and not at all unusual or remarkable actor's exclamation or noise/signifier for pain, grief, heightened passion, especially associated with dying.[12] There is a telling example in Middleton and Rowley's *The Changeling* (1622). Beatrice has been mortally wounded by De Flores, and we hear her and her bloody paramour *"within,"* as an offstage chorus to the public clarifications of her father, Vermandero. Beatrice's "Oh, oh, oh!" (V.iii.139)[13] represents reality finally breaking in on the stolid and complacent Vermandero, who doesn't seem to hear his daughter until the second outcry: "Oh, oh!" (l. 140). The father finally reacts: "What horrid sounds are these?" (l. 141). "Horrid" is an extremely strong word in Elizabethan usage, with its Latin sense of "horrifying," "causing horror," rather than the modern comic sense of cute but unacceptable childish behavior. At this horrid, climactic moment, De Flores brings in the wounded Beatrice. Her "O's" are a sufficient indication, at a moment when the resolution must move swiftly, that Beatrice is dying.

Similarly, in *The Revenger's Tragedy* (1606) the wounded Lussurioso peppers his dying discourse with O-groans (I count seven between V.iii.48 and V.iii.79 in the Revels edition). Spurio clearly alerts us to the beginning of the sequence by asking, "Whose groan was that?" (l. 49,[14] and as Vindice reveals that he has murdered him, and his father too, Lussurioso can only answer with "O's" (l. 79). What seems on the printed page to be a failure of eloquence on the part of a dramatist who was rarely

---

12. See E.A.J. Honigmann's radical account of the O-groans in "Re-Enter the Stage Direction: Shakespeare and Some Contemporaries," *Sh S*, XXIX (1976), 117–125. Honigmann argues that the "O's" in dramatic texts are not words but merely "crypto-directions" for the actors to ad-lib. Unfortunately, the author weakens his own authority to speak about stage directions by almost totally ignoring their relation to performance.

13. Thomas Middleton and William Rowley, *The Changeling*, ed. N. W. Bawcutt, The Revels Plays (Cambridge, Mass., 1958).

14. Cyril Tourneur, *The Revenger's Tragedy*, ed. R. A. Foakes, The Revels Plays (London, 1966).

at a loss for words, must, in performance, have appeared quite adequate
for the emotional needs of the occasion. In Ford's *'Tis Pity She's a Whore*
(1632), the beautifully lyrical Annabella dies with Shakespearean repetitions, but her very last sounds are hypermetrical "O's" like Hamlet's:

> Forgive him [=her brother, murderer, and lover Giovanni], Heaven—
> and me my sins; farewell.
> Brother unkind, unkind!—Mercy, great Heaven—O!—O!—[15]
>
> (V.iii.92–93)

The "O's" give the impression of suspended discourse rather than of a
speech that has been completed. In this love tragedy, they also have a
certain sense of puzzled rapture and ecstasy, when the soul leaves the body
to unite with the object of contemplation (as in the long tradition of
Petrarchan and religious eroticism).[16] "The rest is silence" only in this
world that the lover is forsaking.

Aside from Falstaff's rather casual "O's," the other examples we have
considered—Hamlet, King Lear, Othello, Lady Macbeth, Titus Andronicus, Anne Frankford, Beatrice, Lussurioso, and Annabella—are all
part of a meaningful system of emotional expression in the tragedies of
Shakespeare and his fellow dramatists. To accept some of these examples
and discard others as the grotesque and unseemly interpolations of actors
seems to me an arbitrary and capricious way of dealing with Shakespeare's
text. It is apparent that strong value judgments lie behind these
seemingly objective textual decisions. The strongly anti-theatrical bias of
this kind of criticism may be illustrated from Harold Jenkins's precisely
argued essay, "Playhouse Interpolations in the Folio Text of *Hamlet*."[17] It
is distressing to find Jenkins constantly covering his tracks by giving

15. John Ford, *'Tis Pity She's a Whore*, ed. N. W. Bawcutt, Regents Renaissance
Drama Series (Lincoln, Nebr., 1966).

16. I am indebted to Lester Beaurline for this link with the Petrarchan and religious
traditions. Beaurline notes the *OED* reference (B2) to the *O's of St. Bridget* or *Fifteen O's*,
which were "fifteen meditations on the Passion of Christ, composed by St. Bridget, each
beginning with *O Jesu*, or a similar invocation." I must also acknowledge Professor Beaurline's kindness in reading my manuscript and suggesting ways in which the argument
could be made more convincing to textual critics. Robert K. Turner, Jr., also made
sensible contributions to this noble aim.

17. Harold Jenkins, "Playhouse Interpolations in the Folio Text of *Hamlet*," *Studies in
Bibliography*, XIII (1960), 31–47.

theatrical reasons for choices that show an open contempt for the play in performance. All of what he identifies as playhouse interpolations are, of course, to him playhouse corruptions that cheapen and coarsen Shakespeare's true text.

Jenkins's remarks on Hamlet's "Mother, mother, mother" (l. 2381), spoken offstage at the beginning of the Closet Scene (and recorded only in Folio), are entirely typical:

> I infer that Q omits it because it was not in Shakespeare's manuscript and that the actors put it in. Indeed this is the sort of literalism in production from which we sometimes suffer in the modern theatre, as though we are not capable of imagining that the characters in their world of the play may see or hear things that are not made visible or audible to us. Such things are at best superfluous and at worst merely crude. What sort of prince is this who cannot come to his mother's chamber without announcing his arrival by calling "Mother" three times in the corridor? It is a small thing, but it degrades the play for a moment. . . .[18]

Hamlet's O-groans are, of course, an example of the extra dialogue with which the Folio text unnecessarily embellishes the stage business, a superfluity that cheapens Shakespeare's text. Jenkins fulminates against these "inane repetitions"[19] in strongly moralistic tones, and with a polemical vigor unusual in scholarly discussion. "All these things, no less than the dying groans, should be recognised for the stage accretions that they are. As such they have no claim to be admitted into an edition of *Hamlet* which aims at fidelity to its author."[20]

Without indulging in a point-for-point reply to Jenkins, I share the dismay expressed by Terence Hawkes at the implications of this kind of textual criticism. In his witty Modern Language Association paper expounding on T. S. Eliot's line, "O, O, O, O That Shakespeherian Rag," Hawkes asks Jenkins some embarrassing questions:

> Terms as confident in their presuppositions as "intrusive matter," "actor's interpolations," "stage accretions" deriving from "corruption through performance" remain the common coin of one kind of Shakespearian criticism.
> But "intrusive" *into* what? "accretions" *onto* what? "corruptions" *of* what? There is no pristine manuscript of any of Shakespeare's plays. And if there were,

18. *Ibid*, p. 35.
19. *Ibid.*, p. 38.
20. *Ibid.*, p. 42.

on what basis would we grant it stronger authority, say, than the text of a prompt-book which relates, with some immediacy, to an actual contemporary performance in which the author's acquiescence was not improbable?[21]

One cannot help feeling that the argument lies well outside the limited precincts of textual criticism, and that Jenkins's distaste for the coarsening and cheapening effect of *Hamlet* in performance echoes Pope's supercilious observations about Shakespeare's actors in the preface to his edition of the plays (1725):

Having been forced to say so much of the Players, I think I ought in justice to remark, that the Judgment, as well as Condition, of that class of people was then far inferior to what it is in our days. As then the best Playhouses were Inns and Taverns (the *Globe*, the *Hope*, the *Red Bull*, the *Fortune*, &c.), so the top of the profession were then meer Players, not Gentlemen of the stage: They were led into the Buttery by the Steward, not plac'd at the Lord's table, or Lady's toilette: and consequently were intirely depriv'd of those advantages they now enjoy, in the familiar conversation of our Nobility, and an intimacy (not to say dearness) with people of the first condition.[22]

I don't mean to exaggerate the fierceness of my own conviction that Hamlet's O-groans must immediately be restored to any genuine edition of the play. The Quarto 2 and the Folio texts obviously represent two different *Hamlets* that cannot comfortably be conflated into a single, hypothetical version. I would not question the assumption that Quarto 2 is closer to Shakespeare's manuscript and his original intentions, while Folio reflects the theatrical history of the play during a period of about twenty years. I am not trying to construct a definitive textual argument to guide future editors—this argument must still be worked out in all of its detail—but I am merely trying to sketch some of the problems raised by the O-groans. I have been implying, with more or less obviousness, that opinions about the O-groans seem to depend on what moves us in the theater, how we define dramatic poetry, and the way we conceive Hamlet as a dramatic character.

The O-groans are painful, not mellifluous, and this applies equally to

21. Terence Hawkes, "'That Shakespeherian Rag,'" *Essays and Studies 1977*, ed. W. Moelwyn Merchant (London, 1977), p. 34.

22. Quoted from *Eighteenth Century Essays on Shakespeare*, ed. D. Nichol Smith, 2d ed. (Oxford, 1963), p. 55.

Hamlet, King Lear, Othello, Lady Macbeth, Titus Andronicus, and Falstaff. They are cries of anguish and perturbation. When rendered effectively on stage, they are disturbing without being quotable and belong naturally with the uncelebrated eloquence of Shakespeare's "unpoetic poetry." [23] The argument over Hamlet's O-groans forces us to reconsider what is the authentic text of Shakespeare and by what assumptions we edit that text to suit our own preconceptions of what Shakespeare should be like. Unfortunately, it seems to make a great deal of difference whether we like our Hamlet—and our Shakespeare—rough or smooth, and whether we insist that the audience be "people of the first condition."

23. See Maurice Charney, "Shakespeare's Unpoetic Poetry," *SEL*, XIII (1973), 199–207.

Ben Jonson's Satiric Choreography

PATRICK R. WILLIAMS

> When I cannot shun you, we will meet.
> *Every Man Out of His Humour*,
> I.i.225

ALTHOUGH BEN JONSON is commonly regarded as among the most accomplished and versatile playwrights in the language, the four-hundredth anniversary of his birth passed recently without a major theatrical event. Perhaps this is so because literary criticism, following the normal procedure of applying rediscovered critical techniques first to Shakespeare, has only just begun to investigate the theatrical composition of Jonson's plays.[1] Indeed, students of Jonson observed the quatercentennial extensively in a number of anniversary periodicals and colloquia, and

---

1. A farsighted article that maps the way for investigation into Jonson's theatrical technique is William A. Armstrong's "Ben Jonson and Jacobean Stagecraft," in *Jacobean Theatre*, ed. John Russell Brown and Bernard Harris (New York, 1960), pp. 45–61. The only book-length study in the field is Franz Fricker's *Ben Jonson's Plays in Performance and the Jacobean Theatre* (Bern, 1972).

in these, two noteworthy views recur: that there is a need to see Jonson as humorous, if satirically so; and that Jonson requires—and deserves—staging.[2]

I suggest that an attempt to discover an approach to Jonson's plays that accounts both for their theatrical characteristics and for their satiric humor, one in terms of the other, will answer this call. In fact, if we look briefly at the early investigators into Shakespeare's stagecraft, an approach both literary and theatrical is precisely what they suggest. John Russell Brown concludes his *Shakespeare's Plays in Performance* with a recommendation for cooperation between literary and theatrical research: "For this to happen, literary critics must learn to consider the full theatrical life of the plays they study, so that they can analyze and judge a play as well as a poem, and speak of an image of life as well as of a theme, or pattern, or moral statement."[3] Similarly, J. L. Styan, whose *Shakespeare's Stagecraft* can profitably be read as a complement to Brown's study, affirms: "To reconcile literature and theatre is not to lose something from each, but rather to understand what dramatic dialogue is and does, why words on the page are not the same as words on the stage."[4]

What I will attempt, then, is a brief investigation into one aspect of Jonson's literary and theatrical technique, or, if you will, his satiric stagecraft. As it presents a technique for analysis, satiric stagecraft is inherently both literary and theatrical; by definition it counters the bifurcation of literary and theatrical analysis, since it describes the translation of a literary genre's conventions to the visual and aural medium of the stage. It obviously responds both to those insisting on attention to Jonson's stage technique, and to those calling for attention to Jonson's humor. We will discover, one hopes, what Richard Levin insists upon as essential to our appreciation of Jonson: "what perspective to apply during

2. See, for instance, Clifford Leech, "The Incredibility of Jonsonian Comedy," in *A Celebration of Ben Jonson*, ed. William Blissett, Julian Patrick, and R. W. Van Fossen (Toronto, 1973), pp. 23–24. There is also a useful discussion among a Jonsonian actor (Colin Blakely), a director (Terry Hands), and an editor (Peter Barnes) with the *Gambit* editors in "Ben Jonson and the Modern Stage," *Gambit*, VI, no. 22 (1973), 5–30. Similar studies include: S. Schoenbaum, "The Humorous Jonson," in *The Elizabethan Theatre*, 4th ser., ed. G. R. Hibbard (Hamden, Conn., 1974); and Richard Levin, "'No Laughing Matter': Some New Readings of *The Alchemist*," *SLI*, VI, no. 1 (April 1973).

3. John Russell Brown, *Shakespeare's Plays in Performance* (New York, 1967), p. 237.

4. J. L. Styan, *The Elements of Drama* (Cambridge, Eng., 1960), p. 2.

our experience of a play . . . how we know when we should laugh."[5]
Because of the restrictions of space, I will limit my analysis to an early
play, *Every Man in His Humour*, two comedies from the middle period,
Volpone and *The Alchemist*, and Jonson's final, if premature, triumph,
Bartholomew Fair.

Among the most formative characteristics of a successful play, one
which both distinguishes it from other writing and decides its success
with its audience, is the eventual translation of its words to sights and
sounds onstage. As the playwright anticipates performance, he shares in
the directorial task by integrating with the words and sequential activity
of the play a schematic order adaptable to conveying meaning onstage.
Within this order, the organizing of the actors' placement onstage is of
first importance. Where the audience looks, what it sees, and where the
actors are onstage all clarify and develop the play's meaning. Although
directing is most immediately concerned with controlling the positioning
of the actors onstage and manipulating the audience's attention, a mature
playwright assumes the responsibility for organizing place in terms established by the text itself. Just as one does not view actors within a dramatic
context merely as mouthpieces for a variety of ideas, neither should one
underplay the connotative significance in their spatial relationships.[6]
Specifically, in analyzing Jonson's plays, one wants to describe those
spatial relationships among the various characters, and the response they
create in the audience, as they relate to our understanding of the play's
satiric framework. Admittedly, this involves a good measure of interpretation, but it is essential to our understanding of Jonson, just as discovering
the scheme of ordering place in the text is essential to the success of the
play in performance.

At the most basic level, that of character depiction, Jonson's thematic
intent manifests itself spatially. The characterization is marked by an
antipathy between the gull and knave, types that reduce the human
personality to caricature, irrationality, and material drives. Satire points
up the self-destructive nature of this folly, presenting us with an image of
society's hostility to unhealthy and unnatural activity. Both in its inciden-
tal effects and in its more sweeping movements, Jonsonian satire inclines

5. Levin, "'No Laughing Matter,'" p. 97.
6. See J. L. Styan, *Shakespeare's Stagecraft* (Cambridge, Eng., 1967), pp. 82 ff.

toward the depiction of a stasis, contrast, or tension, a dramatic measure of the gap between human aspiration and achievement, between what people say or think they are like and the more disconcerting reality.

The feature of the Elizabethan stage that attracts immediate attention in this context is its flexibility. Exempt from the limitations of the verisimilar theater, the conventions of Jonson's stage incline to the nonillusory: stage area is free from undue definition and is easily adaptable to narrative demands, as imaginary distance takes precedence over real distance.[7] The audience credits a highly unrealistic illusion of place wherein those on stage not meant to be seen by others simply step to the side or the rear; locale is established by the presence of characters, who seem to transport geography with them.

The exploitation of this fluid illusion to satisfy the demands of the merely exotic or novel does not characterize Jonson's major comedies. Always, the convention bears significantly on character and meaning. In Act II of *Every Man in His Humour*, Kitely retires into his house as Brayne-worme enters from the other stage door, and, in soliloquy, establishes the new locale as "More-fields" (II.iv.9).[8] He retreats to the rear of the stage unobserved, as young Kno'well and Stephen enter, then, approaching them in his disguise of a maimed soldier, enters into their service, and all three exit (II.iv.). Old Kno'well then enters and sets the locale as another part of More-fields in a soliloquy on parental responsibility. Brayne-worme, apparently moving about at random, reappears and, maintaining his disguise, enters into the service of his old master, pausing at the end of the scene to congratulate himself before the audience (II.v).

This is an economical bit of stage business, first portraying the house within the town to which the travelers are going, then presenting them en route. But more importantly it emphasizes the ubiquity and facility of a central satiric character, the knave Brayne-worme. He speaks the opening and closing lines of the scenes in More-fields, thereby bordering an imaginary context corresponding to the geography, repeats a successful disguise on both his young and old masters and the gull Stephen, and progresses

7. For these conventions, see Bernard Beckerman, *Shakespeare at the Globe*, 2d ed. (1966; rpt. London, 1969), pp. 162–164.

8. All textual references are to *Ben Jonson*, ed. C. H. Herford and Percy and Evelyn Simpson, 11 vols. (Oxford, 1925–1952), with the usual letters normalized. The edition of *Every Man in His Humour* is that of the *Folio* of 1616.

from a hesitating novice to a practiced performer. We do not ask how Kitely's house becomes More-fields or how Brayne-worme moves about and speaks to the audience unnoticed. We accept the fluid transformation of the environment as Brayne-worme's knavery controls it. In all the plays, the knave—expert, flexible, and dexterous—controls place and positioning just as surely as he controls the mechanical, irrational gull.[9]

Bartholomew Fair, with its intricate web of characters, incidents, and relationships employs the stage's flexibility to maximum advantage. While it is true that specific locales of thematic significance can be assigned to many scenes in this play,[10] there is a sense, as the play progresses, in which vagueness of locale is desirable. In Act IV, when all normal human relationships are at sixes and sevens and the fair has undermined the pretensions of its visitors, the characters seem to be in an unlocalized limbo of folly. Cokes is gulled, for what seems to be the hundredth time, as he wanders about aimlessly, stripped of guardian, fiancée, family, and possessions (IV.ii). Immediately, Quarlous and Win-wife, the former friends and critics of the fair, enter with swords drawn, vying for the hand of Grace (IV.iii). At the end of the scene, when the pickpocket Edgworth has agreed to steal the marriage license from Wasp, the combatants proceed to Ursla's booth where Wasp is in his game of vapors:

QUARLOUS

Lead, which way is't?

EDGWORTH

Here, Sir, you are o' the backside o' the
Booth already, you may heare the noise.

(IV.iii.129–131)

Here, imaginary distance is substituted for real distance. If the directing has conveyed the irrational element in human endeavor throughout the

9. For more on the distinction between gull and knave see Jonas A. Barish, "Jonson and the Loathed Stage," in *A Celebration of Ben Jonson*, p. 42.

10. For thematic undertones of locale in *Bartholomew Fair*, compare: Eugene M. Waith, "The Staging of *Bartholomew Fair*," *SEL*, II (1962), 181–195, and, in slightly altered form, in 'Appendix II: "The Staging," *Bartholomew Fair*, ed. Eugene M. Waith (New Haven, Conn., 1963), pp. 205–217. R. B. Parker notes his qualifications to Waith in "The Themes and Staging of *Bartholomew Fair*," *UTQ* (July 1970), pp. 293–309.

previous scenes, the lack of logical transition in moving from place to place, as well as the illogical atmosphere of an unspecified locale, will underscore this very irrationality for the audience's perception.

As a permanent feature of this stage, and the wall from which all exits and entrances are made, the tiring house proves adaptable to a variety of narrative demands and satiric emphases. John Russell Brown has written of the Shakespearean stage as an alternatingly closed and open composition, corresponding to action close to the tiring house and close to the audience.[11] Perhaps it will be useful to adopt these terms in our present discussion. There is a dynamic, visual tension on stage throughout the play, emphasizing and clarifying both the satiric tension between the characters' ambitions and achievements and the personal tension between the antagonistic knave and gull. The tendency in Jonsonian satire to move characters offstage, that is, to what Brown calls a closed composition, near the tiring house, results from the outnumbered knave's attempts to keep the majority of gulls occupied elsewhere while one or two others are being fooled. The tension is created chiefly by the gull's desire to be onstage, expanding in his characteristic daydream, or attempting to control the action. A gull allowed the luxury of a free moment is always in danger of meeting another gull or discovering the knave; the knave's ability to keep the procession of gulls inward, toward the tiring house which can be imaginatively transformed to suit the moment's purpose, is a measure of his success, communicated visually by a closed composition.[12]

The flexibility of the tiring house, and the thematic uses to which it can be put, are evident in the opening scenes of *Every Man in His Humour*. First we have an open composition, Old Kno'well outside his house with the gull Stephen (I.i), then a closed composition inside the house where Young Kno'well, who is studying, and Brayne-worme make fun of Stephen (I.iii). Next, we see Cob outside his house with the gull Matthew (I.iv), then look inside the house at the hung-over Bobadill and Matthew making fun, ironically, of themselves (I.v). Next we have an open scene outside Kitely's house, with Kitely and Downe-right, the only remaining

11. Brown, *Shakespeare's Plays in Performance*, pp. 131–136.
12. By "closed," I do not mean, as directors often do, "near." Indeed, when characters are closer to the tiring house, they may appear closer together than they would near the audience because of perspective. I use "closed" to mean near the tiring house, not near to another actor.

gulls (II.i), their meeting with Bobadill and Matthew (II.ii), and Kitely's jealous retreat into his house (II.iii). Abruptly, Brayne-worme, making the journey over More-fields to London, occupies the stage alone for his knave's soliloquy and transformation to an actor (II.iv).

The situations parallel and comment on each other visually as well as verbally, and establish a kind of spatial idiom in which place clarifies character and relationship. In the open compositions, Old Kno'well, whose wisdom and gentility set him apart from most aged fathers of Jonsonian comedy, is compared to Cob and Kitely by virtue of their presence in front of their respective houses. Cob is more the gull; his minor suspicions and jealousies of his wife Tib strike a mean of sorts between Old Kno'well and the completely jealous gull, Kitely. The spatial movement of these three men, each seen initially outside his house, is inward, corresponding to their increasing folly. Old Kno'well is relatively liberal; Cob, busy about his chores, is somewhat closer to his house; Kitely, who enters with the angry Downe-right, is drawn irresistibly into his house to spy on his wife and tend to business.

Furthermore, each man is joined outside his house by a gull, and these, too, progress in folly. Stephen, the amateur gull, greets Old Kno'well outside his house and goes inside where he is mocked by the knaves. He is imaginatively linked to the more practiced gull, Matthew, who greets Cob and enters to the master gull, Bobadill. Inside, Bobadill's and Matthew's behavior is implicitly contrasted, because of their identical location onstage, with that of Young Kno'-well, Brayne-worme, and Stephen. Specifically, Young Kno'-well, who has been studying and planning the day's fun, is contrasted with Bobadill, whose drunkenness renders him immobile at the same hour. The gulls continue their domination of the stage area outside Kitely's house; this time, not one but two gulls—Matthew and Bobadill—greet the master of the house.

The movement throughout this sequence can be described, in terms of space, as a progressive contraction of movement toward the tiring house in the scenes outdoors before the three houses, and a corresponding expansion away from the tiring house in the scenes indoors. Significantly, as the gulls dominate the action, the open compositions become increasingly contracted, and the closed compositions, expansive. Carefully worked out in the early scenes, this choreographed activity establishes a dramatic shorthand by which the playwright informs the audience of the characters' relations and successes in future encounters: unchecked folly, open composition; folly checked by knavery or by its own self-destructive ineptness, closed composition. The fluid stage, with its imaginatively flexible rear wall, provides the playwright a medium for displaying his thematic choreography.

Volpone and *The Alchemist* employ the tiring house in very similar ways. We see, repeatedly, Mosca or Dol or Face rushing to the tiring house to look "out doors" and identify the gull, as Volpone, Subtle, or Face assumes his costume. Moreover, in both plays there is a repeated tendency to marshal the gulls toward the tiring house in one of its many disguises: outdoors, some inner room in the house, toward some promised treasure. The action of these two plays seems to be a contest for control of the tiring house, and the character's success is measured by his ability to stay onstage for a long period of time.

As a corollary to this rule, both *Volpone* and *The Alchemist* employ open compositions to signal the knave's reversal. In *Volpone*, the initial scenes of Volpone's successes are followed by a scene on the street with Peregrine and Sir Pol. Here, as Volpone leaves the safety of his bed and sallies forth into society to see Celia, he brushes with defeat; he is driven off the stage by Corvino, and subsequently beaten by Bonario. The next scene on the street is Mosca's soliloquy on parasites (III.i), and again this signals danger for the Fox. Inevitably, Volpone's undoing is intelligible in terms of place, as his desire to torment the bounty hunters leads him out of the house for the final time, into the unlocalized confusion of the Venetian streets, and to trial. Each instance of an open composition, a scene out of doors where the gull's movements are expansive and away from the tiring house, is a further step in Volpone's failure.

The principle is much the same, but in more compact form, in *The Alchemist*; here, the rear wall, which had been only one of a few walls inside Love-Wit's house through Act IV, suddenly becomes the front of his house. Coinciding with society's revolt against the knaves as seen in the six neighbors, Love-Wit's return terminates the knavery of the three knaves as a group. Until then, the knaves had controlled a closed world; the social perspective subjects them to intolerable scrutiny, and the play ends.

Several literary theorists have noted that satire measures dramatically the distance between human expectation and accomplishment, between what men aspire to and what they actually achieve.[13] The flexible Elizabethan stage is receptive to the portrayal of the heights of human emotion and activity, as witnessed in Shakespearean drama. Jonson, the satirist, wants a control. He wants his audience reminded always that Bobadill's lessons in gentility and courage are undercut by their spokesman's ridiculous lodgings, that Mammon's visions of timeless sensuality in his "Novo Orbe" are bounded by the alchemist's shop, that Volpone's imaginative transformation of gold to an object of religious and amatory idolatry is limited to his decadent bed chamber.[14] The tendency to a closed composition, inward, toward the tiring house, is one such control.

But even more important in establishing a tension between human aspiration and realization in terms of space is Jonson's adherence to the unity of place. Here is the Jonson of tradition, Jonson the classicist. Having inherited a stage conventionally adaptable to portraying widely separated locales, and a corresponding adaptability to greatly divergent forms of human activity, Jonson chooses to confine the range of locales in his plays to one house or, at most, one town. Shakespeare moves from Egypt to Rome in an instant; Jonson spends two hours in a room. Yet as satire seeks to discredit global aspiration and romantic love, the unity of place is appropriate. By severely restricting the choices of environment open to his characters, on a stage that resists restriction, Jonson hits upon a most effective means of establishing satiric tension and portraying ironic discrepancy. Here, as is often the case, we see the artist committing himself to a convention and finding great freedom within it.

Gail Kern Paster, in "Ben Jonson's Comedy of Limitation," explores this topic at length.[15] Paster demonstrates that Jonson, by presenting no alternative locales to his characters, entertains no themes related to a variety of analogous or complementary places. The tangible, familiar

---

13. For a concise statement, see Northrop Frye, *Anatomy of Criticism: Four Essays* (Princeton, N.J., 1957), pp. 229 and 233. Specifically related to Jonson see Harry Levin, "An Introduction to Ben Jonson" (original title: "Introduction"), from *Selected Works of Ben Jonson*, ed. Harry Levin (New York, 1938), rpt. in *Ben Jonson*, ed. Jonas A. Barish (Englewood Cliffs, N.J., 1963), pp. 48–49.

14. See Eugene M. Waith, "Things As They Are And The World Of Absolutes In Jonson's Plays And Masques," in *The Elizabethan Theatre*, pp. 106–126.

15. Gail Kern Paster, "Ben Jonson's Comedy of Limitation," *SP*, LXXII, no. 1 (January 1975), 51–71.

settings of Jonson's plays, as they are restricted spatially, measure the moral dimension of their inhabitants. In treating their small section of the world as central, the characters' blindness to more comprehensive concerns elsewhere insures defeat. While this spatial restriction prohibits thematic catholicity, it is perfectly suited to the satiric limitation of the genre and its parochial inhabitants; the very idea of a "humour" character implies the same sort of restriction.

To a certain degree, it is a circular argument to say that characters are limited by the dimensions of their settings, inasmuch as the characters themselves establish settings by their presence.[16] The familiar marginal note, "To them," indicates that the playwright conceives of his characters as entering not so much to a place as to a person.[17] *Every Man in His Humour* suggests in its title that each character is a center of activity, and the unity of place in that play arises from the inability of the characters to conceive of activity beyond the perimeters of their own imaginations. Similarly, in *Volpone* and *The Alchemist*, the most compact of plays in their observation of the unity of place, the control exerted by the title characters over the others determines their adherence to a limited region. Everyone wants something from Volpone or Subtle, so everyone gathers around them. Only *Bartholomew Fair* is named after a place, and in that play the characters are seen as related by their common human frailty; no individual dominates the action, and the fair is varied enough to accommodate its diverse visitors.

To further illustrate this point, one notes that Volpone's chamber assumes its unique atmosphere because of Volpone's activity within it. The play opens with him entering to his gold (not a person for once!) and establishing the limits of the stage by his particular imagination. Or one might cite the opening of *The Alchemist*, in which the three knaves enter not so much to a room in the house as to a quarrel with each other during which, because of their petty yet expert schemes, the stage becomes circumscribed by the intensity of their commitment to underhanded dealings.

An element so recurrent as to be termed characteristic of Jonson's style in maintaining the illusion of the unity of place within the narrative is

---

16. Brown, *Shakespeare's Plays in Performance*, p. 131.
17. Beckerman, *Shakespeare at the Globe*, p. 174.

the tendency of characters always to go inside a house and, once in, further in. *The Alchemist* is most thorough in this respect. Invaded by gulls, the knaves pigeonhole Mammon with Dol in a bedroom, Dapper in the privy (a locale fixed definitely by having all the knaves leave with Dapper and return from the other door with Mammon), and Pliant and Surly in the garden. Here, Jonson reverses his procedure and heightens the intensity of locale, by showing the front of the house last, in Act V, after the inner rooms have been probed.

Exits and entrances are, of course, instrumental in establishing locale, and Jonson molds the necessary departures and arrivals to his thematic purposes. The time required to enter or depart the large Elizabethan stage provides opportunities for long speeches during which, in addition to character, place can be established. In this context, we note Justice Overdoo's wonderful opening soliloquy in which he not only reveals his presence in the fair and his attitude toward it, but also provides time for the fair vendors to set up their booths behind him and for him to assume his disguise (II.i). Mammon's first arrival at the alchemist's employs another long speech, during which he dreams of future pleasure while, behind the scenes, the knaves rehearse their chicanery (II.i). Kitely's long speech on jealousy (II.iii.57–74) gains in intensity from the space he has to cover between the front of the stage and the rear, where, supposedly, his wife and money need attending. His jerky, agonized departure is followed immediately, and implicitly contrasted, by Brayne-worme's soliloquy on knavery, and again the size of the stage empowers him to elaborate on his cunning, as he moves from the rear of the stage to the front.

Always in control of the action, the knave orchestrates arrivals and departures for his own ends. When an unexpected gull arrives, the knave simply directs traffic. When Drugger arrives early, Face dismisses Dapper, admonishing him to prepare for the Fairy Queen (I.ii). When Mammon's arrival is expected, Drugger is sent to solicit Kastril and Pliant (I.iii). Every exit and entrance makes a satiric point. The need to get characters on- and offstage becomes a means of establishing a hierarchy of folly in *Volpone*. In Act I, first Voltore enters to Volpone, then Corbaccio, and finally Corvino. At the will scene (V.iii), they are dismissed in reverse order. Voltore, a lawyer, is the most calculating of the three, and makes the best first impression; there is something satisfying in saving his humiliation for the last. Corvino is the pettiest, and is felt as inconsequential. At his first arrival, he is merely the third in a series; at his dismissal, the least threatening. Cobaccio's physical infirmities emblematize the moral infirmities in all three, and he is placed, as a touchstone, in the middle.

The tension between a flexible stage and the playwright's insistence on unity of place upon that stage is a major weapon in the satiric playwright's artillery, and helps create the humorous perspective for the audience. The rule of the game now is that no one leave the board or playing field for long, despite its diminutive boundaries. There is a feeling of entrapment about these characters. It is remarkable, therefore, that the characters, though confined, are at pains to maintain a distance between themselves and others. Onstage, the characters' spatial relationships should signify thematically; the playwright wants to communicate a personal separation in a physical one. The exigencies of blocking so that no character is obstructed from the audience's view, or the tendency of Elizabethan acting to emphasize delivery, minimizing the relationships between characters, are the results, not the causes, of separation among Jonson's characters. [18] The satiric personality is highly subjective; each character is a center of activity, sealed off by his obsession in a self-contained world that prohibits trespassing. In Shakespearean comedy, there is a feeling of characters forever touching, drawing nearer, striving to lift the veil. Jonson denies intimacy. His characters posture and pretend, spy and sneer, arresting each other at arm's length. Antipathy and aberrant personality are the blocking principles in satire; what touching there is commonly takes the form of a beating. The gull's entry into the knave's sphere of influence is perceived by the audience as ironic: he is being drawn in only to be repulsed.

Even in so antiseptic a play as *Every Man in His Humour*, the characters tend to minimize contact. Bobadill's cowardice naturally keeps him away from Downe-right at their first meeting:

> DOWNE-RIGHT
>
> Why, doe you heare? you.
>
> BOBADILL
>
> The gentleman-citizen hath satisfied mee,
>   Ile talke
> to no scavenger.

18. *Ibid.*, p. 132.

DOWNE-RIGHT

How, scavenger? stay sir, stay?

(II.ii.10–13)

The posturing of the gulls keeps not only the knaves who mock them, but also the other gulls, who imitate them, at a critic's distance. Stephen and Matthew, the minor gulls, naturally step aside to observe the master, Bobadill:

(Matthew: 'Pray you, marke this discourse, sir.
Stephen: So, I doe.)

BOBADILL

Observe me judicially, sweet sir, . . .

(III.i.135–136, 140)

Bobadill's beating of Cob (III.v), and Downe-right's of Bobadill (IV.vii), are the only genuine instances of contact in the play. Young Kno'well and Bridget, who become introduced, engaged, and wed in the course of the action, never speak to each other on stage.

In *Volpone*, all the gulls are encouraged to draw near to the dying Fox. "Bring him neere, where is he?" (I.iii.14), Volpone says to Mosca at Voltore's visit. "You may come neere, sir" (I.v.55), Mosca tells Corvino, encouraging him to shout in Volpone's ear. "Please you draw neere, sir" (III.vii.70), Mosca says to Corvino, who has brought his wife. Only Bonario, who beats Volpone, and Celia react judiciously. "Nay, flie me not" (III.vii.154), Volpone's words to Celia, strike the ear as unique.

An additional recurrent and humorous means of keeping people at a distance is through an intermediary.[19] The birds of prey rarely speak directly to Volpone, but are forced to approach him through Mosca. This device places the gulls at a further remove from the real source of their deception, and renders them more gullible. The distancing effect is identical in *The Alchemist*, where Face stands between Subtle, supposedly too committed to alchemy to speak directly to visitors, and the individual gull, relaying information from one to the other. The funniest instance of this device occurs in Busy's disputation with the puppet in *Bartholomew*

19. Gabriele Bernhard Jackson notes the use of a go-between in the Introduction to her edition of *Every Man in His Humour* (New Haven, Conn., 1969), p. 8.

Fair. Here, Lantern Letherhead acts as the intermediary in a *reductio ad absurdum* of logical debate:

> BUSY
>
> First, I say unto thee, Idoll, thou hast no *Calling*.

> PUPPET
>
> *You lie, I am call'd* Dionisius.

> LANTERN
>
> The *Motion sayes you lie, he is call'd Dionisius* i' the matter, and to that *calling* he answers.

> BUSY
>
> I meane no *vocation, Idoll*, no present lawfull *Calling*.

> PUPPET
>
> *Is yours a lawfull Calling?*

> LANTERN
>
> The *Motion* asketh, if yours be a lawfull *Calling?*

> BUSY
>
> Yes, mine is of the Spirit.

> PUPPET
>
> *Then* Idoll *is a lawfull* Calling.

> LANTERN
>
> He saies, then *Idoll* is a lawfull *Calling*! for you call'd him *Idoll*, and your *Calling* is of the spirit
>
>   (V.v.52–63)

As if disputation with a puppet were not ridiculous enough, the puppeteer points up the absurdity of the debate by speaking the puppet's lines and his own. The gravity Busy places on the debate by allowing the distance and moderator that are proper to formal debate between two equal disputants undercuts his position before he can establish it.

The mutual antipathy of characters within a closed environment does not exhaust the sources of spatial tension in the plays. Although the characters are physically and emotionally repulsed by each other, they are drawn, nevertheless, to an area of mutual interest—in Wallace Bacon's descriptive phrase, a "magnetic field." [20] In Jonson's later plays, where we see so often the forms and patterns of his earlier work without the imaginative energy, this magnetic field is embarrassingly mechanical, almost allegorical—and not only in the aptly titled dotage, *The Magnetic Lady*. Lady Pecunia in *The Staple of News*, who represents not only money but also love and religion, draws all to her. Or worse, Lady Loadstone in *The New Inn*, as her name indicates, attracts all the characters (or, at any rate, the playwright seems to be laboring to give her that power). But in the great satires the technique is realized imaginatively and humorously. All seem drawn or herded to an area where their particular folly is brought into focus and, implicitly, evaluated. Consistent within the analogy, the magnet repels those it attracts after too immediate or extended a contact.

Love-Wit's house is the obvious center of attraction—the only locale, in fact—in *The Alchemist*, and this fact serves to unify an already brilliantly unified action: everyone journeys irresistibly, and for different reasons, to the house, is gulled, and admonished. *Volpone* is a slightly different case. Volpone's bed is the apparent center of attraction, but it is not the only one. Scoto of Mantua draws a large crowd, and all are taken in by his hawking. Furthermore, at two important times during the play, all the major characters congregate at court. The element common to all these incidents is not locale but the title character himself. Volpone's credible performances attract everyone and, almost immediately, repel them. After each encounter at Volpone's house or in his presence, there is a general dispersing of characters, like an infection drawing to a head, bursting, and flowing out into the social body.

Bartholomew Fair would seem to have several centers of attraction, notably Ursla's booth and the puppet show, and Letherhead's booth and the stocks. But again, the title encourages scrutiny. It is the business of the entire fair to attract visitors: the opening act at Little-wit's house seems designed to show to the audience everyone outside the fair first; then, in the rest of the play, everyone is drawn uncontrollably to the fair. Among them is Zeal-of-the-Land Busy, ostensibly trying to keep others away from the fair, and its many attractions, then drawn by his nose to feast on Ursla's pig, by his choler and drunkenness to overturn

20. Wallace A. Bacon, "The Magnetic Field," *HLQ*, XIX (1955–1956), 121–153.

Letherhead's and Trash's shops, by his obtuseness to argue with the puppets. Or Justice Over-doo, who aims at maintaining the judicious distance
of the observer, inevitably trapped, fettered in the stocks. Or Win and
Mistress Over-doo, drawn to Ursla's privy and enlisted in Knock-hum's
harem. Cokes makes apparent the childish reality others try to mask. He
is intoxicated with the fair before he even sees it. Once in, he runs to the
shops, encourages the ballad singer (who is helping to rob him), and at
last tries to get behind the miniature tiring house to talk to the puppets.
When, at the play's conclusion, the fair disperses its visitors back into
society, its influence is perceived as lasting and restorative. After all,
Cokes wants to bring the puppets back with him.

This description of characters confined yet antipathetic, all drawn powerfully to a point of common interest and repelled by one another, approx-
imates a useful translation, in terms of stagecraft, of what others have said
in terms of plot or theme: that Jonson's characters do not act upon each
other, but merely "fit in"; that meetings in Jonson's plays are accidental
and result in isolation and fragmentation; that in Jonson's world characters confront each other in shifting configurations of confusion.[21] The
audience perceives these encounters visually, in terms of space, as mechanical, repetitious, and irrational, patterns corresponding to the behavior of
the gulls. The large, shifting, spatial patterns throughout the play are
complementary or analogous to the alterations, in terms of character, of
the individual performer, and cast the play into a complex order of essentially disharmonious elements.

For instance, the gull tends to assert his ego, expanding to grotesque
proportions until the knave pricks his expansion and the gull contracts,
only to expand again; this process continues throughout the entire play
until a final deflation and leveling. The stage, too, fills and empties
throughout the play, becoming increasingly full until the final procession,
but with periodic emptyings. There is more of the atomist than of the
anal-erotic in Jonson; he expands his scenes by adding one character at a
time until the stage and action can sustain no more.[22]

21. See the following: Jackson, Introduction to *Every Man In His Humour*, pp. 1–34.
T. S. Eliot, "Ben Jonson," *Selected Essays 1917–1932* (New York, 1932), rpt. in *Ben Jonson*,
ed. Barish, p. 8. Jonas A. Barish, *Ben Jonson and the Language of Prose Comedy* (Cambridge,
Mass., 1960), pp. 79–80.

22. Alvin B. Kernan notes that the scene of satire is always crowded in *The Cankered
Muse: Satire of the English Renaissance* (New Haven, Conn., 1959), pp. 7–14.

Even so tightly structured and sparingly peopled a play as *Volpone* shows a repeated tendency to fill the stage and empty it. The undiscriminating crowd, whose common voice cries, "Follow, follow, follow, follow, follow" (II.ii.28), is drawn to Volpone as Scoto of Mantua. The packed stage is emptied by Corvino, to whom the crowd's hostility, and ours, is directed. At Volpone's beating by Bonario, the three birds of prey flock onto the stage, united by their greed, and are summarily dismissed by Mosca to perjure the noble youths. We see their rapid influx and departure as a dynamic image of the unthinking evil and haste in their common will. The actual legacy scene is most effective in this respect: each gull enters individually to collect his booty until all, including Lady Pol, are present; then each is dismissed with nothing. Again, this expansion and contraction of the stage image renders tangible the fragmented, isolated will, and its speedy, inevitable deflation.

It would be reassuring to see, in the image of a crowd, society's restorative influence on those whose aberrations threaten its survival. Satire does not always see it that way. The crowd in *Volpone*, intoxicated with promises of a panacea, sounds the more frequent note. Still, an equable reading of *The Alchemist* includes some recognition of society's ability to correct its course. In Act V, as we have seen, the neighbors besiege Love-Wit's house, which contains within it every socially destructive force, presented satirically. When Love-Wit secures entry and opens the doors, the stage is flooded again, as though society were filling the vacuum created by cheating and foolish aspiration. But actually, what we see in *The Alchemist* is a version of the legacy scene in *Volpone*. Mammon and Surly enter and are dismissed, then the Puritans, and finally Drugger, and Dol and Subtle. The new society that crystallizes on the purged stage round Jeremy, his master Love-Wit and his new mistress Pliant, and her brother Kastril, is inauspicious and completely in keeping with the amoral tone of the play.

Bartholomew Fair presents this image in reverse: at the beginning of the play the supposedly normal people fill the stage, gathering around their friends and relatives at the Littlewits'. When the stage empties, and everyone goes to the fair, fragmentation and isolation result; the play seems to be saying that that is not how society really works, and the fragmented, isolated figures on stage reinforce this feeling, and insinuate a more essential fragmentation within the individual. One character does try to bring order:

To see what bad events may peepe out o' the taile of good purposes! the care I had
of that civil yong man, I tooke a fancy to this morning, (and have not left it yet)
drew me to that exhortation, which drew the company, indeede, which drew the
cut-purse; which drew the money; which drew my brother *Cokes* his losse; which
drew on *Wasp's* anger; which drew on my beating: a pretty gradation!

(III.iii.13–20)

That is Justice Over-doo, and we know where his attempts at establishing
order lead.

The stage is organized on spatial principles other than a series of crowd-
ings and emptyings, however. Coherent, recurrent patterns of satiric
grouping are discernible in all the plays. The most frequent and effective
of these is the split scene which denotes a division of perception or
sensibility.[23] Symmetrical balance is the most basic ordering principle in
art, and Jonsonian satire, which takes its impetus from the struggle
between gull and knave, employs this type of balance extensively.[24]
Characteristically, the stage becomes a balanced picture with the gull on
one side and the knave on the other, or a knave in the middle flanked on
both sides by gulls. Of course, there are many variations. In the first
meeting between the young knaves and the three fops in *Every Man in His
Humour*, for instance, we have first a strictly divided scene in which Young
Kno'well and Well-bred occupy one side to observe Stephen, Matthew,
and Bobadill on the other. Then the picture shifts as Bobadill assumes the
center stage for one of his great daydreams; the stage remains balanced,
however, as the knaves on one side mock him, while the gulls on the other
side admire him (III.i).

The middle scenes of *The Alchemist* employ symmetrical balance extensively before the general chaos of Act IV. With Dapper or Drugger, the
knaves occupy one side of the stage, the gull the other, or else Face bisects
the stage, acting as a go-between for Subtle and the gull. As the gulls
become more substantial, the balance becomes slightly more complex and
effective. At Mammon's first daydream, he is flanked on one side by
Subtle and Face, and on the other by Surly, marking a division in perception of Mammon's aspirations. Then, Subtle assumes the central position
between Mammon and Surly, each of whom likewise perceives the al-

23. Styan, *Shakespeare's Stagecraft*, p. 124.
24. See Beckerman, *Shakespeare at the Globe*, p. 165.

chemist's jargon differently (II.iii). At the Puritans' arrival, the stage picture echoes these scenes, as first Tribulation Wholesome divides the stage between the churlish Ananias and Subtle, then, again, Subtle assumes the central position (III.i). As the symmetrical balance of the stage picture duplicates itself, the spectator is urged to entertain a thematic connection: Mammon wants to buy piety so that he can be rich; Tribulation wants to buy wealth so that he can spread holiness.

It is well to bear in mind, however, that these balanced stage pictures are abstractions, and do not really exist for long in performance. The stage picture is ever shifting—rapidly in satire—and momentary order is extremely ephemeral for most of the play. The crowding and expanding, followed by contraction and isolation that we have already posited is the usual movement. Characters tend to move quickly, regroup, and merge, until a final order, comprehended spatially, is established in the judgment scene at the end. Here, finally, is a formalizing tendency, symptomatic of either society's ability to check abnormal behavior, or the suicidal nature of folly. Of the conventional actions on the Elizabethan stage that Bernard Beckerman describes as suited to ceremonial or formal arrangements, several seem to characterize the final scene in Jonson's plays: the combat, a struggle between gull and knave; the revealed mystery, the knave's willful unmasking; the judgment, always the revealed knave's responsibility; and the parade, the procession offstage, crowned by the knaves.[25]

At the end of *Every Man in His Humour*, Justice Clement occupies a middle position, seated in his chair, and brings order to the group of characters who surround him, seeking justice. As he sentences each character, he arranges the stage so as to disentangle the relative merits of the participants. Bobadill and Matthew are positioned on one side, with Formall who is to preside over their punishment. They are joined by Stephen and, perhaps, Downe-right, who must learn to live in the same society. Since Stephen is to entertain Cob and Tib, they are situated next to him as they are reunited, as is the next couple, Kitely and his wife. On the other side of Clement, we imagine, are his friend Old Kno'well, who is never a gull, then Brayne-worme the central knave, who makes the spatial transition between his old and new master, Young Know'-well, with his bride, Bridget. Well-bred, the final knave, stands next to his

25. *Ibid.*, pp. 207–209.

friend, in appreciation of the marriage he helped to arrange. The stage is a picture of social order and symmetry, and the procession offstage, led by the gulls and capped by Clement and Brayne-worme, cements that order in the audience's final estimation.

Volpone is the least affirmative of all Jonson's plays, and especially in its final, violent order. *Volpone* himself establishes order by unmasking, and assumes the central position, obscuring the Avocatori who, as decadent representatives of the social order, deserve obscuring. Mosca joins the birds of prey on one side; Celia and Bonario, cardboard virtues, are on the other. This is hardly a balance, and there is no procession. The noble youths return to their homes, the criminals are taken individually to their punishments, and Volpone is left alone, lying against the light, to solicit the audience's approval in the epilogue. The final order seems to insist that the society in the audience consider carefully its healthy condition.

The Alchemist has no comparable final order, insofar as the stage represents it spatially. In a concluding action somewhat reminiscent of *Every Man in His Humour*, Love-Wit, as both judge and bridegroom, exists with his new wife and brother-in-law, leaving Face, like Volpone, alone. The recommendation here is for a purge, lest Mammon's threat, "The end o' the world, within these two months" (V.v.82), prove prophetic.

Trouble-all, the madman, chases everyone to judgment at the puppet show in *Bartholomew Fair*, where Justice Over-doo tries to bring order to the assembly, but is merely reunited with his drunken wife. A reunion based on a reordering of one's self-perception seems to be the organizing principle when Quarlous finally leads Over-doo through the maze of folly. The Little-wits and Over-doos are reunited, Quarlous and Win-wife get Purecraft and Grace, and the indomitable Cokes rejoins his haggard mentor, Wasp. A diffuse symmetry of couples is the desirable order; after all, everyone and everything in society is related. Everyone, that is, but Busy, to whom Jonson does not extend even his most comprehensive sympathies. Nor should the procession offstage be too formal. The fair lingers after the visitors leave, and some recognition of the ineradicable presence in society of childish contrariness and prerational desires is in order.

The most common catchword in treatments of spatial ordering in the theater is "focus." Actually, at all times throughout the play the audience's attention is directed for a particular purpose; in Jonson, the purpose is usually humor. Complementing the filling and emptying of the stage is the alternatingly wide and narrow focus.[26] In general, a narrow focus is directed at an object of ridicule or a center of knavery, while a wide focus signifies the satiric tendency to point up the artificiality in social distinctions, leveling, and society's flexibility for integrating abnormal behavior into its fabric.[27] A narrow focus is more common early in the play; a wider focus is appropriate for later complications and judgments.

The solitary figure is rare in satire, and when it occurs there is an important reason. Brayne-worme has the most time alone with the audience in his play because he more than any other character directs the audience's response, and embodies the knavery that drives the play together. Old Kno'-well has a surprisingly long soliloquy on the relationship of parents and children which, in part, establishes a theme of the play, but more importantly frees him from the stereotype of a foolish old father. He contradicts the stereotype, both by the good sense of his statements, and by his solitary presence. As we soon discover, a gull is very rarely alone onstage, and Old Kno'well's isolation communicates that.

Indeed, the gull is almost always accompanied by someone who focuses his stupidity. This is both a consequence of the knave's ability to draw gulls into traps, and of the gull's own need for an audience. Kitely does express his jealousy directly to the audience on a rare occasion (II.iii), but the more humorous scene is created when he calls his servant Cash to watch over the house (III.iii). Cash's bemused observations of his master, who is torn between revealing his concerns to his servant and preserving his dignity, heighten the comedy by casting it in a social context. The presence of another person forces the tentative, disingenuous gull to reveal his folly, and the audience's amusement is heightened.

Similarly, Bobadill is never alone in the play. If he were, he would not be Bobadill. Matthew's presence in the bed-staves scene (I.v) evokes Bobadill's pretense, and splits the focus between the master gull and his pupil. Once in society, Bobadill's relentless efforts to be the center of attention, to focus the audience on him, prove his undoing. Although always at the center of the stage, he never controls the audience's response.

26. See Brown, *Shakespeare's Plays in Performance*, p. 116.
27. Beckerman, *Shakespeare at the Globe*, pp. 171–173.

In his greatest acting scenes, the battle of Strigonium (III.i) and the plan for twenty men to preserve the commonwealth (IV.vii), the young knaves are present, puncturing his expansion with asides to the audience, and thereby controlling its response. The audience's attention is deflected, passing through the distorted mirror of the knaves' asides, and lighting on Bobadill from their vantage point.

The realization that a solitary figure is rare lends substantial value to soliloquies. There are none in *The Alchemist*, in which the center of activity is increasingly a solitary knave set upon by gulls and society, or a solitary gull besieged by knaves and gulls alike. The classic example of a gull as the focus of interest is Surly, the one character who is on to the knaves, and upon whom the other gulls descend at the moment of his apparent triumph (IV.vii). The more dexterous Face proves his mettle and his claim to survival when, from the front of the tiring house, he keeps gulls, neighbors, officers, and his master at bay outside, and keeps the other knaves busy inside, until he can secure Love-Wit's confidence. This image, of Face at the rear of the stage with the load of hostile attention directed at him, yet maintaining his sympathy with the audience, enforces his solitary ingenuity, and foreshadows his final victory.

Mosca's soliloquy on parasites is all the more chilling because, alone with the audience, he permits us to see his cunning to a greater extent than does any other character in the play (III.i). In this, his fascination is that of Iago. Jonson permits the extended, narrow focus as a means of creating the illusion of a fair contest between Mosca and Volpone. It is, however, an illusion; Volpone is supremely the focus. Propped up in his sick bed, carried into court on a pallet, elevated again on his stage to woo Celia, and again on his bed to seduce her, and for a final time peering over the arras to direct our response at the delightful legacy scene, "Looke, see, see, see!" (V.iii.17), Volpone is guaranteed the center of attention whenever he is onstage. For a character to rise above the level of the stage once is rare. For him to be elevated five times is unique indeed. He enjoys the most intense and consistent focus in the Elizabethan drama, except for Hamlet's soliloquies.

The unmistakable characteristic of a practiced playwright is his ability to work within a convention. The sign of real expertise is inverting a convention to reverse the audience's expectations. Surly, in *The Alchemist*, reverses our expectations. We identify asides to the audience as signs of a shared knowledge, and Surly frequently lets the audience know that he knows what it knows. And so his defeat by the knaves and the gulls, whom he has tried to enlighten, and in the presence of Dame Pliant to whom he has sworn service, reverses our expectations, in the most humorous scene in the play.

The best example of this type of intentionally misdirected focus is Justice Over-doo. Here is a character who lets the audience, and the audience alone, in on all his altruistic and secret plans. He speaks more lines to the audience than he does to characters in the play; yet he fails repeatedly, and we laugh at him more as he tells us each new plan. Our feelings toward him are a mixture of gentle ridicule and sympathy; we all have one friend who is forever on to some get-rich-quick scheme he is sure we'll want to know about, though it somehow always falls through. Yet this inverted ·focus is not so rare in *Bartholomew Fair* as it is in other plays.[28] This play tends to spread out its indictments evenly, obscuring any intense focus. For instance, when Cokes is being gulled by the cutpurse, we want to look at him; but we are also interested in the interplay between the cutpurse and the ballad singer, in Over-doo, who is trying to discover the culprit, and in Grace, who is being admired by Quarlous and Win-wife (III.v). *Bartholomew Fair* is a tapestry in which whatever we look at, or whoever is on stage, catches our eye. There are, of course, scenes of more carefully directed focus: Busy's attack on the vendors, Cokes's final, solitary gulling, the scenes in the stocks. But by comparison with the other plays, *Bartholomew Fair*'s tendency to fill the stage with concurrent points of interest is noteworthy.

Perhaps that is so because satire eschews perspective. The emphasis is on adding by individuals, crowding, and emptying. Measuring his characters by the size of their environment, the satirist avoids, until the end of the play, a tableau more complex than a two-dimensional frieze. Having said that, we must, nevertheless, acknowledge the occasional, effective use in Jonson's plays of the type of activity in which we see people watching people watching people. The least we can say is that Jonson experimented with a variety of techniques. In *Every Man Out of His Humour*, Mitis and Cordatus are positioned onstage throughout the entire

28. Eugene M. Waith notes the lack of focus in the Introduction to his edition of *Bartholomew Fair*, p. 2.

play, and their ongoing response to the action adds a critical if annoying dimension to the play. Similarly (one might almost say, repetitively), in *The Staple of News*, four gossips sit onstage and, like the characters in the play, speculate on the meaning of the latest news, both related to the play and in general.

Jonson is usually better than that. In *Volpone*, the presence of Peregrine and Sir Pol contributes significantly to our perception of Volpone's performance as Scoto of Mantua. Not only do their comments break up Volpone's long, entertaining speech, but they also sharpen the scene by giving voice to the faceless crowd that surrounds Volpone. Sir Pol is completely taken in by the act; Peregrine, not at all. Before we rush to the conclusion that Peregrine is correct (although in a sense, of course, he is), we should hold these views in tandem until we see who delivers the epilogue. But by providing these two vocal spectators at Volpone's first great acting scene, the playwright entertains for us a variety of responses.

Bartholomew Fair begins on a stage, moves to the proctor's house, and proceeds to the fair. The Induction is important in establishing a type of perspective in the play by which the audience is made to feel, increasingly, at one remove further from reality. This feeling, cemented in the early acknowledgment of the stage as a stage, followed by a complete act at Little-wit's house to which we never return, and finally by our entrapment in the confusing, irrational fair, is important to our understanding of the final scene at the puppet show. Here we have genuinely significant perspective, as the stage moves out into the audience in expanding ripples of reality. The puppets, pure fantasy, are at the center and rear of the stage. The child, Cokes, who handles them and speaks with them, is next, followed by the other characters, who are really players. We are compelled to ask, if we want to escape Busy's fate, whether the fantasy ends with the stage, whether the play is really only ineffectual entertainment. Perhaps, like Cokes, we want to take part of the play home.

In concluding our analysis of spatial relationships in Jonson's plays with a brief look at perspective, we are reminded that discovering "the proper perspective to apply to our understanding of Jonson's plays" has been our goal throughout this study. Although this verbal coincidence seems merely fortunate, it is not entirely coincidental. A recurring word in this analysis has been "tension." We have discovered tension in the movement of characters away from the tiring house yet drawn inward, tension in a stage designed to be expansive yet restricted by the unity of place, tension between antipathetic characters drawn to a point of common interest, a dynamic tension between a crowded and a relatively empty stage, corresponding to a wide and narrow focus. This tension, literally a stress, is not unlike our own opinion, on leaving the theater, of society and our place within it. If we are satisfied with the outcome of any of these plays, even as we laugh, we may well be comforting ourselves too easily. The multiple, complex tension on the stage, as it helps produce a provocative, constructive uneasiness in the audience, is one of the most basic criteria we can bring to our understanding of Jonson's plays in performance.

Volpone

in Performance: 1921-1972

R. B. PARKER

ALTHOUGH VOLPONE dropped out of the English repertory in the late eighteenth century,[1] it has become the most frequently revived of all Elizabethan plays with the exception only of Shakespeare's most popular works.[2] In the fifty years between its resurrection in 1921 and Jonson's quatercentennial in 1972 it had at least thirty-five professional productions,[3] and at the present time it has recently appeared at the

1. For earlier stage history see R. G. Noyes, *Ben Jonson on the English Stage, 1660–1776* (Cambridge, Mass., 1935), pp. 41 ff., and *Ben Jonson*, ed. C. H. Herford and Percy and Evelyn Simpson, 11 vols. (Oxford, 1925–1952), IX, 196–208. References to the text will be from the Herford and Simpson edition.

2. See William Hindle, "Shakespeare's Contemporaries in the Theatre, 1890–1968" (unpublished M.A. thesis, University of Birmingham, 1969).

3. The productions are as follows: 1921, Phoenix Society, Lyric Theatre, Hammersmith, revived 1923; 1923, Marlowe Society, Cambridge; 1930, Cambridge Festival Theatre; 1935, Birmingham Repertory Theatre, transferred to the Malvern Festival in July of this same year, with Wilfred Lawson replacing John Clifford as Volpone; 1938, Westminster Theatre, directed by Michael MacOwan, with Donald Wolfit as Volpone; 1940, Cambridge Arts Festival, directed by Wolfit himself, subsequently revived in 1942, 1944, 1947, 1949, and 1953, and toured to the provinces, to Canada, to the U.S.A. and

National Theatre in England, with Paul Scofield as Volpone and Sir John
Gielgud as Sir Politic Wouldbe. There have also been numerous university productions, versions adapted for radio and television, productions in
translation,[4] and some very successful modernizations and rewritings. *Sly
Fox*, adapted by Larry Gelbart, and starring George C. Scott as "Foxwell
J. Sly," is a recent Broadway hit; and Stefan Zweig's version of 1926 ("nach
Ben Jonson"), which was translated into French by Jules Romains and
into English by Ruth Langner, has a list of revivals and adaptations which
surpasses even that of Jonson's original—including a 1940 film of the
French version, with Harry Bauer in the title role and the great Louis
Jouvet as Mosca.[5] Another, very free film version was *The Honeypot* of
1966, adapted by Joseph Mankiewicz from a play by Frederick Knott
called *Mr. Fox of Venice* (London, 1959), which was itself based on Thomas Stirling's novel *The Evil of the Day*. There have also been at least three
musical adaptations: a 1960 German opera with music by Frances Burt; a
1964 English opera with music by Malcolm Williamson; and a musical
comedy version called *Foxy*, set in the Yukon gold rush and starring Bert
Lahr, which opened the Dawson City Festival in 1962 and was moved to
Broadway in 1964.

---

to Egypt; 1944, Stratford-on-Avon, directed by Robert Atkins, who also played Volpone;
1948, New York City Theatre Company; 1951, Princeton Theater Intime; 1952,
Stratford-on-Avon, directed by George Devine, with Ralph Richardson as Volpone; 1955,
Bristol Old Vic, the Marlowe Society at Cambridge, and a production by Joan Littlewood
at the Theatre Royal, Stratford-East; 1960, Manitoba Theatre Centre; 1963, Actors'
Workshop, San Francisco; 1964, Minneapolis, directed by Tyrone Guthrie; 1965, Shake-
speare Festival at Ashland, Oregon, and Nottingham Playhouse; 1966, Oxford Playhouse,
directed by Frank Hauser with Leo McKern as Volpone, a production that was moved to
London in 1967; 1967, the New York Shakespeare Festival; 1968, National Theatre,
London, directed by Tyrone Guthrie; 1969, Birmingham Repertory Theatre; 1970, Great
Lakes' Shakespeare Festival; 1971, Stratford, Ontario, directed by David William; and
1972, Bristol Old Vic, directed by Richard David to celebrate Jonson's quatercentennial.
For help with this list I am indebted to Professor Ejner Jensen of the University of Michigan
who is working to bring Noyes's study up to date.

4. A list of French productions can be found in M. T. Jones-Davies, *Ben Jonson* (Paris,
1973), pp. 186–187; and there is a discussion of German versions and productions in
Walter Pache, ed. *Volpone oder der Fuchs* (Stuttgart, 1974), pp. 330–336.

5. There were two productions of the Zweig version in English in 1968 and another in
1972, Jonson's quatercentennial; and it was Romains's translation of Zweig which also
provided the text for Gerard Vergez's spectacular production at the Comédie-Française in
1972.

With such a record of performance and adaptation, there can be no doubt of *Volpone*'s continuing vitality; but an examination of exactly how it has been staged shows that the play poses several difficult problems for a modern director: difficulties in choice of décor; in the casting and interpretation of certain key roles; in the relation of subplot to main plot; in the amount of self-consciousness between the audience and the actor playing Volpone; and in the exact tone and management of the denouement. Directors have met these problems in various ways, and their solutions not only help to uncover some of the theatrical, as well as dramatic, cruces of the play, but also reveal it as a work that is peculiarly dependent on the dimension of performance.

I

The problem in design is how to provide décor and costumes that will help a modern audience grasp the meaning of the play most readily. Solutions to this problem have fallen into four phases, or, more accurately, four trends. Initially, the interpretative aspect of design was ignored. Under the influence of William Poel, there was a tendency to use sixteenth-century costuming with a minimum of props, and to set the play in curtains on a playing area distinguished as closely as possible into what was then considered the standard Elizabethan combination of upper, inner, and apron stages. This kind of design was used in the Phoenix Society revivals of 1921 and 1923, the 1930 Cambridge and 1935 Birmingham Repertory versions, and the 1944 Stratford-on-Avon production (for which Robert Atkins had the Memorial Theatre's apron especially raised to the level of the main stage);[6] and, basically, it continued to be the form of Donald Wolfit's many productions from 1940 on.[7] Its chief advantage was that it was practically efficient, with the fluidity necessary for *Volpone*'s rapid scene changes; its limitation was that the design made no comment on the action.

A second tendency, therefore, has been to exploit the Venetian setting and evoke an ornate richness that sets the play specifically in time and place and at the same time comments on the materialism and greed that

6. For a picture of this set, see Ruth Ellis, *The Shakespeare Memorial Theatre* (London, 1948), p. 97.

7. A detailed study of Wolfit's production can be found in "Wolfit's Fox: An Interpretation of *Volpone*," *UTQ*, XLV (Spring 1976), 200–220.

Jonson is attacking. Peter Goffin's "gold-encrusted baroque" for the MacOwan-Wolfit production of 1938 can be seen as establishing this trend,[8] and the same solution was adopted in Hutchinson Scott's set for Oxford in 1966 and in Tanya Moisewitch's designs for Guthrie's two productions, based on Titian and Crivelli. At one extreme, this kind of setting can move toward outright symbolism, as in the 1965 Nottingham production, which had a backdrop of gold coins; at the other, it can strive for as realistic an effect as possible. The most elaborate example of the latter was Malcolm Pride's design for George Devine at Stratford in 1952, which the critic Alan Dent compared to Longhi's glowing canvases in the Academy at Venice.[9] Following the lead set by Komisarjevsky in his production of *The Merchant of Venice* in 1932, Pride made much use of the Memorial Theatre's lift stage and side rollers, so that Volpone's bedroom (with a treasure "shrine" that opened when one of the gilded pineapples on his bedpost was twisted) sank out of sight as a detailed reproduction of the Piazza di San Marco, complete with painted backcloth and practical gondolas, slid in from either side. One of the proscenium doors on the apron was then identified as Volpone's house, the other as Sir Politic-Wouldbe's; and for the Scrutineo scenes the whole piazza rolled sideways to stage right and the wall of the Scrutineo rose to reveal its interior. The designs were practicable and visually gorgeous, but they also had certain disadvantages. Despite heavy cutting, the changes made the production last three hours; the roller stages were noisy and met with a clang in mid-stage (*Punch* was reminded of municipal tram cars); and on one occasion an electrical failure paralyzed the lift stage in mid-descent, marooning Ralph Richardson in the top half of Volpone's bedroom.

A third solution has been to experiment with modern dress, or with transposition to a period which is neither modern nor Elizabethan: both modes that are very familiar from recent productions of Shakespeare, with dangers that are obvious. In Joan Littlewood's 1955 production at Stratford-East modernization had the effect of emphasizing the play's farcical element. Among its props were an accordion, a telephone, a cocktail shaker, a bath chair, and a frogman's suit (to replace Sir Pol's

8. A rare, colored picture of Goffin's set can be found in Christopher Hassall, "Notes on Verse Drama," *The Masque* VI (London, 1948), facing page 21; his costume sketches are in *Far and Wide* (January 1947).

9. *News Chronicle*, 16 July 1952. For photographs of set and costumes, see Ivor Brown and Angus McBean, *The Shakespeare Memorial Theatre*, 1951–53 (London, 1953).

tortoise shell); Mosca entered on a bicycle, wearing a wide-shouldered "spiv" jacket, with a cigarette clinging to his lower lip; and Celia's tight sweater, short skirt, and stockings embroidered with stars completely misled at least one French reviewer, when the production was taken to Paris (see *France-Soir*, 26 May 1955). More subtly, David William pointed up the play's sense of blasphemy and sexual decadence by setting the 1971 Ontario production in the Venice of Thomas Mann and Henry James, with the Wouldbe's transmogrified to loud Texans meeting a very Jamesian Peregrine in a crowded café ("L'adizzione, s'il vous plaît").

Perhaps most interestingly from the interpretative point of view, there have been occasional attempts to use design to re-establish the bestiary level of *Volpone*.[10] In the earlier revivals such an approach was usually confined to costuming effects. In the MacOwan-Wolfit version, for example, a russet-bearded Volpone was enveloped in fox furs, Voltore and Corbaccio were birdlike in costume and mannerisms, and the bespectacled Avocatori were represented as owls (a nice extension of Jonson's symbolism). The effect was confused, however, by having Mosca imitate a serpent rather than a fly, and Corvino a bull instead of a crow; and, as is the way with stage tradition, the bull image was then perpetuated in Wolfit's revivals and adopted by both the productions at Stratford-on-Avon with predictably unhappy results. The 1955 production at Bristol Old Vic developed the bestiary elements further, but was in turn outdone by Sir Tyrone Guthrie's two versions, particularly his 1968 production for the National Theatre. Besides furs for Volpone and a shiny black costume for Mosca, pinched in at the waist and tight on arms and legs, Tanya Moiseiwitch gave six-inch beaks to the birds of prey with feathered capes and gloves with talons[11]—so that every time Voltore grasped Mosca's shoulder the parasite perceptibly winced. Voltore was particularly spectacular, jumping straight on to the end of Volpone's bed to glare down at

10. For a discussion of the play's debt to the bestiary tradition, see D. A. Scheve, "Jonson's *Volpone* and Traditional Fox Lorve," *RES*, N.S. I (1950), 242–244, and Robert Knoll, *Ben Jonson's Plays: An Introduction* (Lincoln, Nebr., 1964), pp. 79–104; later articles on particular detail are: Malcolm South, "Animal Imagery in *Volpone*," *TSL*, X (1965), 141–150; Lloyd L. Mills, "Barish's 'The Double Plot' Supplemented: The Tortoise Symbolism," *The Serif*, IV (1967), 25–28; Ian Donaldson, "Jonson's Tortoise," *RES*, N.S. XIX (1968), 162–166; P. R. Doob and G. B. Shand, "Jonson's Tortoise and Avian," *Renaissance and Reformation*, X (1974), 43–44. For a discussion of its relation to the beast epic, see "*Volpone* and *Reynard the Fox*," *Ren D*, N.S. VI (1976), 3–42.

11. For pictures, see *Plays and Players* (March 1968), pp. 14–17.

him and swooping offstage with his feathered cloak floating out behind him "like a great bomber taking off." [12] Actors were sent to study bird behavior at the zoo in Regents Park; Colin Blakely copied his vocal effects for Volpone from records of real foxes; [13] and it was Guthrie who first took up the scholars' suggestions that the Wouldbe's should be represented as parrots.

The effect of so much invention was finally distracting, however, and the play's moral symbolism was undercut because, as Robert MacDonald complained in *The Scotsman*, "it is difficult to condemn real vultures for behaving like vultures." [14] The bestiary element was more discreetly handled by Richard David, whose quatercentennial production for the Bristol Old Vic was something of a model for this approach (though he overdid it, rather, when Celia appeared on her balcony cradling a lamb). The costumes in this version still recalled animals, but, learning perhaps from Guthrie's mistake, their business was never overdone. Moreover, this production was unique in reflecting bestiary influences more largely in the *mise-en-scène*. The constructivist set was basically three tall, spindly platforms, with the one at stage left towering as high as twenty feet up into the flies. The birds' entrances to Volpone's bedroom were made by swooping down from this height along intersecting diagonal ramps, which not only established the image of circling predators but also allowed some interesting overlappings of scenes, of the kind suggested by Jonson's own use of "One knocks without," to indicate new arrivals before the previous scene has finished. Other bestiary features were a large, round, burrowlike opening over the middle platform and a downstage trap into which Bonario and Celia were thrust to prison. In the scene where Corvino interrupts "Scoto's" wooing of Celia, Mosca slid into this trap head foremost like a fly into a sewer, while the crow harried Volpone up the ramps and into the burrow. The whole set was painted a curious greenish gold with lumpy encrustations, simultaneously suggesting ordure and decaying wealth, and it was appropriately dominated by a large hanging image of the Lion of St. Mark.

One final peculiarity of Volpone's structure, which can have an effect on design, may be noted. The climactic trial scene of the play (V.x.xii) is

12. Ronald Bryden, *The Observer*, 21 January 1968.
13. See Blakely's discussion of the production in *Gambit*, VI (Winter 1972), 7, 15.
14. *The Scotsman*, 22 January 1968.

interrupted by a short sequence out of court (V.xi) in which Volpone hears
from his freaks that Mosca has betrayed him. As V.x and xii are continuous (in fact V.xii is renumbered V.x in the 1607 quarto), the difficulty for
directors is how to break the scene without disrupting the court sequence.
The most drastic solution to the problem has been to cut V.xi completely,
as was done at Stratford-on-Avon in 1944; but a more usual method is to
black out the main stage briefly and have the encounter between Volpone
and the freaks in a spotlight, either before the curtain or at stage front. (At
Bristol in 1955 the transition was emphasized by a gong before and after
V.xi). However, a more interesting and visually beautiful effect was introduced in Frank Hauser's Oxford production and copied in both the
Guthrie versions, whereby the court merely froze into tableau under diminished lighting while the encounter took place. This is probably the
solution most like what we know of Jacobean technique, and several
reviewers remarked on its effectiveness [15]—though it was somewhat di-
luted in Guthrie's case by also using freezes for Volpone's asides to Voltore
and Mosca in the same scene.

II

As is to be expected with a play so rich in implications, the major roles
have been given very various readings. The interpretation of Volpone
himself, for instance, must take into consideration how old he should be
made, how aristocratic, how his malevolence and his humor are to be
balanced, and what emphasis should be given to Jonson's undercutting of
the character with self-condemnatory imagery and failures of nerve.

Volpones have ranged in age all the way from John Clifford's very
young magnifico (Birmingham, 1935) to the genuinely aged, almost
senile foxes of Robert Atkins and Ralph Richardson in the two productions at Stratford-on-Avon.[16] The consensus, however, is to follow

---

15. *Oxford Times*, 23 September 1966; *Cherwell*, 10 October 1966; *Glasgow Herald*,
18 January 1968. Guthrie also used the situation to indicate the passing of time. Having
opened the action at sunrise, he had the clock strike three at the end of the first trial scene,
and, as the lights came up in V.xii after the freeze, torches were brought in as if to account
for the change in illumination.

16. Harold Hobson compared Richardson's "pasty deliquescence" to "a corpse dressed
up for a party." *Sunday Times*, 20 July 1952.

Wolfit's line and show Volpone as in early middle age, a man in the prime of life whose senility, like his diseases, is wholly a pretense.

Understanding of the fox's basic motivation has been much more tricky, but again Wolfit's interpretation can stand as the nearest reading so far to a norm. Developing a line set down by Wilfred Lawson (Malvern, 1935), Wolfit saw the key to Volpone's character as life-greediness, an overweening virility, sexual in origin, which imposes itself relentlessly and cruelly on its surroundings but also has enormous *joie de vivre* (the "gusto" on which Wolfit's reviewers constantly remark). The limitation of this approach, of course, is that it evades too many of Volpone's weaknesses. A vigorous late reading in the same vein by Eric Porter (Bristol, 1955), who had been a member of Wolfit's company, drew the criticism that it was more "lion" than fox;[17] and Wolfit himself went to the length of cutting out several passages in which the fox is shown as ludicrous or ineffectual.

Ralph Richardson's eccentric interpretation at Stratford-on-Avon in 1952 seems, in part at least, to have been in reaction against these omissions by Wolfit, though it may also have been influenced by Atkins's previous reading of the role at Stratford and by the Volpone of the Zweig adaptation, who is represented as a bored aristocrat, disdainful of the weakness of mankind. Far from Wolfit's aggressive exuberance, Richardson's fox was weary, ironic, and withdrawn, so etiolated that in one absurd scene the militantly righteous Celia had to bend over his prone body to beg him not to assault her. This reading seems only to have attained full stature at the end, when Richardson's Volpone stood in chains "silently expressing scorn for the bunch of well intentioned zanies who have sentenced him."[18] A related but much sharper and more aggressive line was taken by William Hutt at Ontario, in which the fox's key was icy, introverted disdain for the immorality he encouraged out of boredom and contempt; the influence here was De Sade.

A third way of interpreting the title role has been to emphasize its element of boisterous comedy, the "broad gusty humour" that Wolfit claimed to have added to Lawson's aggressive savagery.[19] At its extreme

17. Peter Rodford, *Western Daily Press*, November 1955.

18. T. C. K[empe], *Birmingham Post*, 16 July 1952.

19. Donald Wolfit, *First Interval: The Autobiography of Donald Wolfit* (London, 1954), p. 180.

this leads to an infantile Volpone, an Ubu Roi or "monstrous baby"[20] surrendered to the id without discipline or self-knowledge. Leo McKern's interpretation (Oxford, 1966) was perhaps the epitome of this roaring, jovial reading of the part, but both of Guthrie's Volpones were of the same cloth: Douglas Campbell boohooed and pounded the floor when Celia was rescued from him, and Colin Blakely gleefully used his bed as a trampoline at the very mention of "massy plate." However, such an emphasis not only sacrifices the fox's aristocracy and reduces his poetry to mock-heroic but, what is even more serious, can destroy Jonson's careful moral placing. Campbell, for example, was so funny as a seducer that the Minneapolis audience actually applauded his attempt at rape.

III

Volpone's relationship with several of the other characters has also been interpreted very variously and even contradictorily, particularly his attitude to Nano, Castrone, and Androgyno, to Celia (and Bonario), and, of course, to Mosca.

The problem with the three freaks is that their function is largely symbolic, rhythmic, and atmospheric; they are not needed in the action except as a minor aid in the Scoto scene and as a convenient instrument to disabuse Volpone in V.xi. Their parts have therefore sometimes been cut. At Bristol in 1955 Androgyno and Castrone were dropped completely and Nano's role was reduced merely to his involvement in the plot; Joan Littlewood, in the same year, dispensed with Castrone. More often, all three roles are retained but their songs and entertainments are cut and reduced. Thus in many recent productions there has been only one song in the Scoto episode and only the first entertainment for Volpone (I.ii), with the latter's passages on metempsychosis also excised.

However, other productions have exploited the freaks for atmospheric effects of eerie decadence; some have even added to their action; and their costuming in particular has given scope for much grotesque invention. In the MacOwan-Wolfit production, for example, Nano was red-haired (to support Mosca's contention that the freaks are the fox's children), with a bag dangling from his belt in front like a diseased scrotum (Wolfit occa-

20. *The Daily Mail*, 1 February 1967.

sionally assigned the role to an actress); Castrone was the fool of the trio, a mute in harem costume of fez and galabieh; while Angrogyno had one side costumed like a man and the other as a woman, with instructions to do most of his acting in profile, emphasing first one side then the other. At Bristol in 1972 the freaks were distinguished by garish circus costume and make-up, with Castrone convulsively clutching his pants' front and Nano as a monopode, bouncing monstrously across stage. In the 1971 Ontario production Castrone was strikingly fat and bald, dressed all in white satin, Androgyno had naked female breasts and male genitals of mutant size and coloration, and the dwarf emerged from a huge, Castrone-like egg that the other two wheeled in for Volpone's breakfast.

One particularly interesting device has been to key the freaks to discordant music. MacOwan introduced this by identifying each freak in I.ii with one of the instruments in the "sour consort of woodwind" (James Agate) written by Edmund Rubbra as background music for the play, so that thereafter the imaginative effect of the freaks seemed present in the music even when they were not on stage. Other productions have had the freaks themselves play instruments, in an extension of Volpone's own misuse of music in the song to Celia. In the Scoto scene of the second Stratford-on-Avon production, for example, they played on harp, glockenspiel, cowbell, triangle, jingle bells, cymbal, rattle, and trumpet. The Oxford and 1969 Birmingham Repertory productions also expanded the text's hint that Volpone means to have the freaks watch his lovemaking with Celia (cf. III.vii.219–221), so that at Birmingham they watched the attempted rape with leering approval and at Oxford took an active part in it by cutting off Celia's attempts to escape—an invention that also had the advantage of breaking up Volpone's long speeches.

Volpone himself has been given quite different attitudes to these entertainers, the extremes of which can be seen in Wolfit and Guthrie. Wolfit's promptbooks refer to them always as the "queers," and his attitude on stage was one of malevolent contempt. His Volpone neither liked his entertainers nor found them amusing, but treated them roughly and kept them merely as butts for his black humor. Guthrie's promptbooks, on the other hand, refer to them as "the children" or "the kids," and in both his productions they were definitely the fox's children, of whom he was indulgently fond, petting them, feeding them candy, romping with them on his bed, and personally conducting their entertainments. (One side effect of this was to diminish Volpone's discomfiture after the first trial, since his jolly welcome home by "the kids" obliterated all sense of the loss of nerve suggested by Jonson.)

IV

Another critical area for stage interpretation is Volpone's relationship to Celia and hence her characterization. Not only must it be clear from the reading of Volpone himself that his transfer of interest from gold to Celia is another aspect of the same libidinal aggression (not, as Dryden thought, a complete switch), but certain basics about the characterization of Celia must also be decided on: specifically, whether she is a strong character or wholly a victim; why she drops her handkerchief to Scoto; and how close she is—if at all—to succumbing to Volpone's seduction.

In Devine's 1952 production at Stratford-on-Avon Siobhan McKenna gave the role a great deal of positive energy. She laughed gaily at her window, openly enjoying Scoto's antics, and in the seduction scene her strong-minded, Sabrina-like defense of virtue completely overpowered Ralph Richardson's unconvinced attack. At the other extreme, Rosalind Iden played the role for Wolfit as a completely innocent victim, very young and bewildered, panicking at the fox's assault, her plump, blonde submissiveness provoking sadism in both the fox and her husband, Corvino.

Celia's characterization cannot be assessed separately from Corvino's, in fact; and here again there has been surprising variety. The first line for Corvino was to play him as a bull-like fool with a northern tradesman's accent, unaware of his degradation and brutal only when thwarted. This line continued at least to Devine's production, where, with Richardson's withdrawness, it had the effect of deflecting emphasis onto Celia's firm virtue. In Joan Littlewood's version Corvino was characterized physically as repellently sweaty and fat—"an adipose young monster" (*France-Soir*, 26 May 1955)—puffy and thick-tongued, gripping his interlocutors with tiny hands; but in more recent productions there has been a concentration rather on the character's neurosis, his *awareness* of shame, torn between ambition and jealousy, social climbing and class resentment, and his expression of these tensions in a mixture of cajoling cowardice and sadism. The most interesting characterization from this point of view was Leonard

Rossiter's much-praised reading of the role at Oxford, which represented Corvino as an effeminate and vulgar dandy of "tortured affability,"[21] pretending with high-pitched laughter that insults are merely jokes, cooing "Celia, I shall grow violent" *sotto voce*, smirking and breathing hard, with his sadism so bottled up that he kept hitting his own body in transports of rage. Something of the same social tension was also projected by the East-end Jewish lisp into which Corvino occasionally fell in Guthrie's 1968 version, while it was rather the sexual ambiguity of his position that Roland Hewgill emphasized at Ontario, making it clear that Corvino derived a sadomasochistic pleasure in procuring his wife, quite apart from any gain he expected to get by it.

This sexual nastiness seems justified by the perverse innuendo of Corvino's threats to Celia (II.v.60–61) and by the chastity belt which, it should be noted, he has ready to hand before there is any question of a liaison with Scoto to excuse it. Productions have often omitted this "lock" as altogether too unpleasant. It figures in neither of Guthrie's versions, for instance, and in the 1955 Bristol production it was transformed (presumably by mistake) to a door chain, wrapped pointlessly around Celia till Corvino removed it as part of his cajolery. MacOwan and Wolfit, however, had a suitably repellent-looking hoop wrapped in surgical bandage with a piece to go between the legs; and the suggestion of sexual sadism it conveys was further pointed in the Ontario production by giving Celia two wardresses who struck her and forced her brutally to kneel before her husband.

The seduction scene itself allows a wide range of interpretation. Richardson and Hutt were detached and unenthusiastic rapists, in Hutt's case clearly more interested in the rhetoric than the lady. Wolfit, on the other hand, stressed the rampant sexuality of the scene, and in Atkins's production (Stratford, 1944) on the eve of the Second Front this element was so unqualified by poetry or humor that two soldiers walked out in protest when the fox began to stroke Celia's breasts (cf. Voltore's sarcastic "pray you, mark these hands. / Are they not fit to stroke a lady's breasts?" IV.vi.27–28).[22] In Guthrie's productions, however, the seduction was choreographed as a bouncy *pas de deux*, thus safely removing it from any suggestion of real threat.[23]

21. Ian Donaldson, *The Guardian*, 21 September 1966.
22. Ruth Ellis, *Stratford-on-Avon Herald*, 8 June 1944.
23. Volpone's song "Come my Celia" can pose problems if the actor is not a singer.

One of the complexities introduced by MacOwan, then developed by Wolfit, Hauser, Guthrie, and David, has been the idea that Celia should almost succumb to the seduction. Wolfit, Guthrie, and David understood this merely as a daze (literally mesmeric in some of Wolfit's productions) brought on by the barrage of flattery, threats, promises, and gifts with which Volpone bombards the girl. Hauser's reasoning was different, however; as he explains:

The point I wanted to get across in the actual staging of it was that she *is* seduced, not wholly seduced, but tempted by it. . . . She has to be very, very strong. It's conceivable she might yield. And this of course immediately makes it dramatic. Jonson's not doing it in order to have lovely poetry, Volpone's doing it to lay her, and some part of her mind is toying with the idea. . . . The reason he is saying all these lines depends as much on her character as his.[24]

The director's decision here may be related to his choice of when Celia should appear at her window in the Scoto scene and what her reaction to the mountebank, which culminates in the dropping of her handkerchief, should be.[25] It has been usual to have her appear during the freaks' song (II.vii.292 ff.), but this means that, unless the succeeding spiel is cut, we must watch her enjoying Scoto's performance before deliberately dropping her handkerchief, an action which may seem flirtatious (especially if Scoto reveals his real identity to her, as both Wolfit and Campbell did). This was certainly the reaction of Harold Hobson to Siobhan McKenna's Celia, whom he compared to the "sort of girl who entices strangers to her bedroom and then screams for help" (*Sunday Times*, 20 July 1952). Hauser cleverly reduced this danger by having Celia appear at II.ii.215 in sympathy with Scoto's plea to his audience for some token "to show I am not contemn'd of you," so it was clear that she dropped her handkerchief only as part of the crowd's encouragement; and the Ontario production of 1971 adopted the same timing.

Hauser also insisted that Celia's naïveté must not persuade the director to attempt to guy her, because this reduces the audience sympathy for her,

---

Wilfred Lawson cut it, and many Volpones have shortened it to a single quatrain. In a 1935 production at Harvard it was sung by the eunuch and dwarf; and Wolfit tried doing it as recitative, miming to a guitar played offstage. The *Daily Telegraph* (13 October 1953) reported, "Passion may be comic, but Volpone's serenade to Celia should not be so!"

24. *Isis*, 5 October 1966.

25. Cf. Peter Barnes, "[Celia] isn't just a wronged girl. She throws a handkerchief to Volpone, and it's never explained why she does." *Gambit*, VI (Winter 1972), 11.

which in turn diminishes the real nastiness of the fox's attack.[26] On the other hand, he considered that there is enough parody in Jonson's text to justify interpreting Bonario as a fool. Accordingly, Bonario's rescue leap at Oxford got him entangled in Volpone's bedclothes (an invention also borrowed by Ontario), and his inopportune outbursts before the court were treated comically. Though such a reading remains doubtful, it does avoid Coleridge's well-known regret that Celia did not finish as Bonario's wife (as she does in Ludwig Tieck's 1793 adaptation).

Volpone's own reaction to the rescue can also vary from abject fear and near collapse (e.g., Stratford 1952, Bristol 1972), to the petulance of a thwarted child (e.g., Oxford 1966, and both the Guthrie productions), to Wolfit's savage sexual frustration, expressed by a hissing intake of breath with the eyeballs showing white, which only Bonario's drawn sword could hold at bay, and which was released in physical violence to Mosca at "Th' hast made me miserable" in the next scene (III.viii.9).

V

Volpone's relation to his parasite, in fact, is the key relation of the play, but the character of Mosca is another area where there have been considerable differences of interpretation. Again there are three main aspects which we may distinguish from the many readings.

One interpretation has been to show the audience from the beginning that Mosca is treacherous. There was a touch of this in Stephen Murray's "oily, silkily ingratiating schemer"[27] in the first Birmingham production, while in MacOwan's production Alan Wheatley, "a visible hypocrite from the start, rather emphasized this aspect of the character, perhaps as a clue to the sequel."[28] Anthony Quayle's reading at Stratford in 1952 was perhaps the most notable example of this approach. His Mosca was a mixture of a Puritan, Uriah Heep, and Iago, hypocritically smiling, cringing with servile back and meek knees, his hands unctuously soaping one another, and only his physical largeness and occasional "phosphorescently"[29] fixed stare betraying his underlying menace. There was a class

26. *Isis*, 5 October 1966.
27. *Birmingham Mail*, 25 March 1935.
28. Herford and Simpson, IX, 205.
29. Harold Hobson, *Sunday Times*, 20 July 1952.

element in this reading which was also to be seen in Frank Wylie's Scots-accented Mosca for Guthrie in 1968, which one reviewer compared to "some repellant insect hatched in the Gorbals,"[30] and in Lewis Fiander's street-Arab rendering at Bristol in 1972. The most extreme class emphasis, however, was to be found, not surprisingly, in Joan Littlewood's production, where Mosca was unmistakably a postwar "spiv," elaborately coiffed and dressed in ever flashier suiting as his fortunes rose, to end the play in an extravagantly draped white tuxedo.

The opposite line has been to hold the audience as much in the dark as Volpone, keeping the parasite noncommital so that his final treachery comes as a shock. This may be done for very different reasons however. Frank Wylie's underplaying may have had no better reason than a problem with voice production, whereas Wolfit deliberately kept his Moscas from being too prominent in order to throw attention on his own role as the fox. Wolfit always cast rather light-voiced actors for the part, and had them play it in an epicene, attitudinizing style, first established by MacOwan in 1938. Wolfit also cut many of Mosca's caustic asides to the audience and much of his independent plotting, and added business to bring attention back to Volpone at the ends of scenes where Jonson has left the parasite dominant (e.g., II.iv, III.ix). Significantly, he obscured his own eyes with ointment instead of having Mosca do it for him, and the parasite's key soliloquy, in which he reveals for the first time his total egotism and self-interest (III.i), had to be delivered while he leaned languidly against the proscenium arch, picking petals from a flower, and scene changing behind the curtain effectively drowned out many of the words. Such cavalier treatment of a key speech may be contrasted to its careful pointing in the Minneapolis production, where it came immediately after the first interval and the ushers were forbidden to let latecomers back to their seats until it was concluded; or, even more strikingly, to the 1972 Bristol production where, not only was it given prominence as the last speech before the interval, but Lewis Fiander delivered it intimately to the audience, sitting on the edge of the stage with his legs dangling into the auditorium.

The blandness of Wolfit's Mosca was also quite different from the "dry, sly fly"[31] of Alan Dobie in 1955 at Bristol and 1966 at Oxford, though

---

30. Philip French, *New Statesman*, 26 January 1968.
31. *Cherwell*, 10 October 1966.

these performances, too, drew the criticism of understatement. Dobie was deliberately underplaying to establish Mosca's watchful, deadpan contempt, but, as Daphne Levens pointed out in the *Oxford Magazine*, far from lulling the audience into security, the understatement in this case alerted them to the parasite's treachery.[32] Zoya Mohyeddhin, who took over the role when the Oxford production moved to London, was criticized for rather different reasons. Instead of projecting Dobie's aloofness, Mohyeddhin stressed Mosca's charm and *joie de vivre*, the quality that misleads Volpone and constitutes, perhaps, the most orthodox emphasis in the role. A similar "Mephisto-like gaity" had characterized Alan Wheatley's reading in the MacOwan production, but to this Mohyeddhin—an exceptionally lithe and handsome actor—added a quality of ingenuous-seeming youth. The *Observer* critic described him as "the sort of incredibly ravaged and debauched Venetian urchin who accosts you, with eager charm, to offer his thirteen year old sister" (5 February 1967), and remarked on an unexpectedly touching quality in the portrayal. Similar emphases were adopted by Fiander at Bristol in 1972 and Douglas Rain at Ontario, though the latter added to the impression of youthful charm a menacing quality of absolute stillness and—like Quayle—an occasionally unnerving, wide-eyed fixity of gaze.

If Mosca is not to be seen as treacherous from the start, the director has to decide at what point his treachery shall become unambiguously clear to the audience. A discouraging number of modern productions have pruned away the acerbities and asides which give warning gradually of the parasite's independence. Wolfit did this most thoroughly of all, and insisted that the idea of deceiving his master only came to Mosca opportunistically when Volpone said he would make him his heir. In Atkins's Stratford text the promptbook direction "Mosca moves D. R. pondering" at the same point suggests a similar solution. The most obvious place for open acknowledgment is, of course, the fly's soliloquy in III.i, but the 1972 Bristol production created an interesting alternative by allowing Mosca's anger to break through much earlier at "He's the true father of his family, / In all, save me . . ." (I.v.48–49), the effect of which was to suggest that Mosca loathed Volpone for "forcing him to show a love their relationship doesn't justify, and thus making him the parasite he is"[33]—a reading

32. *Oxford Magazine*, Michaelmas, 1966.
33. *New Statesman*, 17 March 1972.

which Volpone's quasi-homosexual advances might also help to support (cf. I.iii.79, I.iv.137, V.iii.103–104).

A final decision about Mosca has to be to what extent he, too, should be included in the general bestiary effect. Picking up "I could skip / Out of my skin now, like a subtle snake" (III.i.5–6), MacOwan had the parasite played sinuously like a snake, an interpretation anticipated by Stephen Murray's "viper-like" reading in the first production at Birmingham and developed later by Wolfit. The most flylike representation to date was probably that of Anthony Quayle, who replied to an objection that he was too large to suggest a fly with the comment, "Then I shall play him as a bluebottle."[34] Quayle combined physical agility with shiny black clothes, rubbed his hands together in a motion that was part Uriah Heep, part a fly massaging its legs, stressed his sibilants, and gave a curious buzzing whenever he laughed. At his moment of triumph in the will scene (V.iii) he even seemed to have eight limbs, since he was seated at a table whose legs were carved into black stockings and shoes to resemble his own. Buzzing was also used by George Grizzard at Minneapolis and by Lewis Fiander; and Rain's curious bouts of stillness were anticipated by Frank Wylie, though in his case, instead of Rain's menace, they gave an impression of lassitude: "halting his insect scurrying for a sudden fit of weariness or a rare gleam of ambition."[35]

The establishment of a physically bustling, buzzing, persistent fly, contrasted with the prone "deaf" fox, was almost certainly intended by Jonson, since it helps prepare for the reversal in Act V, where it is Mosca who pretends to be deaf and rests motionless at his desk or on the stool provided for him in court, while Volpone as *commandatore* dashes around, buzzing asides, and annoying his dupes with a crazy, flylike persistence. Before we examine this aspect further, however, we should glance at the problems of the subplot.

VI

The Wouldbe plot has probably been the greatest single embarrassment for modern directors of *Volpone*, because not many of them have seen its relation to the main plot,[36] and even when they have, its difference in

34. *The Scotsman*, 15 July 1952.
35. *Sunday Telegraph*, 21 January 1968.
36. See Jonas Barish, "The Double Plot in *Volpone*," MP, LI (1953), 83–92, and Judd

tone and the contemporary nature of many of its references have still created problems.

The simplest and most drastic solution has been to cut it completely, as MacOwan and Hauser did and as Wolfit came to do after replacing it in his 1940 production at Cambridge and experimenting with various abbreviations of it in 1942 and 1944. Even when the Wouldbe's are not wholly omitted, it has been usual to curtail the Sir Pol and Peregrine dialogue, and this has sometimes been done so completely that the two characters are reduced merely to members of Scoto's crowd—in some of Wolfit's versions, for example, they are doubled with two of the Avocatori. Such cuts almost invariably omit Sir Pol's travel advice and his contemporary gossip—though at a time when the Alger Hiss scandal was still remembered, Guthrie was able to get a clever laugh by substituting "pumpkin" for Sir Pol's comment about secrets hidden in cabbages. The extracts from his diary are shortened, and his inventions often reduced to the single scheme for detecting plague. The tortoise scene (V.iv) presents a particular difficulty, especially for productions in which the bestiary element has not been developed. It is often omitted (though this leaves the Wouldbe's and Peregrine falsely in harmony), and even when it has been retained—as it was by Devine, Guthrie, David William, and Richard David—it has never been received with enthusiasm by the critics.[37] The only positive response to the scene was for Joan Littlewood's ingenuity in transforming the tortoise shell to a modern frogman's suit and having Sir Pol exit by a dive into the orchestra pit.

Sir Pol has been characterized variously. As was mentioned earlier, the Ontario production portrayed him as a loud, big-hatted Texan, an "ugly American" whose naïveté betrayed him to the local police spies while he boasted of his shrewdness. Another interesting line was established at Stratford in 1952, when Michael Hordern connected the character's absurd inventions and misfortunes with the sweet dim-wittedness of Lewis Carroll's White Knight—a lead taken up three years later by John Hum-

---

Arnold, "The Double Plot in *Volpone*: A Note on Jonsonian Dramatic Structure," *SCN*, XIII (1965), 47–52. A complementary argument is developed by Dorothy E. Litt, "Unity of Theme in *Volpone*," *BNYPL*, LXXIII (1969), 218–226.

37. Cf. Nicholas Boileau, *The Art of Poesy*, trans. Sir W. Soames and John Dryden (London, 1683):

When in the *Fox* I see the tortoise hist,
I lose the author of the *Alchemist*.

phries at Bristol. Sir Pol's connection with an imitative parrot was not exploited till the Guthrie productions, however, particularly the National Theatre one of 1968 in which Graham Crowther, pigeon-toed and dressed in garish colors, presented a Sir Pol with "withered, parrot, slow winking eyes, leathery tongue clicking and whistling in a dry mouth, feet restlessly clawing at an invisible perch"[38]—a clever but too elaborate portrayal that was adapted more discreetly at Bristol in 1972.

Though her part is often reduced, Lady Pol is cut less frequently than Sir Pol and Peregrine because her action is involved with Volpone himself. She is usually played with shrill-voiced gentility—"all gaucherie and Girton," as one reviewer described the Joan Littlewood version[39]—though the Ontario production made her into a hysterically "feminine" southern belle. It is a role that can easily be broadened out of control, and at Stratford 1952 Rosalind Atkinson was accused of acting it like a pantomime dame[40]—an interesting comment since, at the suggestion of John Meynard Keynes, Wolfit actually cast a don, Donald Beves, to play the role at Cambridge in 1940, and it is again attributed to a man, Eric Maxton, in his 1944 program (though the promptbook shows that the role was eventually cut). It seems probable that the part was taken by a man, not a boy, in the original 1605 production.

Lady Pol has certain obvious comic business—with her reticule, her medicines, her books, and the cap she has knitted for Volpone—and she usually manages to climb onto, or even into, the fox's bed. Her kissing of Volpone in the first court scene, however, which is referred to later at V.ii.97, has often gone unnoticed by directors. Actresses have also added individual business: Joan Littlewood's Lady Pol was a mistress of the obscene nudge; in both Guthrie's versions she constantly curtsied as she talked down the judges; and there were great laughs at Stratford 1952, Oxford 1966, and the National Theatre 1968 at her belated "I pray you, lend me your dwarf" (III.v.29), when she had already in effect shanghaied him.

VII

The more farcical nature of the subplot is a reminder not only that *Volpone* is highly theatricalist in style but also that acting is thematically

38. Alan Brien, *Sunday Telegraph*, 21 January 1968.
39. *Times*, 4 March 1955.
40. *Manchester Guardian*, 16 July 1952.

important in the play, as many recent critics have demonstrated.[41] This element of self-conscious "performance" was a key factor in Wolfit's success in the title role, and more recently was crucial to both of Tyrone Guthrie's versions, to the 1969 production at Birmingham, and to Richard David's quatercentennial version.

A sense of acting *within* the play is an element that affects many aspects of *Volpone* (our recognition of Mosca's hypocrisy, for example, or our response to the freaks' entertainments), but it is particularly important for deciding whether the worship of gold in the opening scene is seriously intended by Volpone or is a mocking blasphemy; in the handling of the Scoto scene; in the episodes in which Volpone, disguised as a *commandatore*, persists in teasing his dupes; and in the control of tone in the final scene, especially as it relates to the epilogue.

Though the first scene can be taken completely straight (as it was by Wolfit), with the worship of gold intended seriously and Mosca seen merely as a henchman, directors can also establish a critical context to match the way that Jonson has booby-trapped the fox's lines with self-condemnatory imagery; and this can be variously toned to represent the scene as a serious or a comic blasphemy. For example, a certain comic degeneracy can be established in the way that Volpone is awakened. In the Ontario production a whore slid out of bed as Mosca entered to wake his master, an effect made more luridly (but also more comically) at the New York Shakespeare Festival of 1967, when both a man and a woman were rousted out. More farcically, at Minneapolis Volpone was awakened by Mosca tickling his nose, then holding a drink beneath it which brought his master upright, still with closed eyes, following the liquor.

There are also degrees of religiosity and blasphemy possible in the worship of gold. In the 1972 Bristol production the note was one of perverse but serious religiosity. Mosca made much play with a rosary and crossed himself repeatedly; the treasure "shrine" was located behind a private altar, which swung open to allow Volpone to kneel among his gold; and after his discovery by Bonario, Act III closed with Volpone kneeling at prayer, clasping a jeweled crucifix. Guthrie's productions, on

---

41. E.g., Alvin Kernan, Introduction to *Volpone* (New Haven, Conn., 1962), pp. 7–26; Jonas Barish, "Double Plot in *Volpone*"; C. G. Thayer, *Ben Jonson: Studies in the Plays* (Norman, Okla., 1963), pp. 59–66; Alexander Leggatt, "The Suicide of Volpone," *UTQ*, XXXIX (1969), 19–32.

the other hand, concentrated more on the aspect of deliberate mockery. After waking, Colin Blakely as the fox literally washed "himself with gold coins, shaking the small change out of his ears"[42] (presumably an expansion of the suggestion at I.iv.74). At Minneapolis there was worship of a dangling sun-jewel, to the tinkling of sacring bells; while at the National Theatre a coin was elevated like the host, then fed wafer-like to the kneeling Mosca at "Hold thee, Mosca, / Take of my hand, . . ." (I.i.66–67)—a brilliant piece of stage symbolism. The quality of blasphemy was altogether more sinister, however, in the thundering baroque organ music to which Volpone awoke at Ontario, and the treasure "shrine" was not behind an altar in this production but Freudianly beneath Volpone's circular bed, which gradually opened like a bivalve, with light streaming perversely from below and Volpone astride the opening like a grave.[43] The blasphemy was then continued by an orgy, with which this production replaced the freaks' first entertainment. A procession of penitentes—including figures representing the Virgin Mary, Mary Magdalene, and the pope—entered chanting and flagellating themselves, only to strip off for sexual congress to the thunder of the *Dies Irae*, while Volpone in black pyjamas commented "Now very, very pretty!"

Volpone's playacting is unambiguous during the visits of the three legacy hunters which follow; and Wolfit set a high standard of comic invention in exploiting the link this can establish between the fox and audience. There was his initial, breathlessly fast disguising, smearing his face grotesquely with ointment; his funny old man's voice, with overtones of Mrs. Gamp at "I am sailing to my port"; his sly relishing of Voltore's plate, and "dead man's" grasp on Corbaccio's "chickens" (*cecchines*); and a particularly noteworthy piece of business when he hid Corvino's pearl in his mouth, to regurgitate it wetly once the dupe had gone: a splendidly empathetic image of self-indulgence. He wriggled his toes with glee beneath the coverlet, exaggeratedly mimed all the symptoms attributed to him by Mosca, nodded senilely as Mosca and Corvino bawled insults at him, and coincidentally murmured "Corvino" at appropriate places in Mosca's account of his master's care for the merchant.

42. *Sunday Telegraph*, 21 January 1968.

43. The same symbolism was suggested in Guthrie's two productions by using a treasure chest as Volpone's "coffin." In the 1969 Birmingham production Volpone shot his loot through a trap device to a cache beneath his bed.

Subsequent productions copied this mischief—though never quite with Wolfit's flair—but the Guthrie versions show a curious and significant variation on the approach. During all the visits, but especially Corbaccio's, Guthrie's Volpones took risks that went beyond the bounds of any possible realism. During Corbaccio's visits, for example, Volpone left his bed to roam about the room, fetching candy and offering some to Mosca as the latter was speaking to Corbaccio, kicking away the old man's walking stick, throwing his opiate back and forth with Mosca, and, at the National Theatre, eventually pouring it loudly into a chamber pot. This might be rationalized on the grounds of Corbaccio's blindness were it not that Volpone took the same risks with other characters too: sitting up to examine Corvino's jewels so that the crow twice caught sight of him, and at Minneapolis (though not at the National) anticipating the shock of his resurrection by letting Celia also catch him sitting up when she is first brought to his room; hiding behind a screen at Lady Pol's return in III.v; and surreptitiously shaking Mosca's hand from his hiding place during the will-reading scene. The effect of such business was not only to increase the general playfulness of the presentation but also to make it a particularly *theatrical* playfulness, a comic understanding with the audience, not realistically contained within the boundaries of the play—just as the purblind Corbaccio was directed on several occasions to stumble off among the spectators. This movement beyond the action to a direct involvement of the audience was also, much more subtly, a key to Wolfit's success, and it becomes particularly important in relation to the Scoto scene and the tone of the final denouement.

The Scoto scene cries out for directorial invention, and all productions have elaborated business for it.[44] Scoto's spiel is usually trimmed (most severely at Oxford), and the actor often tries to incorporate elements that appeal directly to the modern audience as well as to the onstage crowd. Wolfit, for example, delivered the spiel at great speed with the broad accent of a market huckster in the Newark of his youth, and invariably got a laugh by delivering the line "Let me tell you" (III.ii.40) in the Lancashire voice of "Enoch," a character in the BBC's variety show "Hippodrome" at that time, whose entrance line it was. More blatantly, Richardson imitated Groucho Marx, a trick which was combined at Min-

44. For Wolfit's rewriting of the opening of this scene, see "Wolfit's Fox," n. 20.

neapolis with echoes of W. C. Fields and at Ontario with a parody of the ex-prime minister, John Diefenbaker.

Guthrie introduced further theatricalism by having Scoto and his minions hum the *Don Giovanni* aria "Deh, vieni alla finestra" as he mounted the ladder to Celia's window. Then Corvino appeared at his wife's window, instead of in the piazza, in order to push Volpone's ladder away and give occasion for a spectacular backfall into the arms of his attendants. This was followed by an almost miraculously rapid clearing of the stage which drew applause both in Minneapolis and London.

A sense of playacting has also been used in some versions of the seduction scene (though not in Wolfit's). Guthrie's choreographed rape, for instance, reduced the scene to a romp, while the aloofness of the Volpones in the 1952 Stratford production and at Ontario in 1971 put the emphasis on rhetoric rather than action. The relation of acting to the series of scenes in which the disguised Volpone taunts his dupes (V.vi, vii, viii, ix) has not been so generally grasped, however, with the result that they have usually been clumsily cut. Reduction and rearrangement can eliminate their repetitiveness while still retaining a sense of Volpone's vindictiveness, but Jonson's comment on the transfer of the fly's stage persistence to the fox is lost by such cutting, as is the manic acceleration of the play's repetitive rhythm. At Bristol in 1955 the scenes were dropped completely, and though Guthrie kept them at Minneapolis, he altered them considerably for the National Theatre, so that Volpone's teasing was omitted.

The *commandatore* scenes also create particular difficulty if Sir Pol's tortoise scene is cut, since there is then no time between Volpone's announcement of his intention to disguise and his appearance as the *commandatore*. This problem is recognized in the Wolfit promptbooks by a direction for "2 mins. wait for Mr. Wolfit's change" in the 1942 version and by the 1944 promptbook prefacing Jonson's V.v with a short interpolated sequence between Mosca and the real *commandatore*, drunk and suitless, which served the same purpose. The Oxford promptbook relies on an enigmatic "clap" (applause?) to bridge this gap; but the cleverest solution was that of the 1972 Bristol production, where Volpone merely assumed his disguise onstage as Corbaccio and Corvino made their prolonged entrances from the tower above. This repeated an effect in I.ii where Volpone was elaborately made up as an old man as his first visitor, Voltore,

planed slowly down the long entrance ramps; and there were similar
onstage makeup sessions to repair Volpone's disguise before the entrance
of Corvino, and for Lady Pol to apply cosmetics from a bag held by her
maid. Taken together with the use of an onstage wardrobe, such business
clearly established acting as a major theme of the play, on a par with the
bestiary and blasphemy emphases of this particularly intelligent production.

VIII

The importance of the theatrical dimension of Volpone stands out most
strikingly in the denouement, which also poses for a director the knottiest
problem of the play. As Jonson himself recognized in his Epistle Dedicatory to the 1607 quarto, it is difficult to reconcile the nearly tragic tone of
the fox's recognition and punishment with the comedy that precedes it
and the impudent epilogue that comes after.

Volpone's decision to unmask is a highly dramatic climax which lends
itself to spectacular stage effect. Wolfit, for example, introduced a startling vocal effect at this point. After he had been harshly and impressively
sentenced, he held his hands, palm outward, over his eyes and gave a
strangled, sobbing, animal howl, rising on a long intake of breath to be
expelled hissingly with "This is call'd mortifying of a FOXE," prolonging
the last sibilant. J. C. Trewin likens the effect to the curling, breaking,
and ebbing of an enormous wave.[45] This was invented for MacOwan's
production; but in his own, independent productions later Wolfit tried to
offset the seriousness of the effect by making the Avocatori farcical—a
disastrous idea which too easily got out of hand and degenerated to
slapstick. Miraculously, however, he still managed to pull the tones together by his handling of the epilogue. He spoke it in his own person: not
in character as Volpone, but as a variant of his own familiar hanging-
from-the-curtain call. With his face relaxed, the make-up could be seen as
make-up; the actor was visible through the role; and, as he gracefully
begged the audience's applause in his Volpone "poetry" voice, the defeat
of the fox was absorbed into the success of the actor, and the link between
Volpone-as-performer and Wolfit-as-performer was finally consolidated.

Other directors have had much less success with the conclusion. For
Guthrie the severity of the end was a particular problem because his

45. In a letter to the writer.

emphasis in both productions had been to see the action as a romp. In the Minneapolis version he ended by having the cast surprisingly unite to sing a madrigal before Volpone's epilogue. For the National Theatre he dropped both masque and epilogue to emphasize what his program note calls "the delicious sadism" of the conclusion, by having the senile court laugh uproariously at each appropriate sentencing. This provided no more suitable a conclusion than the madrigal, however, and left reviewers baffled.

Richard David found the problem so difficult that there are three different endings for the Bristol quatercentennial production. At the beginning of the run Volpone bribed his guard during the epilogue and was allowed to escape, slamming down the trap door at the concluding "clap your hands." This was then changed diametrically, so that the guard refused the bribe and the epilogue was repudiated by thrusting Volpone down to prison at its conclusion. (There were similar repudiations of the epilogue at Bristol in 1955 and Oxford in 1966.) Finally, David decided to leave the problem unresolved, so that, as the dungeon trap was banged back, all other characters froze and Volpone stepped forward to speak the epilogue without any indication of its outcome.

The only recent version to find a solution comparable to Wolfit's was David William's production at Ontario, and this too relied on a recognition of the play's theatricality. Jonson's anticlimactic order, in which the minor characters are sentenced after the protagonist, allowed Volpone to leave the stage while they were being condemned, to reappear on the balcony for the epilogue, very much at ease in an Edwardian smoking jacket, overseeing the denouement. Whereas Wolfit had solved the tonal problem by obliterating the gap between role and actor, William's effect was to identify Volpone with the director—rather like the conclusion of John Fowles's novel *The French Lieutenant's Woman*, which had just then recently appeared.

Theatricality would therefore seem to be essential to *Volpone*. The play gives considerable scope for directorial interpretation, but the most successful productions have all been slightly stagey, distancing the audience by use of the bestiary tradition or by a direct relationship established between the audience and the actor playing Volpone. And, seemingly, only when such a dimension of performance is included, can the play come to a satisfactory conclusion.

Ideally, one would like somehow to combine Wolfit's understanding of

Volpone's dynamism and his command of the audience, with, say, Quayle's—or Rain's—independent Mosca, Rossiter's Corvino, Moisewitch's designs, Hauser's interpretation of Celia, William's freaks, and John David's handling of the bestiary element. But any such list would prove immediately centrifugal, and other readings would clamor for inclusion. *Volpone* has proven one of the most stimulating of all Elizabethan plays for modern designers, actors, and directors, and will undoubtedly continue to provoke a rich variety of performance.

Afterword

Peter Hall's production at the National Theatre was as different as could be from Guthrie's version nine years before. Whereas the latter slowed the pace with overelaborate business, the new version was notable for speed and "attack" from the moment that Scofield burst in through the center doors with an exuberant "Good morning to the day . . ." The stripped-down classicism of John Bury's set allowed remarkably rapid changes: three paved avenues radiated off into the blackness through pointed iron archways, whose reversible swing doors instantly converted the playing space from bedchamber to street to senate house. (A colored picture of the model for this set can be found in *Tabs* XXXV [Autumn, 1977], p. 12.)

Moreover, whereas Guthrie's version emphasized the play's bestiary element, Hall's eschewed this completely in favor of gorgeous Renaissance costumes and psychological realism. Scofield's Volpone was a true grandee, languid but formidable, with immense aristocratic pride (especially at the end) and a genuine gift of poetry—expressed particularly in the seduction scene where he shifted with virtuoso skill from one extreme to another of his enormous vocal range and sang "Come, my Celia" unaccompanied in a strong, sweet baritone—something no previous Volpone seems to have been capable of doing. The other noteworthy characterization was John Gielgud's Sir Pol, which, in spite of plus fours, a feathered tam, a camp stool, and an ever-ready traveler's shoulderbag, Gielgud presented as a believable English tourist, officious and dunderheaded but kindly—though the tortoise scene was strained with such a reading. Elizabeth Sprigge's raucous Lady Pol and Ben Kingsley's quick, avaricious Mosca were successful, if more standard, characterizations; but the aim to avoid caricature deprived the predators, the freaks, Celia, and Bonario of any chance to make a particular impression (except that Nano was played by an actual dwarf).

The production's virtues of pace, fine speaking, visual beauty, and psychological realism were offset, in fact, by its lack of any real sense of corruption; it was entertaining, but not especially funny; and it lacked close involvement with the audience. Scofield played lines directly out to the audience, but the combination of his own curious aloofness as a person and the separate identity built up for Volpone prevented the personal rapport which Wolfit had established seemingly without effort.

Ben Jonson's Stagecraft in Epicoene

FRANCES TEAGUE

I N LATE 1609 AND EARLY 1610, the Children of the Queen's Revels produced Ben Jonson's *Epicoene* at the Whitefriars Theatre.[1] We know little about this original production, but the information we do have (or can deduce) about its features suggests that Jonson maintained a tight control over the play in performance. He seems to have exploited the physical features of the playhouse for maximum effect and to have designed the play to show off the company to the greatest advantage. In short, an analysis of the features of the original performance of *Epicoene* shows Jonson to be a highly skilled practitioner of stagecraft.

Although little information is available about the Whitefriars, Jonson has made use of several of the playhouse's features which we do know about. First of all, Jonson fitted the events of his play to the physical limitations of the theater in his manipulation of noise level. The Whitefriars was an enclosed theater and small in comparison to the open-air public playhouses like the Globe; the Whitefriars hall was approximately 85 feet

---

1. C. H. Herford and Percy and Evelyn Simpson, *Ben Jonson* (Oxford, 1925–1952), IX, 208 (hereafter cited as H & S).

long and 35 feet wide.[2] If we adopt the plausible ratio of 8:5 (for length of stage to depth),[3] we may posit a depth of 22 feet and a length of 35 feet for the Whitefriars stage. Subtracting the depth of the stage from the length of the hall, one arrives at a maximum seating area 63 feet or 21 yards long; the length may have been less if the tiring house was within the hall.[4] Therefore, when Jonson filled the Whitefriars stage with characters chattering, music of all sorts, and drums and trumpets, the audience shared Morose's discomfort, for they all sat within 21 yards of the stage. The aural effect of such a scene would have failed at the larger Globe, as would the humor of Epicoene's quiet whispering when Morose first inspects her in II.v or the shock of Truewit's noisy entry into Morose's room in II.ii. *Epicoene* could have been written only for a small playhouse like the Whitefriars; Jonson takes advantage of the small size of the playhouse to win the response he wants from his audience.

A less obvious example of his use of stage features occurs in IV.v. Although most of the action takes place on the main platform of the stage, in this scene Jonson makes use of several peripheral stage areas: the upper stage or gallery, the alcove, and the stage doors. One stage direction says that the Collegiates stand on an upper stage area at the start of IV.vi, *"Hauing discouered part of the past scene, aboue"* (IV.vi.s.d. at beginning). Presumably the six women enter during scene v, although they do not speak until scene vi. In another Whitefriars play, John Marston's *The Insatiate Countess*, a stage direction confirms the existence of the acting area above; Mendoza tries to climb up to Lady Lentulus:

He throws up a ladder of cords which she makes fast to some part of the window, he assends, at top fals.[5]

2. Glynne Wickham, *Early English Stages, 1330–1660* (London, 1959–1963), II, ii, 123.

3. The 8:5 ratio is discussed in Richard Hosley's "The Playhouses and the Stage," *A New Companion to Shakespeare Studies* (Cambridge, Eng., 1971), pp. 15–34.

4. A smaller stage than this would cause the company problems, because the seating on the side of the stage would reduce the acting area. Wickham explains that the seating area on the side of the stage restricted the actors to a square acting area, rather than a rectangle, and the side of the square, in this case, would be 22 feet.

5. John Marston, *The Insatiate Countess*, in *The Blackfriars Dramatists: The Plays of John Marston*, ed. H. Harry Wood (London, 1939), III, 37. (I was directed to this play and to Barry's play by William Armstrong's *The Elizabethan Private Theatre*, Society for Theatre Research Pamphlet #6, 1958.)

The Whitefriars also had an acting area at the back of the stage, probably an alcove, covered in *Epicoene* by the arras behind which Clerimont and Dauphine hide. This same area, again covered by an arras, may have been used the following year in the Whitefriars production of Lording Barry's *Ram Alley*, in which a stage direction says:

Enter Throte the Lawyer from his study, bookes and bags of money on a Table, a chaire and cushion. [6]

Finally, Jonson uses the three stage doors as screens to hide characters rather than as means of exiting and entering, changing the doors into a kind of peripheral stage area. The audience has its attention focused on these three doors rather than on the stage platform when the disguised Dauphine issues through the third door like a vengeful jack-in-the-box to administer six kicks and a nose tweaking to Truewit's gulls. Jonson's use of these peripheral stage areas in IV.v suggests the state of affairs which leads to the final denouement in Act V: every corner of Morose's house has been taken over by the intruders from the city.

Jonson may have made special use of other aspects of the Whitefriars stage in *Epicoene*, and some of his experiments may have failed; without further knowledge of the playhouse, no one can say with certainty whether Jonson's use of the theater's physical features was skillful (although the small evidence available suggests that it was). Clearly, however, Jonson had no interest in writing a play which confined itself to the central acting area on the platform, despite Jasper Mayne's praise that Jonson "laid no seiges to the musique-room." [7] In *Epicoene*, Jonson tried to use peripheral stage areas or to exploit the theater's small size when he thought it might further the dramatic action or ensure that his audience would respond as he wanted them to.

Perhaps because the Whitefriars stage was small, Jonson's use of setting in *Epicoene* differs markedly from the way he used it in other plays. The most obvious difference is that, unlike *Volpone* or Jonson's later comedies, *Epicoene* makes no use of stage furniture in establishing setting. The shrine of gold stands ominously behind all the action of Volpone's bedroom,

6. Lording Barry, *Ram Alley*, in Tudor Facsimile Texts #129, ed. John S. Farmer (1913; rpt. New York, 1970), B3v.

7. Jasper Mayne, "To the Memory of Ben Ionson," in H & S, XI, 453, l. 86.

bogus laboratory equipment surrounds Face and Subtle, and stocks appear on the grounds of Bartholomew Fair so that Justice Overdo can sit in them, but Morose has no such objects as these to distinguish his house. In a play with so much talk about appearance and dress, it might seem that a large mirror should stand on the stage to act as an emblem for the play; no such emblem is mentioned in the text. The settings in *Epicoene* seem at first curiously insignificant, but they actually have as much importance as in the other plays. Instead of physical objects that signal setting, behavior distinguishes the various settings of *Epicoene*.

Epicoene has only two distinct settings: Morose's house and London. Whether Jonson localizes the London setting in Clerimont's house, Daw's, the Otters', or in an open street does not matter much, for all stand open to visitors and all are characterized by the same behavior.[8] The visitors sit about, hear the latest news, plan fresh amusements, and enjoy conversation. The interest in the London scenes is largely verbal as Clerimont's boy sings a new song, Daw recites a silly madrigal, and Mrs. Otter berates her husband. Thus, the comic force in the London scenes generally depends on the wit (or lack of wit) each character displays.

Morose's setting reflects the nature of his role as the play's blocking figure. His house stands in contrast to the rest of the city, for those who enter it do not come to visit, but to invade. Concerned only with keeping the rest of London out of his house, Morose delivers monologues to underlings who must respond with farcical miming. The rest of the city circles his house, trying to enter and change it to a normal London household by means of their verbal wit.

Most of the first half of the play uses the London settings, and thus depends on verbal rather than visual comedy. Morose's house is the setting only in Act II, scenes i–ii, and v. Yet in these few scenes in Morose's house, the audience sees far more stage activity—with Truewit's ranting

---

8. William Gifford places III.i–iii, in "A Room in Otter's House" (H & S, V, 199), and later editors have followed his scene direction. The scenes have no references to suggest that they are inside a house, however, and the continual exits and entrances of characters who are never announced make me think that the scene's actual location is the street outside the Otters' door. Mrs. Otter's line, "Will it please you to enter the house farther, gentlemen?" seems to support my scene location. The point is not a quibble; if Mrs. Otter's loud berating of her husband takes place in their doorway before the eyes of all passers-by, her lack of decorum is even more remarkable than if she were inside.

and the elaborate dumb show accompanying Morose's frenzied monologues—than in the London scenes. The closest approach to farce in the London scenes occurs when Mistress Otter threatens her husband with a beating that she does not carry out. (The action approaches farce as the setting approaches Morose's house.) But the rest of the scene at the Otters' remains static. The characters converse, Mrs. Otter describes her dreams, messengers bring news, and the Wits lay the ground for a series of plots which will not culminate until the second half of the play. Jonson has established the contrast between the London characters and Morose's household, and in the rest of the play he moves all the city into Morose's house. The exposition is over and a carnival atmosphere explodes onstage.

The movement of London into Morose's house begins in Act III, scene iv, when Morose discovers that the Parson can cough and his new wife can chatter with the best. Truewit enters in scene v, and blocks Morose's attempts at monologue, taking from him the little power of speech he has left. In the next scene Morose watches appalled as the procession of uninvited wedding guests arrives. Daw and the Lady Collegiates stream in, administering kisses and catechizing the bridegroom; they are followed by Clerimont with a band of musicians, LaFoole with a wedding dinner, fine Mrs. Otter, and finally the Captain, who enters and greets the horrified Morose with, "I have brought my bull, beare, and horse in priuate, and yonder are the trumpetters without, and the drum, gentlemen." Morose, reduced to inarticulate moans, flees as the other characters chase him like a nightmare, shrieking, "follow, follow, follow!" Ludicrous action allies itself with unceasing conversation when the two worlds in the play unite in a single setting. More important, the two modes of comedy, wit and farce, which alternate in the first half of the play, combine to produce a third. Conversation is physical assault for a man who will not endure noise, and farce which relies on physical assault becomes slapstick. The audience is invited to laugh at the sight of characters chased with swords, thwacked on their bottoms, tweaked by their noses, and engaged in mock duels, to a constant and unchanging accompaniment of the conversation that Morose finds worse than any physical violence.

Jonson's use of setting in *Epicoene* is experimental, for the settings are associated with the behavior of the characters, rather than with tangible emblematic stage furniture or decoration as in his other comedies. This experiment with setting has led critics astray in discussing the structure of

the play. Dryden praised its classical comic form, and his analysis of the
play makes clear that he regarded the gulling of Morose with Epicoene as
the main plot, while the gulling of the Collegiates and of Daw and
LaFoole seemed to him subplots.[9] Other critics followed Dryden's analysis
until 1947 when Freda Townsend took issue with it in *An Apologie for
Bartholomew Fayre*:

Each [of the three lines of action] is developed for its own sake, though each is
closely connected with the other [*sic*]. Interdependency is secured, in part,
through the resolution of all three actions by means of one "engine," i.e., the
unmasking of Epicoene. . . . Summary analysis of the component parts of Jonson's play bears out . . . the view that the play is compounded of three major
elements, and that there is no subserviency of any of these to a main action.[10]

An analysis of the play by setting shows that the first half of the play is
divided between the London settings and the action in Morose's house;
neither dominates. Although the action in the second half of the play is set
in Morose's house, it involves all the characters, not just Morose.

Yet Dryden's reading of *Epicoene* cannot be dismissed. One reason for
thinking of the intrigue involving Morose and Epicoene as the main plot
is that the actions centering in Morose's house command more attention
than the generally static scenes set in the city. In addition, Jonson fails to
establish that Epicoene has a place in London society, for the audience
only sees Epicoene in the London setting once, and that appearance is a
brief one. If Townsend is right, the structure of the play depends on three
interdependent intrigues, each of which is equally important; in this case,
Jonson's correlation of setting and structure seems flawed, although his
correlation of setting and dynamic forces is successful. The first half of the
play pits the force of the city and its drive toward noisy chatter against the
force of Morose's house and the drive toward silence; the second half
merges the settings, and we see open warfare. But Morose's scenes in the
first part of the play assume disproportionate importance because of the
farcical action, and Morose seems to be the play's most important character. In any case, Epicoene, the mediating figure between the two worlds,
is not clearly established as part of the noisy London world until late in the

9. John Dryden, "Essay of Dramatic Poesy," in *Essays of John Dryden*, ed. W. P. Ker
(Oxford, 1900), I, 83–88.

10. Freda Townsend, *Apologie for Bartholomew Fayre* (New York, 1947), pp. 64, 65.

play. The play's structure is weakened, and this weakness has led to confusion among the critics.

Although Jonson's experiment with setting fails, his use of the actors in the Children of the Queen's Revels is successful. A discussion of the way in which Jonson's knowledge of the company (like his knowledge of the theater) affected the way he wrote *Epicoene*, cannot come from concrete details about the individual actors involved in the production, because so little is known about them. According to the 1616 folio of Jonson's *Works*, in *Epicoene*

The principall Comedians were,

Nat Field.	Will. Barksted.
Gil. Carie.	Will. Pen.
Hvg. Attawel.	Ric. Allin.
Ioh. Smith.	Ioh. Blaney.[11]

Although evidence has come to light which suggests that William Barksted played the part of Morose and Hugh Attawell of Sir Amorous LaFoole,[12] no other parts can be assigned. These principals are obscure, save for Nathan Field, who had acted in two earlier plays by Jonson and who would achieve celebrity as an actor and playwright before his death ten years later.[13] We can, however, use the general knowledge scholars have about the children's companies to evaluate Jonson's stagecraft.

To begin with the obvious, members of the children's companies were generally younger than the actors in the adult companies. Nonetheless, the members of the boy companies were not necessarily children. No doubt the audience would have enjoyed the sight of a schoolboy Morose wielding a grown man's sword and pursuing other boys about the stage, but they probably never saw such a performance. Barksted, who may have played Morose, was old enough to have written one long poem, *Mirzah* (1607), and may have had enough stage experience to make additions and changes to John Marston's play, *The Insatiate Countess*.[14] Although Bark-

11. H & S, *Epicoene*, V, 272.

12. James A. Riddell, "Some Actors in Ben Jonson's Plays," *Sh S*, V (1969), 285.

13. Edwin Nungezer, *A Dictionary of Actors*, Cornell Studies in English XIII (New Haven, Conn., 1929), pp. 135–141. (Information on individual actors is also summarized in G. E. Bentley, *The Jacobean and Caroline Stage* (Oxford, 1941–1968), vol. II.)

14. Nungezer, *Dictionary of Actors*, pp. 28–30. In Barksted's poem, "Hiren, or the Faire Greeke" (1611), he speaks of himself to the Countess of Derby, as "Your honor's from youth obliged," suggesting that she had helped him earlier in his youth.

sted could have been a clever boy in his teens, no mention of his youth is made in any of the documents extant about him. Nor would Barksted have been out of place as an adult in a children's company; Nathan Field, another member and principal comedian in *Epicoene*, was twenty-three years old when the play was performed. Child players did exist, since Jonson had eulogized Solomon Pavy who had been acting at the age of ten, and Field himself began when he was only thirteen.[15] For the most part, however, the actors appear to have been in their late teens and early twenties; "the Queen's Revels may have had a larger proportion of boys than usual, but there were at least six full adults, some of them with decades of acting behind them."[16] What is more important than their age or size is the fact that most of the members of the company had less stage experience than members of the adult companies.

This lack of experience may have meant that Jonson took a larger part in preparing his play for production than he could have with an adult company like the King's Men. John Aubrey wrote of Jonson, "Now B. Jonson was never a good actor, but an excellent instructor,"[17] and in all likelihood, Jonson practiced the art of instruction in preparing the Children of the Queen's Revels for their production of *Epicoene*. Since he was a good friend of the company's leading actor, he would be the obvious person for the actors to consult if any problems about the play arose. As Franz Fricker has pointed out, such questions might well arise, for *Epicoene* is not so precisely controlled as *Volpone*, i.e., the action in *Volpone* is more clearly indicated by explicit and implicit stage directions.[18] Fricker argues that Jonson could write a more complexly plotted play for the children's company than he could for the King's Men because he knew that he could supervise actors' work and would not have to trust to their understanding of difficult points in the text. Thomas Dekker's claim in *Satiromastix* that Jonson bullied his actors is interesting to consider in relation to this theory, although Dekker undoubtedly exaggerated.[19] Fricker's theory

15. Nungezer, *Dictionary of Actors*, p. 136.

16. Andrew Gurr, *The Shakespearean Stage, 1574–1642* (Cambridge, Eng., 1970), p. 36.

17. John Aubrey as quoted in H & S, I, 182.

18. Franz Fricker, *Ben Jonson's Plays in Performance and the Jacobean Theatre* (Bern, 1972), pp. 49 ff.

19. Thomas Dekker, *Satiromastix*, in *The Dramatic Works of Thomas Dekker*, ed. Fredson Bowers (Cambridge, Eng., 1953), I, 382.

seems warranted by what is known about Jonson's relationship with the Children of the Queen's Revels, and suggests that Jonson's knowledge of the company influenced his writing of *Epicoene*.

The boy companies had different audiences and repertoires from the adult companies, and these facts also bear on Jonson's writing of *Epicoene*. Unlike the adult companies, the children could perform in indoor theaters located within the city walls, and the audience who attended their plays paid more than at the public theaters. As a result, the private playhouse

probably attracted members of the upper classes who felt their social status to be precarious: withered old-line aristocrats struggling to maintain their standing; or gentry, *nouveaux riches*, and young inns-of-court men striving for higher status.[20]

In the private playhouses belonging to the children's companies, such audiences watched the young actors perform comedies and satires, but only rarely tragedies and romances. Plays which required actors to show depth of emotion were not suited to the less experienced performers of the children's companies and were generally avoided. However, the young actors *were* uniquely suited to satire; the children's companies seem to have had greater freedom than the adult companies in their choice of plays and could perform satires which would have been shut down if the adult companies attempted them. When Jonson wrote *Epicoene*, he created scenes which are farcical, protagonists who are cynical, and a view of fine London society which is satirical. Furthermore, the play calls for its actors to display little depth of emotion. Morose's wailing cannot be taken too seriously by the audience or the comedy turns bitter, while Epicoene's anguish when Daw and LaFoole "betray" her is intentionally contrived and false. In short, Jonson wrote a play which displays his actors' abilities most favorably to the audience, an audience which if displeased would feel no compunction about disrupting the play.

Jonson made brilliant use of his young actors in manipulating his audience's reactions at the conclusion of *Epicoene*. His audience would expect to see a boy acting the part of Morose's wife, and save for her ambiguous name, they have no real hint that this is not the case. But the unmasking of Epicoene at the play's end reveals that Epicoene is a boy

20. Michael Shapiro, "Audience vs. Dramatist in Jonson's *Epicoene* and Other Plays of the Children's Troupes," *ELR*, III (1973), 401.

actor playing the part of a male character. What the audience has seen and disregarded because of theatrical convention, a boy pretending to be a woman, is the real case within the world of the play. Dramatic illusion breaks, and the audience is reminded that they are seeing actors playing their roles. This anti-illusionary moment has been preceded by others in the play when the actors talk about make-up and costumes, masques and pageants, but the unmasking of Epicoene places the audience in a new and unexpected position. By withholding the information about Epicoene's sex, Jonson has played a trick on the audience, and the actors have carried the gulling out. Furthermore, the trick is played in such a way that the audience must remember that *Epicoene* is a play and the characters only dramatic fictions. The actors, thrown out of character for a moment, can laugh at the audience which has been taken in by the entertainment.

This reversal of dramatic convention leaves the audience with two responses: they may be discomposed and silent like the Collegiates, Daw and LaFoole, and Morose, or they may laugh at themselves like the more generous Truewit who says to Dauphine, "but much good doe it thee, thou deseru'st it lad" (V.iv.226–227). Truewit's request for the audience's applause makes this more generous choice an easy one for the audience. When he says, "Spectators, if you like this *comoedie*, rise cheerefully, and now MOROSE is gone in, clap your hands. It may be, that noyse will cure him, at least please him" (V.iv.251–253), he invites them to join with the Wits of London and tease Morose. If the audience applauds the clever trick played on them, they pretend the character of noise-hating Morose actually exists and they maintain the dramatic convention which has slipped out of place. They also follow the example of an attractive character, Truewit, instead of one of the fools at whom they have laughed during the play.

Jonson manipulates his audience so that they will approve his play because he understands a simple fact, that a boy takes the part of a girl on his stage. Of course, such a manipulation did not depend on the children's company for whom he wrote *Epicoene*; any company in Renaissance London could act the play with similar casting and results. The point is, however, that Jonson's consciousness of how his plays would appear on a stage and how they would affect the audience watching them works splendidly in *Epicoene*.

An analysis of stagecraft in *Epicoene* would not be complete without consideration of the visual presentation, the way Jonson's specifications about staging, properties, and costumes affect the audience's understanding of the play. The discussion of the stage and actors covers some elements of the visual presentation, of course; Jonson's correlation of stage setting and behavior would probably fail if the stage were filled with furniture, while the effect of the ending depends on the woman's clothing worn by the actor playing Epicoene. But such a consideration does not exhaust the topic of visual presentation. The staging of the play is remarkable for the ways in which stage business and the characters' speeches are combined and reflect each other, the properties serve both to carry out and characterize the action, and the costumes illustrate visually the sexual and social disorder in the play.

In Act I, for example, the various elements of visual presentation are woven together carefully so that actions which seem casual counterpoint what the characters are saying. An easy way to see how the stage business and speeches are interrelated within the act is to list the actions and the topics of discussion side-by-side in the order in which they occur:

ACTIONS	*TOPICS OF DISCUSSION*
Clerimont and his boy enter	
Clerimont makes ready (gets dressed)	The boy's adventure with Lady Haughty
The boy sings	
Truewit enters	Wasted time
	The Lady Collegiates
The boy sings again	
	Ladies' appearance
	Dauphine and his uncle
Dauphine enters	Morose's marriage
	Sir Jack Daw
Truewit's abrupt exit	
	Truewit's frankness
	Daw
Boy sent for water	
	LaFoole

Boy returns, announces	
LaFoole	
LaFoole enters	Invitation to dinner
	The LaFoole family
LaFoole runs out of breath	
LaFoole exits abruptly	
Clerimont and Dauphine	LaFoole
exit	

The major topic of discussion within the act is appearance—the appearance of Lady Haughty and other women about town, Morose's foolish disregard of appearance with his turban of nightcaps, and LaFoole's attempts to appear a fashionable gentleman. Two extreme attitudes are discussed; the ladies are excessively concerned with their appearance and Morose cares nothing about his. Yet throughout the scene a third attitude is expressed through the action of Clerimont as he dresses. He makes ready during most of the scene, for he has sent the boy to fetch water so that he can wash shortly before LaFoole enters. Yet he is not so obsessed with appearance as the ladies he condemns; neither of his friends twits him about his care in dressing, and he is not upset at having visitors as he prepares himself. Jonson uses the action to point out that there is a median between a too-nice appearance and utter disregard. This middle ground is occupied by Clerimont and his friends who take care of their appearance without overvaluing "gold jerkins" as LaFoole does.

Action and speech are neatly fitted together in other ways as well. Jonson handles the entrances and exits in this act carefully so that they will not seem overcontrived. Clerimont tells Truewit that he has returned from court just the day before and suggests that the two of them visit their friend Dauphine whom he has not seen for three days. Dauphine's entrance a short while later seems natural, for Jonson has already prepared for it. Furthermore, the conversation which prepares the audience for Dauphine's entrance also provides the necessary information about him and his uncle so that the audience can follow the plot. The arrival of LaFoole as Dauphine and Clerimont talk about him is treated as a coincidence, but not a very great one, by the characters; since LaFoole is described as a gentleman who loves giving entertainments, when he comes to invite Clerimont to dinner his action seems normal. The way in which Jonson handles the characters' exits is equally skillful. Both Truewit and

LaFoole exit during the scene, and in both cases the exit is spoken of as "abrupt." But the similarity in their departures points up a difference in their characters. LaFoole leaves abruptly because he is a fool who wants to seem more important and rushed than he actually is, as Clerimont and Dauphine's conversation makes clear. Truewit, on the other hand, has stressed the way he values time to Clerimont; his rapid departure is not devised simply to make an impression on his friends. Thus speech and action work together to suggest indirectly that Truewit's abrupt exit is for a specific purpose and that it will have further consequences in the play.

One other piece of stage business in the first act deserves comment. The song which the boy sings twice at the beginning of the act functions as a comment on the topic of appearance as well as a unifying device within the rest of the play. The use of music in Act I anticipates the horn which Truewit plays in Act II and the musical instruments which appear in Act III, and sets up a contrast between music which is pleasant to listen to and music which becomes merely noise. Clerimont says that he has written the song about overdone cosmetics and costumes to remind ladies that anything carried to excess violates decorum and becomes unpleasant. In the later noisy scenes, the point which the song makes gains force. Having been pleased with the boy's song, the audience may remember it when the noise from other musical instruments assaults their ears, not only understanding the wisdom of the song, but experiencing it physically as well.

The stage business in the first act is almost totally independent of stage properties. The boy may accompany himself on a stringed instrument (like a guitar) as he sings, and he brings a bowl of water in to Clerimont, but these are the only props mentioned in the text. This freedom from props is typical of *Epicoene*; it is interesting to compare the play to *Volpone* which uses a large number of props. The difference in visual presentation in the two plays suggests a major difference in the kind of comedy each play presents to its audience.

In *Volpone* the various props are generally extensions of the character who uses them. For example, Volpone's will is blank, a fact which suggests his isolation from the rest of Venetian society, while Corbaccio's will has the name of his son crossed out and Volpone's name substituted for it, which indicates that Corbaccio's greed has overwhelmed his feelings as a father. When Volpone's will is kept locked in a chest, while Corbac-

cio's will is brought to Volpone's bedside, Jonson has used the two props
to suggest the nature of the relationship between the two men. But the
document which Morose signs in *Epicoene* tells the audience nothing about
his character that is not already known, and instead has the primary
function of giving Dauphine enough financial freedom to unmask
Epicoene. In other words, the prop is more important for the plot than for
anything it can tell the audience about the characters of *Epicoene*.

Volpone is a comedy centered on character; in *Epicoene* the center of
interest is the plot. The audience of *Volpone* watches to learn what will
happen to the individuals, how each character will act and react in a given
situation. Jonson need not conceal all the turns of *Volpone*'s plot, as he does
in *Epicoene*; in fact, it is to his advantage if *Volpone*'s audience understands
clearly what is going on at any given moment so that they can also understand what each character's actions imply about himself. In *Epicoene*'s
comedy of intrigue, plot has more importance than character. The parts
which Daw and LaFoole play in the plot could be interchanged with little
loss to the play, while the parts Voltore, Corvino, and Corbaccio play in
Volpone could not be. Haughty, Mavis, and Centaur are replications of one
another, and the hero of the play, Dauphine, resembles his friend Clerimont far more than he differs from him.

The props which occur in *Epicoene* often serve a dual function. Since
props are mainly used to carry out the action of the plot, rather than to
establish character, relatively few are needed, but those which Jonson
specifies in the text of the play often act as an index to the value of the
action which requires them. For example, when Jonson wants the audience to know that Morose has gone through with the marriage, he introduces a scene in which Morose gives the hoarse preacher several prop coins
as payment for his services. When the preacher coughs, Morose wants the
coins back, for he has always been able to buy silence. The coins represent
the monetary value set on quiet in the play and give information essential
for the ending when Morose must resign all of his fortune to regain the
quiet he desires.

Again in Act III, props are necessary to represent the marriage feast
which some of the Londoners use as a pretext for entering Morose's house.
But the dinner they bring in is an index to the value of the wedding as
well, for the dinner is no more a wedding feast than the marriage of
Morose to a young boy is a wedding. Instead the feast is a ridiculous

dinner party which has simply been renamed and rerouted to Morose's house, and which is presided over by the social-climbing Mrs. Otter and her witling cousin LaFoole. Such a feast is altogether appropriate to Morose's ludicrous wedding.

One of the cleverest uses of props in the play involves the swords.[21] In Act IV, Morose attempts to drive the London invaders out of his house by descending on them with his sword drawn. This action provokes the shrill *double-entendre* from Mistress Otter, "O god, madame, he came downe with a huge long naked weapon in both his hands, and look'd so dreadfully!" (IV.iii.2–4) The incongruity of Morose as a bridegroom is cruelly emphasized by this piece of business. Later in the same act, when Morose makes his entrance, he carries not one, but two swords, and asks, "WHat make these naked weapons here, gentlemen?" (IV.viii.1) This line recalls the earlier *double-entendre*, and makes old Morose seem even more foolish in his role as reluctant bridegroom. Furthermore, it provides Truewit with the opportunity of spinning a story about knights battling for Epicoene's favors. Morose is so dismayed to hear about these duels that he throws himself on the mercy of the young men who have engineered his discomfiture, a move that later leads to his public declaration that he is "Vtterly vn-abled in nature, by reason of *frigidity*, to performe the duties, or any the least office of a husband" (V.iv.46–7). Thus Jonson weaves the swords, with their phallic implications, into the action, to forward the plot and to mark Morose's changes of mood in the play from rage to literally impotent despair.

The costumes and disguises assumed by the various characters have more importance in the play's visual presentation than the properties. As the title suggests, *Epicoene* is set in a world of sexual ambiguity, and this confusion of sexual roles is accompanied by a confusion of social roles as well. Jonson uses the appearance of a character on stage and verbal descriptions of appearance to reflect the sexual and social chaos of the play.

The confusion of sexual roles in the play has been analyzed by Edward Partridge and others.[22] Mrs. Otter, for example, has usurped her hus-

21. Both Edward Partridge in *The Broken Compass* (New York, 1958), and William Armstrong in "Ben Jonson and Jacobean Stagecraft," Stratford-upon-Avon Studies 1: *Jacobean Theatre* (London, 1960), pp. 42–61, discuss the swords.

22. Partridge's discussion in *The Broken Compass* analyzes the sexual inversions in the play, while Ray L. Heffner, "Unifying Symbols in the Comedy of Ben Jonson," *English*

band's role in their marriage, by virtue of her superior financial position. She provides the Captain with his maintenance, as she reminds him, allowing him "your three sutes of apparell a yeere, your foure paire of stockings, one silke, three worsted, your cleane linnen, your bands, and cuffes when I can get you to weare 'hem" (III.i.40–44). His only retaliation to her cankered generosity is to describe her mercilessly to his friends when she is not around, telling them of her grotesque appearance, her bad breath, wig, false teeth, cosmetics, and the way

She takes her selfe asunder still when she goes to bed, into some twentie boxes; and about next day noone is put together againe, like a great *Germane* clocke: and so comes forth and rings a tedious larum to the whole house, and then is quiet againe for an houre, but for her quarters.

(IV.ii.97–101)

Mrs. Otter knows that the only way she can join the Lady Collegiates and advance in the social hierarchy is by maintaining her subjection of her husband; their battle for sexual domination is fought on the grounds of appearance.

Description of the actors' costumes reflects the sexual confusions in *Epicoene* in another way. Although Clerimont and his friends discuss the excessive concern that women have with their appearance, the actual description of an individual's appearance is generally of a man rather than a woman. The audience learns that Lady Haughty is heavily made-up, that Mrs. Otter wears false teeth and hair, that Epicoene is "exceeding fair" and wears a mask, but these comments are the only descriptions given of the women on the stage (I.i.87–88; IV.ii.92–94; II.v.17; II.v.3). More humorous and specific details are given about the men's costumes. The audience hears about and sees Morose's headgear, the Mute's footwear, and Otter's clean linen; LaFoole is a "mannikin" with a gold-handled sword, and Dauphine is "a very worthy gentleman in his exteriors," who is "judicial in his clothes" (I.i.144–145; I.i.188–189; III.i.42; I.iii.25; IV.vi.104; IV.vi.24–26). It is the men who

. . . haue their faces set in a brake! . . . haue euery haire in forme! . . . weare purer linnen than [the women], and professe more neatnesse than the *french hermaphrodite*!

(IV.vi.28–31)

Stage Comedy, ed. W. K. Wimsatt, Jr., English Institute Essays 1954 (New York, 1955), pp. 74–97, describes the association of noise and the battle of the sexes in the play.

By this sort of verbal description, which is carried out by the actual costumes of the actors, the epicene nature of the characters in the play is shown, for the appearance of the males is given more prominence than that of the females.

A number of the costumes specified in the play are disguises, and these disguises always signal the gulling of some other character. The most obvious example is Epicoene's disguise as a woman; other disguises are Otter's canonical gown, Cutbeard's civil gown, and Dauphine's carpet, scarf, and cushion. Less successful disguises are assumed by Truewit and LaFoole. When Truewit pretends to be a post in order to gain admission to Morose's house, he provides himself with a horn to indicate the part he plays. Later, LaFoole is persuaded he must revenge himself on Daw by taking his dinner party to Morose's house. Part of his plan involves his wrapping a towel around his waist so that he can disguise himself as the head server. Truewit and LaFoole assume inadequate disguises, and their plots fail to take in anyone, although Truewit is later able to redeem his failure. The ability to play a role so that other characters are gulled and will behave as the trickster wants has central importance in the social hierarchy of *Epicoene*.

All of the characters in *Epicoene* try to manipulate others, either by trickery or by offering rewards for a directed performance. The Collegiates, for example, have more power than Mrs. Otter, for they can manipulate their husbands more successfully than she. Her husband occasionally tries to stage a revolt against her manipulation; their husbands are such nonentities that they do not even appear. Yet the Collegiates are less powerful socially than Dauphine, for they cannot persuade him to take the role of lover which they have designed for him. Similarly, when Epicoene stops playing a woman, the Collegiates are shown to be failures in choosing Epicoene to "vindicate their fames" (V.vi.217), a failure foreshadowed by the refusal of Clerimont's boy to wear women's clothing and play a feminine role to women who play men. The only characters whom the women can easily manipulate are Daw and LaFoole, whose adherence is worthless, for their refusal to perform correctly in a duel has proved that they are not true knights. Their surrender of their swords is a surrender of the proper costume for the social role they have tried to play. When Truewit and Dauphine use disguise to gull them, Daw and LaFoole lose their power and their desirability.

The only successful players in *Epicoene* are the Wits. Truewit fails to dissuade Morose from marriage in his disguise as a post, but he can persuade Clerimont and Dauphine that they should pretend his scheme was a success. Like his friends, Truewit recognizes that the ideal behavior of society is to play, to act, to do

> . . . nothing: or that, which when 'tis done, is as idle. Harken after the next horse-race, or hunting match; lay wagers, praise *Puppy*, or *Pepper-corne*, *Whitefoote*, *Franklin*; sweare vpon *White-maynes* partie; spend aloud, that my lords may heare you; visite my ladies at night, and bee able to giue 'hem the character of euery bowler, or bettor o' the greene. These be the things, wherein your fashionable men exercise themselues, and I for companie.

(I.i.33–41)

If one is not a fashionable gentleman, one should disguise himself as one and play the part. Jonson structures the play by comic modes (wit alternating with farce, and slapstick), but whatever the controlling mode in a particular scene, the three Wits are able to use the mode to manipulate others. The only garlands to be won in *Epicoene* are for the clever player, as Truewit reminds the audience at the end of the play. When Truewit invites the audience's applause, he asks them to affirm that the world is a stage and that men's occupation is playing, by pretending that the play is real and that Morose may still be tormented.

The Duchess of Malfi *at the Globe and Blackfriars*

R. B. GRAVES

IN HIS ADMIRABLE Revels Plays edition of *The Duchess of Malfi*, John Russell Brown argues that the scene with the "dead man's hand" (IV.i) can only have been effective in a darkened theater and that the play must therefore have been written with the King's Men's indoor Blackfriars theater in mind. But the title page of the 1623 first edition states clearly that the play was *"Presented privatly, at the Black-Friers; and publiquely at the Globe."* Because Professor Brown takes the lighting of this extraordinary scene to be critical to a proper understanding of its original staging and effect, I should like to examine the scene in relation to what we know of the illumination at both theaters. Although I happen to think his interpretation of the facts is not the most plausible one, Brown nevertheless calls attention to an important, perhaps even crucial, point of comparison between the open-air "public" and indoor "private" theaters—namely, their lighting. Recent studies of these theaters have sought to distinguish between them by reference to their repertories or their stages and stage facilities.[1] Yet plays and staging practices are the very things one would

---

1. Largely on the basis of a comparison of the repertories and audiences at the public and private theaters, G. E. Bentley, "Shakespeare and the Blackfriars Theatre," *ShS*, I

not expect to change as the King's Men moved from one theater to another. *The Duchess of Malfi* is but one example of many plays known to have been performed at both theaters; and one imagines that the stages, stage properties, and tiring-house walls of the two theaters resembled each other as much as possible so that the actors could avoid restaging their plays every time they migrated from the summer Globe to the winter Blackfriars. But there were important elements of the production which could not have been so easily duplicated. Among these, lighting and acoustics were largely dependent on the particular performance site and allowed of little or no regulation by the playwrights and actors. In assigning *The Duchess of Malfi* to Blackfriars on the basis of its stage lighting, Brown at least refers to an aspect of production which inheres in the essential form of the playhouse.

For an example of the influence which stage lighting could exert on an audience's response to a play, we need look no further than Webster's other great tragedy, *The White Devil*, performed only a year or so before *The Duchess of Malfi*. When *The White Devil* was produced at an open-air theater (almost certainly the Red Bull) early in 1612, the play failed not because the dramatist or actors were inept, but because the theater was dark and dreary—or so Webster claims in his famous Preface to the first edition. The play was acted "in so dull a time of winter," he complains, "in so open and black a theatre, that it wanted (that which is the only grace and setting out of tragedy) a full and understanding auditory." [2] Those who know London in the wintertime can sympathize with Webster,

---

(1948), 38–50, and Alfred Harbage, *Shakespeare and the Rival Traditions* (New York, 1952), conclude that the two kinds of theaters must have been very different. But extensive research into the staging practices at the two theaters has uncovered little to differentiate them; see, e.g., T. J. King, *Shakespearean Staging: 1599–1642* (Cambridge, Mass., 1971), p. 2. Richard Hosley, "Elizabethan Theatres and Audiences," *RORD*, X (1967), 13–14, points out that the only important difference which affected staging was the use of a permanent music room at the indoor theaters. Originally intended for the music concerts made possible by the better acoustics indoors, the private-theater music rooms were consequently visible to the audience and, hence, available for discoveries "above." But the difference was short-lived: Hosley notes that the practice of discoveries above spread to the outdoor theaters soon after the King's Men began regular performances at Blackfriars.

2. Unless noted, all Webster quotations and line numbers are from Brown's Revels Plays editions—*The White Devil* (London, 1960) and *The Duchess of Malfi* (London, 1964).

although it should be added that many plays did succeed in the winter despite outdoor performance. Still Webster may himself have lived to see the play and his excuses for its failure at an open-air playhouse vindicated. According to the title page of the 1631 second edition, *The White Devil* was later revived and performed "divers times" at the indoor Phoenix theater whose roof and artificial lights presumably afforded the play and its spectators more hospitable accommodations.

No one will doubt that playhouse conditions have a substantial, if not always so determining, effect on the audience's perception of a play. Insofar as the atmosphere in a playhouse may be said to influence a spectator's response, one naturally supposes that plays performed in the public and private theaters evoked responses which, all other things being equal, differed in proportion as the two theatrical environments differed. In assessing the distinctive contributions of the public and private theaters, however, it is extremely difficult to keep other things equal. The success of *The White Devil* in the 1630s may have been due as much to changing literary fashions as to differences between the playhouse structures and their lighting systems. Or the actors and staging may simply have been better. With so many unknown quantities, a theatrical equation is not readily solved; one can never be sure whether Webster's gloomy picture of *The White Devil's* premiere represents an accurate explanation of its failure or is the exaggeration of a disgruntled playwright. But in the case of *The Duchess of Malfi*, several of these indeterminate quantities are conveniently eliminated from consideration. For in examining the staging of the dead-man's-hand scene at the Globe and at Blackfriars, we shall be concerned with the same scene performed at about the same time by the same acting company.

In IV.i of *The Duchess of Malfi*, the Duchess's brother Ferdinand begins his long-delayed punishment of her for remarrying. At the beginning of the scene, we see Ferdinand shortly before he is to visit the imprisoned Duchess. We learn that he has a request to make of her as a condition for their meeting, which he bids Bosola convey to her. Ferdinand retires, the Duchess enters, and Bosola informs her of the unusual request. It is that "neither torch nor taper / Shine in your chamber" during the interview because Ferdinand once "rashly made a solemn vow / Never to see you more" (ll. 23–26). The Duchess agrees to the condition and orders, "Take hence the lights." Ferdinand re-enters, and the darkness is established in an abruptly realistic touch when he is obliged to ask the Duchess, "Where are you?" (l. 29). Ferdinand begins by remarking, "This darkness suits you well," and with ironic and sinister undertones continues, "It had been well / Could you have liv'd thus always; for indeed / You were too much i' th' light" (ll. 30, 40–42), by which he alludes not only to the trick he is about to play but also to several closely interwoven connotations of "light"—her wantonness, her having been too freely exposed to other men, and even the efficacy of darkness to hide his own incestuous inclinations. (I shall return to these points shortly.) There follows Ferdinand's offer of reconciliation; "here's a hand," he says, while in an apparently authorial stage direction, we read that he *Gives her a dead man's hand"* as his own (l. 43). The Duchess dutifully kisses it, but when her lips feel how cold the hand is she cries out, "Hah! lights!—O, horrible!"; whereupon Ferdinand, in one of Webster's most brutal lines, orders, "Let her have lights enough" (l. 53).

Brown believes that the scene must be played in darkness so that the audience will experience the same shock the Duchess does when lights are brought back on and she sees the severed hand. He argues, rightly, that an audience might well laugh to see the Duchess holding a property hand while Ferdinand promises he will "leave this ring with you for a love-token; / And the hand, as sure as the ring" (ll. 47–48). "What would be difficult, clumsy, and grotesque at the Globe," Brown concludes, "could be thrilling and sensitive in the darkened auditorium of the Blackfriars." [3]

But even if we agree that shocking the audience is a desideratum, are we positive that actual darkness could be achieved at the Blackfriars or, if it could, that darkness was the most likely means by which such a shock was produced? When he re-enters, Ferdinand presumably carries the hand in his cloak sleeve to pretend it is his. Darkness would not be required to avoid giving the trick away to either the Duchess or the audience. And when he "gives" her his hand, need we imagine that he passes it to her, that is, actually hands it to her? It seems more probable that when she offers to kiss his hand, he simply extends his sleeve forward. She might then cross to him, kneel, take the hand in hers, and kiss it while he continues to hold the property hand through his sleeve as though it were his own. When she notices its coldness, he could then release it, letting

3. *The Duchess of Malfi*, p. xxiii.

her hold it a second or two in astonishment until in a paroxysm of horror she lets it fall to the ground. Richard Burbage, who created the role of Ferdinand, must certainly have possessed the talents to perform this literal sleight of hand in the Globe daylight. Indeed, as seen in bright light, the moment when Burbage let the hand go would have been substantially as shocking and a great deal more sudden and jarring than the corresponding reintroduction of light on the Blackfriars stage. If anything were clumsy (not to mention distracting), it would have been the rushing in of servants carrying torches and candles from the tiring house at a time when our attention should be focused on the Duchess. I even wonder if the sudden bringing of torches into a darkened auditorium would not have temporarily blinded the audience at the very moment they needed most to see the severed hand. As it is, the stolid tone of Ferdinand's "Let her have lights enough" hardly suggests lights were brought back on in enough of a hurry to startle the audience.

Surely the horror derived as much from the actors' reactions to the hand as from the hand itself—just as it does in such analogous public-theater scenes as Benvolio's cutting off Faustus's head or Lavinia's entering to her brothers with her hands cut off in *Titus Andronicus*. To insist that the effect resided more in a blood-drenched stage property than in the actors' horrified responses (and, just as important in shocking an audience, in preparing the audience not to anticipate those responses) is to underestimate the sophistication of the audience and to overestimate the skills of the Jacobean property makers. It is to start once more down the quaint path which leads finally to little green lights twinkling on the Ghost's helmet in *Hamlet* while the startled faces of Horatio and the watch are invisible on a darkened stage.[4] The dead hand produced its gruesome effect primarily by the words and actions of the Duchess both before and after she kissed it, just as the Ghost in *Hamlet* frightened its original audience because it was seen to frighten the previously calm and unsuspecting Horatio and Hamlet. To produce the dead-hand scene illusionistically in darkness means that the audience can see neither the Duchess's initial shock nor her

4. On the absurdities resulting from too much illusion in the illumination of Shakespearean revivals, see G. Wilson Knight, *Shakespearian Production* (Evanston, Ill., 1964), pp. 63–65. Shakespeare himself ridicules this sort of nocturnal illusionism when he has Bottom suggest that the mechanicals' play be performed in real moonlight shining through the windows of Theseus's great chamber (*A Midsummer Night's Dream*, III.i.41–50).

contrasting self-possession at the beginning of the scene; a little wax hand is made to carry almost the entire burden of this striking effect. If this kind of illusion in the lighting were actually required, one could argue as easily that the shadow Ferdinand throws in the outdoor gallery scene (V.ii.31 ff.) required Globe performance for an effective presentation.

In any case, the dead-man's-hand scene as originally staged in 1613 or 1614 [5] need not have been blazingly lit at the Globe. If Wenzel Hollar's sketch (c. 1644) of the second Globe is any guide, the stage there was completely shaded by a mammoth "heavens" severely reducing the amount of light to reach the actors. The stage was so well protected from the elements, in fact, that if the hall at Blackfriars possessed a typical complement of windows (Richard Hosley estimates at least ten large windows in the auditorium itself),[6] then, depending on the time of performance and the season of the year, it may occasionally have been possible to illuminate the Blackfriars stage with nearly as much natural light as the Globe stage itself. Moreover, the lateness of the scene (Act IV) in this long play (its first quarto reaches to 104 pages, nearly twice the normal length) would have put an open-air performance of the effect close to twilight in spring and autumn, assuming the King's Men followed the practice of Lady Elizabeth's Men in April 1614 at the Hope of beginning plays at 3 P.M.[7]

For that matter, Blackfriars hardly needed the special indoor "lighting device" Brown hypothesizes, either to produce darkness or to inspire Webster to write the scene. Blackfriars plays were given in the winter, and a wintertime performance of IV.i would necessarily be played in

---

5. The date of the original production can be fixed at 1613 or 1614 because the play incorporates material not published until late 1612 and because its cast list includes an actor who died in December 1614. In suggesting that the play could work as well at the Globe as at Blackfriars, I am aware that the Globe fire on 29 June 1613 cut short the first of the two Globe seasons in which the play could have premiered and perhaps delayed the beginning of the second until the new theater was finished. See G. E. Bentley, *The Jacobean and Caroline Stage* (Oxford, 1941–1968), VI, 182.

6. *The Revels History of Drama in English*, III (London, 1975), 202.

7. See the actor's contract in James Boswell, ed., *The Plays and Poems of William Shakespeare* (London, 1821), XXI, 414. The play was printed "with diverse *things* . . . *that the length of the Play would* not beare in the Presentment." It is not always clear why plays had to be cut, but the most frequently mentioned constraint—early sunsets—does not support a theory that the playhouse windows were covered.

twilight because Blackfriars plays apparently began no earlier than 2 or 3 P.M.[8] In advancing the theory that Webster fashioned the play with Blackfriars in mind, Brown hinges his argument on the presumed fact that the "auditorium could be darkened by covering its windows." But even with the windows wide open, little natural light could have illuminated the dead-hand effect at Blackfriars. Had the performance begun even as early as 2 P.M., I do not see how the effect could have taken place much before 4 P.M.—just the time of London's winter sunset. The diminution of light was unique neither to Blackfriars in particular nor to the indoor theaters in general. The early winter sunset managed the effect all by itself. Far from being darkened, the artificially lit Blackfriars stage would have appeared brighter in relation to the rest of the auditorium at the end of the play than when daylight flooded through the windows at the beginning. As the daylight waned and darkness gathered in the pit and boxes, the apparent brightness onstage would have increased because the stage candles would have contributed a greater share of the total illumination. Imagining the effect of the scene indoors, we get a sense of the coolness in the auditorium as the spectators sit in lengthening and then engulfing shadows, until at sunset the candles shining above the stage begin to spread their light and warmth, at first feebly, then with greater power and intensity as night falls around them. If one wanted to argue that *The Duchess of Malfi* was written especially for Blackfriars, one might as well point to the suitability of artificial light to the increasingly "artificial" shows by which Ferdinand entertains the Duchess—the dead man's hand, the wax figures of Antonio and her children, and the masque of the madmen.[9] Not darkness, but artificial light suits the play toward its conclusion.

8. According to a 1619 complaint to the Privy Council, coaches clogged the streets around Blackfriars from 1 or 2 P.M. until 6 P.M. Since one-hour concerts were provided to entertain arriving spectators, the plays must have lasted from 2 or 3 P.M. until 5 P.M. or so; *Malone Society Collections*, I (London, 1907), 91–92. The King's Men's chief indoor competitors (the Queen's Revels Children) began at 3 P.M. in 1611; E. K. Chambers, *The Elizabethan Stage* (Oxford, 1923), II, 369.

9. I do not include in this list the light which Antonio believes he sees over the Duchess's grave in V.iii. Brown (*The Duchess of Malfi*, p. xxxv) takes this hallucination to be a special lighting effect which would have to be "cut for performance at the Globe," although he can hardly believe the dead-man's-hand scene was also cut there. It is questionable whether there is any light at all, but if one were required I imagine a torch held by the Duchess's ghost would have done as well at the Globe as at Blackfriars.

Brown cites no evidence for his assertion that the windows at Black-friars could be covered. Apparently he has inferred it from a passage in Thomas Dekker's *The Seven Deadlie Sinns of London* (London, 1606), sig. D2, in which Dekker describes London at nightfall as looking "like a private Play-house, when the windowes are clapt downe, as if some *Nocturnal*, or dismall *Tragedy* were presently to be acted before all the *Trades-men*." Certainly it would have been possible to clap down window shutters, but Dekker makes it clear that when this was done, the windows were covered when the plays were "presently to be acted," that is, before the beginning of the performance. In that case, it would have been difficult to produce real darkness as property lights were carried offstage or as the time of the play was supposed to change from day to night. Someone would have had to sit beside each window and close shutters on cue as the illumination was supposed to shift from light to dark. I venture to say the expense of hiring apprentices to perform this duty would have eliminated it from consideration if, in fact, the idea ever occurred to the actors at all. Even with the auditorium windows covered, the stage would still have been lit by the playhouse candles we hear about in such Black-friars plays as Fletcher's *The Faithful Shepherdess* (1608) and Jonson's *The Staple of News* (1626). These lights might have been extinguished to darken the scene as well; but then the tireman would have had to lower and extinguish lights while the scene was in progress and relight and raise them sometime later. It is possible that the whole of Act IV was per-formed in darkness, but it must be pointed out that no extant pre-Restoration promptscript even hints that windows were covered or candles extinguished during the act breaks. Instead of decreasing the light, actors at both the indoor and outdoor theaters regularly indicated darkness by carrying stage-property lights with them.[10] Darkness was paradoxically signaled by the introduction of more rather than less light on stage. Even at Court, changes in brightness were effected not by extinguishing candles above the stage but by machines which could be turned or drawn aside to reveal brightly lit and painted scenes.[11]

10. The use of candles, torches, lanterns, and tapers to symbolize darkness at the Blackfriars is found in the stage directions of such plays as *The Elder Brother* (IV.iii), *Love's Pilgrimage* (I.ii), *The Fair Maid of the Inn* (I.i), *The Maid of the Mill* (I.iii; IV.iii), and *The Knight of Malta* (IV.ii), all of which reflect playhouse origin.

11. Sometimes called the "Scene of Light," these discoveries are best described in such

The only convenient way to decrease light (or to suggest that it was decreased) was to remove stage-property lights, and this is the method which Webster's dialogue tells us was used. To produce a really significant change in light, however, would have required a rather large number of such property lights. For if we imagine that some two or three dozen candles burned over the Blackfriars stage,[12] then at least another dozen or so hand-held candles would have been required to produce a discernible fall or rise in the level of illumination as they were removed or brought back on stage. Brown adds a stage direction to his text indicating that Bosola removes the lights, but one doubts he could have removed and then quickly brought back on the large number of lights needed to shock the audience.

It is more probable that two or three lights were brought on stage when the Duchess entered, and that darkness was indicated symbolically by their removal. Although darkness was usually suggested by the bringing in of lights rather than by their removal, property lights held close to the actors may have been able to indicate darkness more realistically by being extinguished, at least toward the ends of plays when the daylight had begun to fade. When Paris enters the graveyard in the last scene of *Romeo and Juliet*, for example, his page's torch is a conventional indication that the scene is presumed to take place at night. But immediately afterward Paris tells his page "put it out, for I would not be seen" (V.iii.2).[13] If the boy had held the torch close to Paris when they first entered, then its

---

Jonsonian masques as *Hymenaei* (1606), *Entertainment at Theobalds* (1607), and *The Golden Age Restored* (1615); *Ben Jonson*, ed. C. H. Herford and Percy and Evelyn Simpson, 11 vols. (Oxford, 1925–1952), VII, 154–155, 239, and 425.

12. There is very little evidence regarding the number of candles used indoors. At Salisbury Court in 1639, approximately 8s. was spent each day on lights, which would pay for about two or three dozen candles, depending on their size and quality. At the Cockpit-in-Court in 1632, where plays were usually, though not always at night, there were two "great" chandeliers (probably holding around a dozen candles each) and ten smaller ones "about and before the Stage," with at least three more great chandeliers "in the front of the stage." See Bentley, *Jacobean and Caroline Stage*, II, 687, and VI, 273. The frontispiece to *The Wits* (London, 1662) shows sixteen candles above its small "droll" stage, which apparently is also illuminated by strong sunlight. In the summer Salisbury Court seems to have dispensed with artificial light altogether; evidently the windowlight there was strong.

13. Shakespeare quotations are from Alfred Harbage's Penguin edition (Baltimore, 1969).

extinction soon afterward might have eliminated some of the highlights on Paris, at least in contrast to the entering Romeo and Balthasar—also carrying a torch—to whom Shakespeare wants the audience's attention directed. Similarly, if a few lights were brought on quickly in *The Duchess of Malfi* and held close to the dead man's hand, then a small increase in light on it is possible to imagine—not enough to jolt the audience, certainly, but enough to suggest that the previous dialogue was presumed to take place in darkness. Whatever the case, the point is that both Paris and the Duchess need to be seen while they are supposed to be standing in the dark. Far from being grotesque in the light, one of the scene's most provocative moments would be obscured if the audience could not see the Duchess kiss the hand "affectionately" (l. 45). I should not be surprised if, instead of concealing the hand as his own, Burbage signaled somehow to the audience during his speech about the ring that the hand was indeed a dead man's hand. Her kiss would then be all the more ironic and degrading. In fact, the irony pervading Ferdinand's speeches suggests that Webster was less concerned with shocking the audience than with creating dramatic suspense, a growing anxiety in the audience that what they fear might happen will happen.

Whether the point of the scene was shock or suspense, whether the darkness was only symbolic or was suggested by a slight diminution of light near the actors, the scene works best when played in enough light to allow the audience to see what is going on. As such, the scene was as effective outdoors as indoors.

I regret having to take issue with Professor Brown in discussing the lighting of this scene, not only because of the excellence of his edition, but also because he is the only editor of the play to venture a playhouse ascription based on specific technical evidence. Others have been happy to relegate the play to Blackfriars on the basis of what they take to be an "indoor" or "oppressive" atmosphere surrounding the play.[14] Indeed there

---

14. See, e.g., M. L. Wine, ed., *Drama of the English Renaissance* (New York, 1969), p. 498, and E. M. Brennan, ed., *The Duchess of Malfi*, New Mermaid edition (London, 1964), pp. 114–115, who, disregarding the many scenes of pretended darkness in public-theater plays, believes Bosola's mistaken killing of Antonio in V.iv was due to the weak light "provided by candles or lanterns which the speakers held." Una Ellis-Fermor, *The Jacobean Drama*, 4th ed. (London, 1957), p. 43, remarks that Bosola's last speech could

has been a tendency to assign bright, happy plays to the public theaters and dark, melancholy plays to the private theaters when no external evidence is available. Such assignments ignore all the countervailing evidence (the Globe's somber *Hamlet* and *Macbeth*, for example, or the popularity of such bright comedies as *Twelfth Night* and *The Comedy of Errors* indoors), and usually argue circularly that the nature of a playhouse's illumination must have been whatever would complement the mood of the play being assigned to it. While Brown gives *The Duchess of Malfi* to Blackfriars because of its "partially darkened stage," for instance, Frank Kermode calls Blackfriars the "natural home" of *The Tempest* because of the "brightly lit stage" there.[15] Their assessments are not necessarily contradictory—the Blackfriars stage could have been both bright and capable of being darkened. But it is clear that neither description can be taken as fact and that both scholars have selected only the presumed characteristics which fit their theories. External evidence for original Blackfriars production—thin enough for *The Duchess of Malfi* and nonexistent for *The Tempest*—has been stretched to fit none-too-compelling internal evidence.

Contrasting with these attempts to see plays as written for specific theaters and lighting arrangements are the admonitions of Clifford Leech and J. A. Lavin that playwrights wrote less to turn a given theater into good account than they wrote to please themselves or, at the least, to follow the prevailing literary fashion.[16] Lavin goes so far as to deny that the King's Men could have seen any aesthetic distinction between the Globe and Blackfriars and will allow their playwrights no accommodation to it. Of course, Lavin's insistence on the interchangeability of public- and private-theater repertory is well taken in regard to the King's Men. But Lavin forgets that playwrights, particularly the Caroline playwrights, tell us that they sometimes wrote with specific theaters in mind, including the

---

not be spoken in an outdoor theater "with that almost inaudible faintness which the implied musical notation demands." She does not insist on a Blackfriars premiere, but in any case one doubts John Lowin threw away these lines to inaudibility at the Globe.

15. Frank Kermode, ed., *The Tempest*, [New] Arden Shakespeare (Cambridge, Mass., 1958), pp. 151–152.

16. Leech, "The Dramatists' Independence," *RORD*, X (1967), 17–23; Lavin, "Shakespeare and the Second Blackfriars," in *The Elizabethan Theatre III*, ed. David Galloway (Hamden, Conn., 1973), pp. 68–81.

Blackfriars. Webster himself participated in adapting a Blackfriars play, Marston's *The Malcontent*, to the resources available at a public theater in 1604, when he was called on "to abridge the not-received custom of music" at the Globe.[17] Whether or not Webster wrote *The Duchess of Malfi* specifically for the Blackfriars, it is easy to see him offering it to the King's Men in 1613 after the literally dismal failure of *The White Devil* in 1612. Besides being better actors than the Queen's Men and able to attract more sophisticated audiences, the King's Men would not have had to perform his new play under a gloomy winter sky. But if Brown and the others are right and a dark theater was essential for a convincing presentation of *The Duchess of Malfi*, then Webster might have done better to have had it produced at the "open and black" Red Bull instead of the summertime Globe and artificially lit Blackfriars.

Leech and Lavin insist that a dramatist's creative imagination always played a larger part in shaping a scene than did the necessities of physical production. The matter is sometimes difficult to settle, turning as it does on the usually unknowable intentions of the playwright. Still in Webster's case, similarities between the dead-hand scene and a scene in *The White Devil* suggest that the darkness implied in both was inspired more by his personal vision than by his taking advantage of special lighting equipment.

For although Webster (and, apparently, his friend Thomas Dekker)[18] had hoped that the premiere of *The White Devil* would take place under fair skies, Webster extinguishes stage-property lights in the play for many of the same reasons they are removed in his supposedly indoor *Duchess of Malfi*. In I.ii of *The White Devil*, Brachiano and Vittoria contrive to spend their first furtive night together. Like Bosola, Flamineo follows orders and arranges that no lights shine during their tryst. He tells the servants, "'tis

17. See the Induction to *The Malcontent*, ed. G. K. Hunter, Revels Plays edition (London, 1975), p. 13. James Shirley "did not calculate" Globe performance for *The Doubtful Heir* (London, 1652), which, he tells us in a prologue, "*should have been presented at the* Blackfriars" (sig. A4). Similarly, Shirley's *The Court Secret* (London, 1653) was "prepared for the Scene at Black-Friers" but never acted, according to the title page. The printer of *The Two Merry Milkmaids* (London, 1620), sig. A1ᵛ, asserted that every playwright "*must govern his Penne according to the Capacitie of the Stage he writes too, both in the Actor and the Auditor*."

18. Dekker wished *The White Devil* a "*Faire* and *Fortunate Day*" in a dedication to his own play, *If This Be Not a Good Play* (London, 1612), sig. A3ᵛ.

his [Brachiano's] pleasure / you put out all your torches and depart" (ll. 8–9). When Brachiano enters, Vittoria (like the Duchess) is immediately told that darkness suits her actions; she hears (again like the Duchess) from her own brother that darkness hides her sin: "Come sister, darkness hides your blush" (l. 198). She is reminded by her own family member (in this case by her mother) that she has been too "light," that is, wanton (l. 269). The nocturnal "witchcraft" that deceives the Duchess (l. 54) is the same "witchcraft" that lures Vittoria (l. 279). And of course, darkness throughout underscores the illicit sexuality of the scene.

In IV.i of *The Duchess of Malfi*, Ferdinand gives reasons for the removal of lights on similar grounds. And while the sexuality there is not overt and is easily overemphasized, it is nonetheless real.[19] What is more, Webster has taken care to link the darkness of the dead-hand scene with Ferdinand's deep involvement in his sister's sexuality. For it was when Ferdinand first discovered her marriage that he jealously made the vow never to see her again, which later provides the pretext for the darkness in IV.i. She had reminded him then of her youth and beauty, but her marriage, as he later admits, "drew a stream of gall, quite through my heart" (IV.ii.287). It was Ferdinand's "too wilful" and rash response to the Duchess's own sexual longings (III.ii.118) that precipitates the darkness of the dead man's hand. Thus, when Ferdinand and the Duchess meet in her dark bedroom at night, and he wishes she could "have liv'd thus always" (l. 41), he alludes not only to the revenge he can exact in darkness, but also to his incipient sexual feelings which can only be expressed in the darkness of a veritable torture chamber.

To be sure, the suitability of darkness to illicit love was a common rhetorical figure. When Shakespeare's Tarquin is about to ravish Lucrece, Tarquin puts out his torch, "For light and lust are deadly enemies" (*The Rape of Lucrece*, l. 674). Similarly, the bed trick in *Measure for Measure* must be "i' th' dark" to work (IV.i.42); Annabella in *'Tis Pity She's a Whore*

19. For a reasonable account of it, see J. R. Mulryne, "*The White Devil* and *The Duchess of Malfi*," in *Stratford-upon-Avon Studies*, I (1960), rpt. in *Jacobean Theatre*, ed. J. R. Brown and B. Harris (New York, 1967), p. 223. Clifford Leech, "Three Times *Ho* and a Brace of Widows: Some Plays for the Private Theatre," in *The Elizabethan Theatre III*, p. 32, points out that the Duchess transcends the prejudice against remarriage in private-theater drama. The sympathetic treatment of Antonio's rise in fortune also seems out of character for a play written expressly for a private-theater "coterie."

blushes after spending the night with her brother only when daylight comes (II.i); and Arbaces in *A King and No King* nearly repeats Ferdinand's words when he tells who he believes to be his sister that if she consents to love him, "thy dwelling must be dark and close / Where I may never see thee" (IV.iv.77–78).[20]

But while the rhetorical figure is hardly unique, Webster's use of it is; it provides evidence that the darkness in the dead-hand scene was not introduced merely to seize an opportunity which the newly opened Blackfriars afforded. For in two separate plays, Webster is the only dramatist of the period to show us the removal of lights for scenes involving improper love. Webster has turned the figure-in-words into a figure-in-action, as H. T. Price describes Webster's persistent practice.[21] In both plays, the darkness protecting illicit love is signaled by the actual extinction of property lights, an indication, I think, that the effect in *The Duchess of Malfi* was not simply Webster's exploitation of a newly available, indoor lighting device, but rather a characteristic stage image which he knew would work as well at the Red Bull and Globe. A glance at the two plays shows that the network of light imagery in them is of a piece. A pervasive gloom strangles the heroine's light and cynically questions whether that light was not illusory all the while. Vittoria likens herself to a glittering jewel: "Through darkness diamonds spread their richest light" (III.ii.294), to which Flamineo later rejoins, "Glories, like glow-worms, afar off shine bright / But look'd to near, have neither heat nor light" (V.i.41–42). Likewise, the Duchess "stains [i.e., eclipses] the time past, lights the time to come" (I.i.209), even though Bosola must remind her, too, that *"Glories, like glow-worms, afar off shine bright, / But look'd to near, have neither heat, nor light"* (IV.ii.144–145). The very texture of the imagery points toward a single conception of the dramatic significance of light and darkness and calls into serious question any effort to see the plays as written with different playhouse atmospheres and lighting systems in mind.

With no compelling internal evidence to suggest that *The Duchess of Malfi* was composed with an eye toward Blackfriars production, we return

20. Francis Beaumont and John Fletcher, *A King and No King*, ed. R. K. Turner, Regents Renaissance Drama edition (Lincoln, Nebr., 1963).

21. "The Function of Imagery in Webster," *PMLA*, XX (1955), rpt. in *Elizabethan Drama*, ed. R. J. Kaufmann (London, 1961), pp. 225–249.

finally to the only pertinent external evidence, the title page of the 1623 first edition. It gives honor of place to Blackfriars, but it does not follow that the King's Men performed the play there as early as 1614. King's Men's plays published in the early 1620s frequently mention the Black-friars on their title pages, even though many of these plays are otherwise known as having premiered at the Globe. The title page of the 1619 first edition of *A King and No King* says the play was acted at the Globe (probably in 1611), but a second edition in 1625 mentions only the Blackfriars, implying a revival there sometime between 1619 and 1625. *Philaster* was published in 1620 as acted at the Globe, even though it is now usually dated to around 1609 and, on internal evidence, assigned to Blackfriars.[22] The second quarto of 1622 mentions both the Globe and Blackfriars, again suggesting an indoor revival around 1621. Or again, the 1622 first quarto of *Othello* names both the Globe and Blackfriars, but we know that *Othello* was performed some four years before the King's Men even began acting at Blackfriars. The name of Blackfriars on a quarto published in 1623, then, proves nothing about where *The Duchess of Malfi* was performed ten years earlier. It remains entirely possible that *The Duchess of Malfi* was premiered *"publiquely at the Globe"* and only eight or nine years later revived *"privatly, at the Black-Friers."*

I take IV.i of *The Duchess of Malfi* to be a crucial instance of how we may use a knowledge of stage conditions to understand the performance and effect of an Elizabethan drama—crucial not only because of the impor-tance of the scene in the play but because the play itself stands just at the presumed shift from "public-theater" to "private-theater" sensibility, from exclusively natural to mixed natural and artificial illumination. I should like to suggest, moreover, that analyses of specific technical prob-lems like lighting and acoustics may more profitably distinguish between the respective contributions of the public and private theaters than can ambiguous comparisons of style and the social composition of the audience. The danger is that if we begin by assuming that performances at the indoor and outdoor playhouses differed significantly, then even the smallest shred of evidence pointing in that direction may be given too

22. See Andrew Gurr's introduction to The Revels Plays edition of *Philaster* (London, 1969), pp. xxxv–xliv, for a balanced assessment of the influence of the Blackfriars on the King's Men's repertory.

much weight. Were we not able to date *Othello*, for example, to before 1605, an attempt to identify its original playhouse might well have yielded the same conclusion as Brown's regarding *The Duchess of Malfi*. For in the last act of *Othello*, there is an important effect which, if it was intended as a lighting effect, would have been difficult to see at the Globe. When Othello enters Desdemona's bedroom *"with a light"* and compares it to her—"Put out the light, and then put out the light" (V.ii.7)—one cannot imagine that either the candle or its extinction could have made much of an effect on the daylit Globe stage. May we conclude, then, that Shakespeare intended the audience to see a lonely candle burning in a darkened hall, poignantly signaling her chastity in a nasty world? Or are we to see it throwing out a feeble light on a bright, open-air stage? Was the scene presented illusionistically at Blackfriars with only Othello's flickering candle lighting the scene? In that case, the audience might have difficulty seeing Desdemona's horrified reactions to Othello's accusations. Or can we rather believe, on the authority of the dead-hand scene, that Desdemona's death scene was performed in sufficient light at both theaters and that the theatrical point of "Put out the light" resided more in the poetry and acting than in the lighting?

We possess no description of the original lighting of *The Duchess of Malfi*, but we do know that when the King's Men performed *Othello* in the Elizabethan Banqueting Hall at Whitehall on 1 November 1604, the Revels Office went to some expense and trouble to provide a large number of lights. The Office paid 30s. "For mendinge of ye old Branches [i.e., branched chandeliers] for a playe on hallomas Night" and apparently purchased six new branches for the performance, as well.[23] Because Inigo Jones's lighting effects had not yet been introduced at Court and because, in any case, Jones is not known to have supervised the production of professional plays, I think we may assume that the nearly two hundred candles shining in the Banqueting Hall were not extinguished and relit as the play moved from day to night. And if a report of the King's Men's performance of *Othello* at Oxford in September 1610 refers to an indoor venue (as it is likely to), then we may believe that such scenes were played in more than adequate light. We learn that the Oxford audience was deeply moved by Desdemona's death scene and especially by the expres-

23. A. E. Stamp, ed., *The Disputed Revels Accounts* (London, 1930), plate V.

sion on her face as she lay dead: "cum in lecto decumbens spectantium misericordiam ipso vultu imploraret."[24] That Desdemona aroused pity *ipso vultu*, "by her face alone," means that the audience could see even the smallest details clearly and that, if the play was indoors, darkness was not attempted by extinguishing the candles. The ability to see such details in nighttime scenes suggests, in fact, that the actors were not regularly obliged to alter their methods of staging as they moved from one theater to another. Some of the smallest indoor halls may have allowed the audience to enjoy subtler acting than was possible outdoors, but Hosley's reconstruction of the second Blackfriars shows that the majority of spectators there were nearly as far from the stage as those in the largest public theaters, where the audience could surround the actors. Hence, if the general illumination were good, audiences at both kinds of playhouse could discern about the same degree of refinement in the acting. The last act of *Othello*, like the dead-man's-hand scene in *The Duchess of Malfi*, could be performed outdoors and indoors, in the afternoon or at night, by daylight or candlelight.

In point of fact, the steady, over-all illumination of the public and private stages, far from imposing a restriction on the actors and playwrights, meant that even in scenes of pretended darkness the audience could see and respond to the visual media of the actors' craft. The King's Men at Oxford, for instance, "moved the audience to tears, not only by their speech, but by their gestures as well."[25] Thus as we read *The Duchess of Malfi* and come across severed hands and wax corpses, we must not forget the expressions and gestures of the actors which so deeply moved the original audiences. The largely ungovernable stage lighting of the era underscores the important, but missing evidence of the acting and confirms indirectly that the staging at the public and private theaters may not have been so different in regard to an aspect of stage production which one might have assumed would define the principal difference between them.

24. Geoffrey Tillotson, "*Othello* and *The Alchemist* at Oxford in 1610," *TLS*, 20 July 1933, p. 494.
25. *Ibid*.

Lamb, Poel, and Our Postwar Theater: Elizabethan Revivals

EJNER J. JENSEN

L ITERARY REVIVALS present the student of cultural history with curious and nearly irresolvable difficulties. Clearly they are most often the product of a variety of causes. The rediscovery of an abandoned or neglected form, the emergence of a particular complex of social or political factors, a nation's or a region's concern with certain moral or ethical issues, a sort of Jungian demand for the one literary kind that answers a collectively felt need, an interest in writers who are easily identifiable as members of a group (women, blacks), a single critic's advocacy of a forgotten figure: any of these causes or any combination of them may be the source of renewed interest in a writer or in a literary kind. Examples come to one's attention almost without bidding. The recent interest in Spenser, or the fact that at the height of the student protest movement nine books on the pastoral had been written or were in train at Berkeley alone, illustrate one sort of revival. The celebration of Frederick Goddard Tuckerman as one of the great American poets is another. The current interest in Kate Chopin, still another. One could multiply instances.

But even in those cases where the source of a revival seems identifiable, it cannot be, by itself, the sole cause. Critical advocacy means nothing if the public is not disposed to read the poems; books on the pastoral are not produced in quantity by professors who dress in Brooks Brothers suits and provide case studies for Vance Packard. Any revival, no matter how minor or short-lived, has behind it a multitude of causes. Searching these out may be a difficult, complex business. And yet, in the cases of poets and novelists, we always know what constitutes a revival. Public critical discussion, new editions or reissues (especially of a writer's minor works), revaluations (or the proud reassertion of ignored earlier estimates)—such are the common signs of a literary revival.

For dramatic literature, however, these are inadequate signs. The revival of a single dramatist includes all of the manifestations of renewed interest just cited, but it must also include stage presentations of his plays. When one talks of a period dramatic revival, all these criteria apply over a broad range of available plays drawn from a particular era. The chances of such a revival's occurring are never very favorable, since few periods appear sufficiently homogeneous for the plays they contain to appeal equally or to satisfy similar needs.

Yet it has become commonplace to hear and read of the Elizabethan Revival, and to discover this term being applied to not one but two distinct periods in later literary history—the revival of interest in early drama initiated by Charles Lamb, and the theatrical revival of the early twentieth century spearheaded by William Poel. In what follows, I want to define the limitations of these so-called revivals and to suggest that it has been only in our own time that the Elizabethan drama—the theatrical world created by Jonson and Middleton, Webster and Tourneur, and their lesser contemporaries—has truly come to life once again.

Before I pursue that course, however, I should mention one earlier attempt to redefine our understanding of the term Elizabethan Revival, an attempt directly contrary to the ideas that I wish to propose in this essay. Over thirty-five years ago, Earl Wasserman wrote an article in which he tried to show that the revival credited to Lamb was not in fact the work of a single zealous advocate but the product of a tradition of scholarship that stressed the need "to see the Elizabethans against an Elizabethan background," to understand major figures like Spenser and Shakespeare in part through the light shed by their lesser contemporaries.[1] For Wasser-

1. Earl Reeves Wasserman, "The Scholarly Origin of the Elizabethan Revival," *ELH*, IV (1937), 217.

man, "The Scholarly Origin of the Elizabethan Revival" is to be discovered primarily in "the transference of the method employed in editing classical texts to the editing of the English classics."[2] In support of his view, he quotes from *An Impartial Estimate of the Rev. Mr. Upton's Notes on the Faerie Queene* (1759): "Within these last few years, Shakespeare, Beaumont and Fletcher, Jonson, and Milton have been published with elegance and accuracy. They have been explained from a diligent examination of their contemporary authors; and in proportion as they have received this rational method of illustration, they have been studied with new pleasure and improvement."[3]

The whole direction of this argument, however, is toward stressing the importance of preservation and accurate historical understanding. These may well be preconditions for a revival, but they are not in themselves the adequate basis for a revival. Something more is needed if the literature of the past is to come to life again and to realize its purposes anew. The attempt to discover in eighteenth-century scholarship the springs of the nineteenth-century Elizabethan Revival tells us something about the history of scholarship but very little about the living history of literature and nothing at all about the life of our earlier drama.

I

When stark oblivion froze above their names
  Whose glory shone round Shakespeare's, bright as now,
One eye beheld their light shine full as fame's,
  One hand unveiled it: this did none but thou.

So begins the dedicatory sonnet that prefaces Swinburne's volume of essays on *The Age of Shakespeare*.[4] The theme it announces is one to which Swinburne returns again and again: Lamb rescued Shakespeare's contemporaries from entire neglect; Lamb alone, with his *Specimens of English Dramatic Poets*, prepared the way for scholars and editors of the nineteenth century who claimed the Elizabethan drama as their special province. Swinburne gives that theme its most emphatic statement toward the close

---

2. *Ibid.*, p. 215.
3. *Ibid.*, pp. 217–218.
4. Algernon Charles Swinburne, *The Complete Works*, ed. Sir Edmund Gosse and Thomas James Wise, The Bonchurch Edition (London, 1926), XI, 270.

of his essay on "Charles Lamb and George Wither." It was Lamb's special gift, argues Swinburne, that "by the heroic or poetic instinct of sympathy with 'high actions and high passions,' with the sublimity of suffering and the extravagance of love," he had "the power to read aright such poetry as to Campbell was a stumbling-block and to Hallam foolishness."[5] The romantic critic becomes for Swinburne a heroic mediator "who has fed us on lion's marrow, and with honey out of the lion's mouth."[6] The panegyric goes on, accumulating details and new figures as Swinburne elaborates still further:

To him and to him alone it is that we owe the revelation and resurrection of our greatest dramatic poets after Shakespeare. . . . He alone opened the golden vein alike for students and for sciolists: he set the fashion of real or affected interest in our great forgotten poets. Behind him and beneath we see the whole line of conscientious scholars and of imitative rhetoricians: the Hazlitts prattling at his heel, the Dyces labouring in his wake. If the occasional harvest of these desultory researches were his one and only claim to the regard of Englishmen, this alone should suffice to ensure him their everlasting respect and their unalterable gratitude.[7]

This view of Lamb as the critic who first revealed the greatness of Shakespeare's contemporaries and as a figure who was uniquely able to interpret their individual qualities has been put more succinctly in our century by Edmund Blunden: "Alone with Webster . . . Lamb was at once right in his delimitation of the kingdom of that dramatist, and unique in his transfusion of Webster's deadly dogged note in his own sentences."[8] By giving himself over to the power of the dramatists, by attuning himself to their differences, Lamb was able to gain a rich awareness of the whole period and the means to communicate his understanding to others. In Blunden's view, "were some future race only to know Elizabethan drama through Lamb's comments, they would be able to . . . scan the lost works as a mountain-range in the crystal glass of this unassuming seer."[9]

5. *Ibid.*, XIV, 284.

6. *Ibid.*, XIV, 285.

7. *Ibid.* This whole passage is worth reading for an awareness of Swinburne's very high estimate of Lamb's worth as a critic.

8. Edmund Blunden, *Charles Lamb and His Contemporaries* (1933; rpt. Hamden, Conn., 1967), p. 99.

9. *Ibid.*, pp. 100–101.

But Lamb's crystal glass, as he himself admits, was a selective instrument. Limited in its powers by the critic's own inclinations and intentions, it focused on the peaks rather than the entire range of the Elizabethan dramatic achievement. The *Specimens*, like any anthology, reflect the taste and habits of mind of the critic who assembled them. James Russell Lowell has described what this involves in the case of Lamb's selection:

Himself a fragmentary writer, he had more sympathy with imagination where it gathers into the intense focus of passionate phrase than with that higher form of it, where it is the faculty that shapes, gives unity of design, and balanced gravitation of parts.[10]

Moreover, Lamb introduces the *Specimens* with a description of two clearly defined aims. He wishes first, he writes, "to illustrate what may be called the moral sense of our ancestors." His second aim, a more practical one, is to place some of the scenes of Fletcher and Massinger, "in the estimation of the world the only dramatic poets of that age . . . entitled to be considered after Shakespeare," in a single volume with "the more impressive scenes of old Marlowe, Heywood, Tourneur, Webster, Ford, and others." In this way, he may hope "to show what we have slighted, while beyond all proportion we have cried up one or two favourite names."[11] There is no question that these aims were in themselves meritorious or that they were to some degree achieved. What I want to emphasize here is that they were also quite narrow and essentially unrelated to the dramatic—i.e., the theatrical—qualities of the plays themselves. In Lamb's selections and in his commentary on his choices we have a very accurate measure of his sense of the values to be discovered in "the old dramatists." He stresses, first of all, the poetry of the scenes; and the poetry he chooses is that which illustrates literature's affective power. He has, therefore, slighted scenes of wit and humor and instead "sought after . . . scenes of passion, sometimes of the deepest quality, interesting situations, serious descriptions, that which is more nearly allied to poetry than to wit, and to tragic rather than to comic poetry."[12] Inevitably, such an emphasis leads to the selection of great scenes, inspired moments, crises of passion and violence; and it involves the same sort of

---

10. James Russell Lowell, from "Shakespeare Once More," quoted in *The Works of Charles and Mary Lamb*, ed. E. V. Lucas (London, 1904), IV, 601.

11. *Ibid.*, IV, xii.

12. *Ibid.*, IV, xi.

misrepresentation illustrated today in long-playing records of the world's great melodies. Artistic structure, any sense of the whole creation, is sacrificed to the emphasis on a single dominant impression. Finally, in those instances where the chosen scene is not charged with passion or poetic energy, it is offered as an insight into a particular issue or as an illustration of some principle or mode of behavior. [13]

A few examples will illustrate Lamb's method and its limitations. Dekker's *Satiromastix* provides him with a scene introduced as follows: *"The King exacts an oath from Sir Walter Terill to send his Bride Coelestina to Court on the Marriage Night. Her Father, to save her honour, gives her a poisonous mixture which she swallows."* Coelestina, after a lengthy apostrophe to the poison ("Thou wholesome medicine to a constant blood"), drinks it down, resisting the frenzied protestations of Sir Walter:

> O stop that speedy messenger of death;
> O let him not run down that narrow path
> Which leads unto thy heart, nor carry news
> To thy removing soul that thou must die.

But the poison is of course not poison, but a "sleeping draught"; and Coelestina awakens later "to the surprise of her husband, and the great mirth and edification of the King and his courtiers." Thus, writes Lamb, "the beauty and force of this scene are much diminished to the reader of the entire play," a loss made especially regrettable, he believes, since "the sentiments are worthy of a real martyrdom, and an Appian sacrifice in earnest" (pp. 56–59). The design of Dekker's play, its over-all tone—these matters count for little; the comic resolution of the plot destroys the power of this moving scene of a virgin sacrificed to honor.

Lamb repeatedly shows in his comments a willingness to accept momentary effects as touchstones of a play's worth, to take the part for the whole. The interview of Vindice and Hippolito with their mother in *The Revenger's Tragedy* leads him to declare that "The reality and life of this

---

13. I am thinking here of the excerpts from *The Case is Altered* or the comments on *Poetaster*, where Lamb claims that in that play Jonson "has . . . revived the whole court of Augustus, by a learned spell" (Lamb, *Works*, IV, 253). All further quotations from Lamb are taken from the Lucas edition, vol. IV, and will be set down without reference to their source.

Dialogue passes any scenical illusion I ever felt. I never read it but my ears tingle, and I feel a hot blush spread my cheeks" (p. 160). He quotes the Prologue from *Antonio's Revenge*, praising "its passionate earnestness" and "the tragic note of preparation which it sounds," and judging it to be "as solemn a preparative as the 'warning voice which he who saw the Apocalypse, heard cry'" (pp. 62–63). In the several pages devoted to *The Duchess of Malfi*, Lamb presents in great detail the accumulated tortures that lead up to the heroine's death, illustrating in this way his claim that Webster's genius was for the creation of just such effects:

What are "Luke's iron crown," the brazen bull of Perillus, Procrustes' bed, to the waxen images which counterfeit death, to the wild masque of madmen, the tomb-maker, the bell-man, the living person's dirge, the mortification by degrees! To move a horror skilfully, to touch a soul to the quick, to lay upon fear as much as it can bear, to wean and weary a life till it is ready to drop, and then step in with mortal instruments to take its last forfeit—this only a Webster can do.

(p. 179)

To praise Webster for such achievements is merely to cite him approvingly as "our Tussaud Laureate," and it is no less misleading than to level that phrase at him with its full pejorative weight.

If the selections just cited show Lamb representing the playwrights in a false light, other examples from the *Specimens* show nothing of dramatic interest at all but rather curiosities that give us a glimpse of Elizabethan fashion and habits. In these instances Lamb assumes the role of antiquarian and gives over his critical function altogether. Marston's *What You Will*, for example, provides a starting point for some comments on fashion and its social meanings:

To judge of the liberality of these notions of dress we must advert to the days of Gresham, and the consternation which a phenomenon habited like the Merchant here described would have excited among the flat round caps, and cloth stockings, upon Change. . . . The blank uniformity to which all professional distinctions in apparel have been long hastening, is one instance of the Decay of Symbols among us, which whether it has contributed or not to make us a more intellectual, has certainly made us a less imaginative people.

(p. 71)

Similarly, a long passage from *The City Madam*, introduced under the rubric, "The extravagance of the City Madams aping court fashions re-

prehended," provides the opportunity for this observation: "This bitter
satire against the city women for aping the fashions of the court ladies
must have been peculiarly gratifying to the females of the Herbert family
and the rest of Massinger's patrons and patronesses" (p. 345).

The antiquarian interest does not, however, become a dominant concern in the *Specimens*. What is dominant, from first to last, is Lamb's
attention to poetry. Dramatic poets—not dramatists—fill page after page
with striking images, tender scenes, memorable figures that blaze into life
from the intense heat of passion. But we learn nothing of the demands of
the stage, of dramatic structure, of the magnificent ordering that unites
violent tragedy and grotesque comedy in a single theatrical design. Along
with others of his time—figures as different from one another as Coleridge
and Thomas Hood, Hazlitt and Thomas Lovell Beddoes—Lamb encouraged a growing interest in things Elizabethan. But he cannot be said to
have initiated a revival of Elizabethan drama, for almost none of the plays
of the period (always excepting Shakespeare's) earned a place on the
nineteenth-century stage. Robert Hamilton Ball, in *The Amazing Career of
Sir Giles Overreach*, has given a detailed account of the stage fortunes
enjoyed by Massinger's *A New Way to Pay Old Debts* in the last century;
but that play's success is an anomaly. Jonson disappeared from the stage
almost totally for nearly a hundred years at just about the time Lamb was
beginning his collection. Webster and Ford, recipients of the an-
thologist's highest acclaim, earned no theater productions as a result of his
advocacy. Middleton, Heywood, Dekker, Chapman—not one of the
dramatists championed by Lamb won the chance to demonstrate his worth
as a theatrical craftsman during the era in which Lamb supposedly
brought them all to public notice once again.

It is true, of course, that Hazlitt, influenced by Lamb and by Barry
Cornwall (Bryan Waller Procter) wrote and delivered his *Lectures on the
Dramatic Literature of the Age of Elizabeth*. But it is a question whether the
Hazlitts and the Dyces dismissed so contemptuously by Swinburne
might not have found Elizabethan literature ripe for harvest even without
Lamb to lead them to the vineyards. In part, at least, the critical activity
of the period may be explained by the burgeoning interest in historical
researches of every sort, a case of scholarship in search of a subject.
Certainly the focus of concern in the editions, from Gifford's *Massinger*
(1805) on, was historical and biographical. When the editors offer critical

commentary at all, it has to do most often with poetic effects or the portrayal of character.

Yet Swinburne was right. Anyone in the nineteenth century who worked in a critical or scholarly way with the Elizabethan dramatists was obliged to honor Lamb's pioneering work.[14] Swinburne himself, who seems to have become acquainted with the *Specimens* at the age of twelve or thirteen, affirmed his own indebtedness to Lamb in a typical rush of excess, declaring to Edmund Gosse, "that book taught me more than any other in the world—that and the Bible."[15] Moreover, although Swinburne's criticism is undervalued at the moment, he ought to be regarded as Lamb's best pupil and the ranking critic of Elizabethan drama of his own age. The essays alone would not assure him that status, but in the sonnets on the Elizabethan dramatists he often strikes off telling and persuasive observations, some of which anticipate in a remarkable way the insights of our most helpful modern criticism.[16]

Nevertheless, Lamb's influence did not inspire others to a view more comprehensive than his own. Swinburne, too, thought of the Elizabethan dramatists primarily as poets. In its early stages, writes Frederick E. Pierce, "the Elizabethan enthusiasm was no great popular wave . . . but the cult of a few comparatively obscure and uninfluential men, who encouraged each other and found little encouragement elsewhere."[17] By the end of the nineteenth century this revival had both grown and enlisted important voices in its support. Yet it remained, as in its beginnings, a critical and scholarly development unrelated to theatrical values and uninterested in finding a place for these neglected playwrights on the contemporary stage.[18]

14. Thus Walter Pater writes of Lamb, "he becomes not merely an expositor, permanently valuable, but for Englishmen almost the discoverer of the Old English drama." *Appreciations, with an Essay on Style* (London, 1918), p. 111.

15. *The Letters of Charles Algernon Swinburne*, ed. Edmund Gosse and Thomas James Wise (London, 1918), I, viii.

16. The sonnet on Webster is perhaps the most remarkable case in point.

17. Frederick E. Pierce, *Currents and Eddies in the English Romantic Generation* (New Haven, Conn., 1918), p. 196.

18. I should point out that the nineteenth century was at times avowedly inhospitable to the Elizabethan dramatists. Jonson was censured for his coarse language and his failure to mete out appropriate punishments. Others were blamed for their freedom in treating sexual matters. In many ways nineteenth-century taste was too delicate for Elizabethan dramatic fare.

II

The second "Elizabethan Revival" to be considered here, that movement nurtured and spread almost single-handedly by William Poel, could hardly have been more different from the first. It was insistently centered on the stage. Poel wanted to return to authentic Elizabethan methods of production—to a stage which emphasized the playwright's words and which, in its simplicity, shifted away from nineteenth-century concern with scenic elaboration toward a concern with the delivery of lines and the verbal shape of the play as a total composition. Over a period of forty years, from 1892 with *The Duchess of Malfi* for the Independent Theatre Society to 1932 with *David and Bethsabe* for the Elizabethan Stage Circle, Poel himself produced no fewer than sixteen non-Shakespearean plays.[19] By the mid-twenties, although he thought himself neglected and unpopular, his production methods and his valuation of the Elizabethan drama were reasonably well established. Thus Robert Speaight writes that "Such of Poel's principles as could be accommodated to the proscenium theatre had been fairly widely accepted. The plays that he had brought back into circulation were now being performed by the Phoenix Society or the Renaissance Theatre."[20] A decade later, when J. Dover Wilson had occasion to look back to the sources of the "new criticism" of Harley Granville-Barker, a criticism that took theatrical values and theatrical experience fully into account, he found that it had been "made possible" in part by "the virtual rediscovery at the hands of William Poel, W. J. Lawrence, Sir Edmund Chambers, and many others, of the character and methods of the Elizabethan stage."[21]

These factors—his activity as a producer, the widespread acceptance of his ideas, and his status as a major figure in the recovery of knowledge about the Elizabethan stage and staging—would seem to substantiate Poel's claim to be the originator of a many-faceted and influential Elizabethan Revival. But William Poel was more of a rebel than an

19. In much of what follows I draw on Robert Speaight, *William Poel and the Elizabethan Revival* (London, 1954). The figures I cite here are taken from Appendix I of Speaight's book.

20. *Ibid.*, p. 239.

21. *Ibid.*, p. 148. This passage is quoted from Wilson's Inaugural Lecture as Regius Professor of Rhetoric and English Literature at Edinburgh.

originator, and like all rebels he was limited by the very thing against which his rebellion was directed. In his case, the target was the nineteenth-century stage with its emphasis on pictorial effects and its consequent inhibiting of the imagination. Poel "feared that the imaginative faculties of modern man—faculties essential for the enjoyment of Shakespeare—were being smothered by the insistent appeal to the eye, which at every turn was recklessly flattered."[22] In Poel's view, "the art of the poet presupposes and comprehends all the other arts. . . . Poetry in fact makes her own pictures as she makes her own music."[23] Such a theory grew naturally out of Poel's researches into the character and function of the Elizabethan stage; in practice, it led to a method of production that was limited both by its antiquarianism and by its adherence to analogies drawn from music.

The antiquarian impulse that led Poel to insist precisely on what he understood to be Elizabethan production methods and Elizabethan stage practices created in turn a kind of antiquarian expectation in those who came to see his plays. One senses that an audience at a typical production took their places with something of the attitude of overawed museum-goers rather than with that lively sense of expectation that an audience brings to a theatrical performance they have reason to believe will be rewarding in its liveliness. A good reflection of this attitude appears in C. E. Montague's review of Poel's 1904 production of *Doctor Faustus*. After comparing Marlowe's play unfavorably with *Everyman* (finding it less "modern," and finding that "time had clawed *Faustus* uncommonly severely in its clutch"), Montague went on to describe the merits of the Elizabethan play as they appeared in Poel's production. His assessment is worth quoting in some detail:

whole tracts and aspects of *Doctor Faustus* . . . were of their own time solely, and now are dead a doornails. . . . yet the performance does give a rare and curious pleasure or blend of pleasures.

There is the pleasure of judging the effect of the Elizabethan platform stage, where the actors stood out "in the round" like statues and the public could see between them and the back cloth or curtains. . . . The platform stage obviously made naturalism in acting impossible and declamation essential. The fact "jumped into your eye" that on such a stage Elizabethan drama had to be a drama

22. *Ibid.*, p. 87.
23. Quoted in Speaight, *William Poel*, p. 87.

of harangues, as on our own stage—an illusive hole in the wall—drama is almost bound over to be realistic. . . .

Like all the Society's work, the performance of *Faustus* keeps you, at any rate while it lasts, in that state of grave and child-like absorption and of freedom from our modern affliction of knowingness that simple and enthusiastic souls can achieve while looking at Giotto's tower with an unclouded faith in Ruskin. . . . Everybody's mind was for the moment simplified—not, indeed, to the point of sharing Elizabethan joy in such a play, but to the point of genuine interest in that joy and partial comprehension of it.[24]

It would be unfair to see Montague's comments as reflecting a universally held reaction to the work of the Elizabethan Stage Society and the other groups for which Poel produced. Many of the reviews testify to the fact that their performances were convincing. But nearly everything that Poel attempted was in its very nature an effort at restoration.

Poel recognized the difficulty of his situation. To bring the Elizabethan plays to life again required, in his view, enormous research and a good deal of well-founded reconstruction. But such activities, insofar as they made his work seem antiquarian or archaeological, prevented the public from attending to the resulting production in a way acceptable to a man of the theater. Thus he protested:

Some people have called me an archaeologist, but I am not. I am really a modernist. My original aim was just to find out some means of acting Shakespeare naturally and appealingly from the full text as in a modern drama. I found that the platform stage was necessary and also some suggestion of the spirit and manners of the time.[25]

Such disclaimers could not, however, alter the public's view of Poel. Although Swinburne might congratulate him "on the benefits you have conferred on all lovers of English dramatic poetry at its best and highest" (through his 1892 production of *The Duchess of Malfi*), and although Shaw praised him for a staging of *Romeo and Juliet* in which "for the first time [the play] became endurable," their support and the support of others like them never succeeded in establishing Poel as a great public force in the English theater.[26] His productions, most often given in out-of-the-way

24. Quoted in Speaight, *William Poel*, pp. 118–119.
25. Quoted in Speaight, *William Poel*, p. 90.
26. The passages quoted here are taken from Speaight, *William Poel*, pp. 73, 192.

halls for a day or two—*The Alchemist* at Apothecaries' Hall for two days in February, 1899; *David and Bethsabe* at the Mary Ward Settlement, Tavistock Place, for one day in November 1932—could not receive great popular favor. Only *Everyman* gained genuine popular acclaim, and after its initial success Poel dissociated himself from further productions of the medieval religious drama.

Guided by his own convictions about the Elizabethan stage and committed to a theatrical purism in matters of presentation, Poel could never present himself convincingly as a modernist. Yet the antiquarian label might not have fastened itself so securely if in his productions he had been able to assert a contemporary applicability of theme or meaning. The truth, however, seems to be that Poel had slight interest in such matters. The correct presentation of a play derived for him from the understanding and reproduction of its verbal music. "For Poel," writes Robert Speaight, "a play was primarily a thing heard. . . . He heard it as precisely as a composer hears the symphony he has just put down on paper."[27] In his 1897 production of *Twelfth Night* Poel orchestrated the voices of the characters as though he were casting parts for an opera. Again and again one sees evidence of Poel's emphasis on the music of dramatic verse— Shakespeare's in particular, of course—and of his understanding of individual plays as poetic-musical structures. It is this stress on musical analogies that justifies in part William Archer's characterization of Poel as a "non-scenic Beerbohm Tree."[28]

What one misses in Poel is the sense that the drama he so passionately cared for had for him an important dimension of meaning. So intent on discovering what a certain dramatic event must have looked like on the Elizabethan stage, so concerned with re-creating the distinctive orchestration that made a play sound just this way and no other, his methods of recovery were always retrospective in emphasis. Such a concern for the past is finally inimical to the idea of a revival. By insisting that a spectator see things as they were, it creates an insurmountable wall between past and present. It encourages exclamatory responses and stresses the quaintness of

27. *Ibid.*, p. 68. Poel himself wrote that "dramatic poetry, so long as it remains unspoken, to a great extent may be compared with a composer's libretto—it is something that is incomplete. The music, which in this case is elocution, must be added." See *Shakespeare's Profession*, London Shakespeare League Pamphlet #2, 1915.

28. Quoted by Speaight, *William Poel*, p. 105.

unfamiliar methods. Finally, such an approach becomes self-defeating. In its scrupulous care for exactness, it makes a statue where it would create a living thing. Thus the Elizabethan Revival of William Poel remained incomplete. As a student of stage history, Poel had a significant influence on the course of dramatic scholarship. As a theatrical producer, his achievement was limited by the necessary imperfection of all attempts to re-create the past. Here a sort of pedantry created an additional barrier to Poel's efforts. Insisting on fidelity to Elizabethan stage practices, he often seemed to make reconstruction an end in itself.[29] The result, predictably enough, was more often an exhibition than a dramatic performance. Drama produced under such conditions and directed to such ends might more plausibly be said to be restored than to be revived.

III

The movements of which Poel was a part, both theatrical and academic, have continued to grow throughout this century. From the Phoenix Society and the Malvern Festival to the whole rich variety of festivals that exist today there has been a continuous and expanding effort to produce the plays of Shakespeare and his contemporaries, often under conditions designed to approximate those of the Elizabethan stage. Furthermore, academic criticism during this same period has developed in an amazing fashion. Historical criticism, theater research, textual scholarship, the new criticism—all the varieties of scholarly and critical activity that have flourished both in and out of our universities—have come together to enable us to see the Elizabethan drama in a richer and more comprehensive way. These developments have provided favorable conditions for the Elizabethan Revival of the last three decades, a revival that has brought Shakespeare and his fellow dramatists into our cultural life with force and meaning.

29. A remarkable instance of this appears in Poel's review of the Marlowe Society production of *Epicoene* in 1909, which was performed with an all-male cast. Since even a National Theatre would not be "likely to include a group of trained youths," wrote Poel, "we must make up our minds to have seen *Epicoene* once and for all." Even granting the appropriateness of boy actors for a staging of this play, their use is hardly a prerequisite for its presentation. The review appeared in the *Times*, 22 February 1909.

Other factors, some of the first importance, have contributed to make the earlier drama more accessible than it was to earlier generations. One of these has been the gradual dissolution during this century of a whole complex of Victorian attitudes that kept such playwrights as Jonson and Ford off the nineteenth-century stage on the grounds of taste and morality. Another change has come about through the displacement of a romantic view of art by a view of art that we call modern. Jonas Barish discusses this shift in relation to Ben Jonson's twentieth-century reputation.[30] Citing T. E. Hulme's essay on "Classicism and Romanticism" as a seminal document in this critical shift, he points out how it legitimized new standards in the judgment of literature, standards that included such qualities as "wit, plainness, and flintiness of texture."[31] I would add that this new attitude allowed other qualities as well, including structural forms that were multiple and diverse, forms that could contain a mixture of attitudes and tones. But the relevant matter is not this attitude alone. It is rather that such a notion of art corresponds directly and in the most striking way to the practice of the great Elizabethan dramatists. One sees this, again, most readily in Shakespeare, and most of all in such plays as *Measure for Measure* and *Troilus and Cressida* which have come into their own only in this century. It is there in Jonson too, and in others, as well, as Ralph Berry has demonstrated in his recent book on Webster.[32]

Still another circumstance has enabled the great Renaissance drama to assume to some degree its rightful place on our stages and thus in our cultural life. The modern theater (the theater of Brecht and Beckett, of Ionesco and Albee and Pinter) and the cinema have conditioned us as spectators in the theater to "read" the way we must do if we are to understand the structure and meaning of the most rewarding Elizabethan

30. Jonas A. Barish in *Ben Jonson: A Collection of Critical Essays* (Englewood Cliffs, N. J., 1963), Introduction.

31. *Ibid.*, p. 9.

32. Ralph Berry, *The Art of John Webster* (Oxford, 1972). Berry defines Webster's plays as "attempts to achieve in literature the effects of the baroque"; in the process, he makes clear how receptive to those effects our modern sensibility can be. Defining *The White Devil* as "a burlesque morality, poised between tragedy and tragi-comedy," he points out that "the 1966–67 revival of *The Revenger's Tragedy* . . . demonstrated perfectly how the genre should be played. The fall of Vindice (as of Flamineo) is, at the end, tragic, and meant to be so received by the audience; but it follows a series of episodes that are witty, outrageous, and sensational" (pp. vii, 19).

plays. Aston's monologue about his confinement and shock treatment in *The Caretaker*, the story of "Jerry and the Dog" in *Zoo Story*, the vaudeville tricks of *Waiting for Godot* help us to understand the grotesque comedy of *The Changeling* and the cynical satiric notes that Bosola sounds among the cries of pain and anguish in *The Duchess of Malfi*.

It is impossible to chart with any exactness the precise course of the revival I am describing. Like any movement in the theater it owes a multitude of debts. For the purpose at hand, I wish to begin with some comments Edmund Wilson made on the George Rylands production of *The Duchess of Malfi* in 1945. Wilson called this staging of Webster's masterpiece "one of the best productions that I have seen of anything anywhere."[33] He found the production "so immensely imaginative and skilful and the acting at the same time so dynamic and so disciplined that it holds you from beginning to end." The play's horrors, unthinkably excessive to earlier critics, took on new validity to a generation that had witnessed the brutalities of Nazism: "One sees . . . the scene where her doom is announced to the Duchess amidst the drivellings of the liberated madmen, at the moment of the exposé of the German concentration camps."

This production at the Haymarket, featuring Peggy Ashcroft as the Duchess and John Gielgud as Ferdinand, has been followed in recent years by no fewer than seven revivals.[34] No one would pretend that these have been uniformly successful; some, in fact, have been outright failures on the testimony of the critics. But the continuing appearance of *The Duchess* suggests that the play answers to some need in modern awareness and that producers and directors have been concerned to explore various aspects of its contemporary significance. In the Aldwych production of 1960–1961, Dame Peggy Ashcroft once again took the title role, with Eric Porter as the lycanthropic Ferdinand. In a performance that seemed both monu-

33. These comments originally appeared in the *New Yorker*, 2 June 1945. I quote from *Europe Without Baedeker*, rev. ed. (New York, 1966), p. 12, both here and in what follows. I am grateful to my colleague Donald B. Sands for bringing this reference to my attention.

34. These begin with an adaptation by W. H. Auden that featured Elizabeth Bergner as the Duchess, John Carradine as the Cardinal, and Canada Lee as Bosola. Later productions include the following: Theatre Royal, Stratford East, 1957; Phoenix Theatre, 1957; Aldwych Theatre, 1960; Royal Court, 1971; Stratford Festival, Ontario, 1971; Royal Shakespeare Company, Stratford-upon-Avon, 1971.

mental and terrible in its intensity—filled, in other words, with the inevitability of tragedy—these two, aided by Max Adrian as the Cardinal, brought Webster's drama to life in the theater. Flawed by the too-affable Bosola of Patrick Wymark, this production nevertheless forced spectators to face up to that malcontent's grim analysis of human life:

> In what a shadow, or deep pit of darkness
> Doth womanish and fearful mankind live.
>
> (V.v. 101–102)[35]

Ten years later, at the Stratford Festival Theatre of Canada, Jean Gascon took another way with Webster. While Donald McWhinnie had stressed the play's language and used to the full the strengths of his leading actors, Gascon emphasized a pictorial approach and created a scene rich to the point of decadence on a thrust stage that made every spectator aware of the stifling excesses of brocade and velvet, of incense and perfume, designed to hide the corruption at the heart of the play's universe. In the same year Clifford Williams directed the Royal Shakespeare Company in a production of *The Duchess* that conjured a world linking sex and death, vitality and cynicism, a world in which the forces of nullity and cosmic horror overran the brilliant but ineffectual representatives of youth and love. Judi Dench was a magnificent Duchess whose death, even in its proud assertion of self, defined Webster's absurd universe and plunged the spectators without hope into the void of the play's conclusion.

Many of the plays that we tend to think of in connection with *The Duchess of Malfi* have also enjoyed revivals in the three decades since the end of World War II. *The White Devil*, with Robert Helpmann as Flamineo and Margaret Rawlings as Vittoria, played for four months at London's Duchess Theatre in 1947.[36] The *Times* reviewer called Michael Benthall's production a "bold and highly accomplished venture" and remarked that a new generation of playgoers had developed, willing and even eager to witness the work of such playwrights as Webster.[37] Other

---

35. Text used for *The Duchess of Malfi* is The Revels Plays edition, ed. John Russell Brown (Cambridge, Mass., 1964).

36. See Don D. Moore, "John Webster in the Modern Theatre," *ETJ*, XVII (December 1965), 318. See also the same author's *John Webster and His Critics: 1617–1964* (Baton Rouge, La., 1966).

37. *Times*, 7 March 1947.

revivals of *The White Devil* include two directed by Jack Landau: the first in 1955 at New York's Phoenix Theatre; the second, ten years later, at the Circle in the Square. The 1955 version was a "Sideshow" production of the Phoenix company for a single performance; the 1966 version had an extended run and a good deal of critical praise. In 1969, the National Theatre presented a highly successful staging of the play; and in the summer of 1976, Glenda Jackson took the part of Vittoria in a production at the Old Vic.

The Changeling, although it has suffered some conspicuously unworthy productions, notably that by the Lincoln Center Company under Elia Kazan's direction in 1964, has received a good deal of helpful attention as well. Robert Shaw created a frighteningly credible DeFlores in the 1961 Royal Court production, and Luca Ronconi directed a sensational version of the play in Rome in 1967. Borrowing from the *Marat/Sade* of Peter Weiss, he focused on the asylum subplot and made the main action a series of events acted out by its inhabitants. *'Tis Pity She's a Whore* has been revived several times, at Nottingham, by the Mermaid and the National Theatre in London, and in this country by the Yale Repertory Theatre. *The Revenger's Tragedy*, arguably the most difficult of all these plays, has been the beneficiary of brilliant productions by the Royal Shakespeare Company featuring Ian Richardson as Vindice.

Other Elizabethan-Jacobean playwrights have enjoyed like attention in recent years. Marlowe and Jonson, although the former must always suffer being labeled Shakespeare's imperfect predecessor and the latter rarely avoids identification as his rule-bound contemporary, have been presented fairly often. Even *Tamburlaine*, in the Old Vic production starring Donald Wolfit and more recently (in 1976) in the National Theatre production with Albert Finney in the title role, has achieved a measure of stage success, while the recent *Jew of Malta* by the Royal Shakespeare Company startled nearly everyone by its brilliance. The City Center's *Edward II*, directed by Ellis Raab, captured the play's design in the swirling, nearly balletic movements of the actors. Jonson's stage fortunes have been increasing steadily throughout this century. Noteworthy postwar productions include John Burrell's 1947 *Alchemist* with the Old Vic Company; the various productions by the Donald Wolfit company of *Volpone*; productions at the Oxford Playhouse of the two plays just mentioned as well as *Epicoene*, all directed by Frank Hauser; and stagings of *Bartholomew Fair* in

1950 by the Old Vic Company, in 1969 by the Royal Shakespeare, and in 1976 at the Nottingham Playhouse.[38] David William's *Volpone* at Stratford, Canada, in 1971, was a compelling exploration of that play's rich variety of tones and effects. Substituting a mimed orgy for the first-act show by Volpone's rout, transforming the Would-be's into inane visitors from Texas in an Edwardian-period Venice, taking full account both of the play's bizarre comedy and its malevolent cruelty, the Stratford production was a thoroughly modern and surpassingly powerful version of the play.

In calling attention to these productions of the last three decades or so, my chief aim is to suggest the range and variety of the postwar Elizabethan revival. The important thing, however, is not that these plays have been available but that they have been available in stagings that have mattered to contemporary audiences. Few persons will have seen even a majority of the productions I have mentioned here. Those who have seen any of the more successful ones will recognize immediately what Mel Gussow was responding to when he wrote, "The subjects discussed, the style of the discussion . . . even the jarring character changes are not alien in the context of modern absurdist theatre." They may have shared a perception like John Russell Brown's, who has suggested that "Possibly new plays like Ionesco's *Rhinoceros* or Pinter's *The Dwarfs*, which use fantastic happenings to present the fantastic unrealities of half-conscious thought, have accustomed actors to playing unrealistic situations boldly." Or it may be that with Peter Thomson they have looked upon one or another of these plays with the realization that "It is impossible to mount a production . . . without intending deeply to disturb your audience."[39] It happens that Gussow's observation refers to Middleton's *Women Beware Women*, in the 1972 production by the City Center Company. Brown is writing about a variety of Shakespearean scenes "which even a few years ago were customarily played with some awkwardness,"[40]

38. On this last production, see my review in *ETJ*, XXVIII (December 1976), 558–559.

39. The quotations come from the following sources: Gussow, *New York Times*, 18 October 1972; Brown, *Shakespeare's Plays in Performance* (New York, 1967), p. 189; Thomson, "Webster and the Actor," in *John Webster*, ed. Brian Morris, Mermaid Critical Commentaries (London, 1970), p. 26.

40. Brown, *Shakespeare's Plays in Performance*, p. 189.

while Thomson's remark refers to both of the great Websterian tragedies. Yet the particular references hardly matter. What our recent theatrical history demonstrates is that the major plays of the Renaissance are accessible to us both through their dominant thematic interests and through their striking and powerful stagecraft. Again and again, the plays can be set over against some of our most significant contemporary dramas with results that are reciprocally illuminating. What we see finally, and what we must respond to, is the sort of theatrical experience that forces us to confront the most fundamental questions about human freedom, about our claims to reason, about our very nature and identity.

In Jacobean tragedy, one of the recurring perceptions we are likely to have, both in reading the texts and in viewing productions, concerns the rigid limitations within which the characters operate. Their field of action (mental as well as physical) seems narrowly defined and inescapable. At times this almost claustrophobic sense of confinement is defined explicitly by stage images as in the narrow castle passageways and the barred asylum of *The Changeling* or in the chessboard stage to which the characters were bound in the Royal Shakespeare Company's *Women Beware Women*.[41] At times it is evoked by more subtle means. In the 1961 production of Webster's *Duchess*, the characters were constrained by darkness throughout the play. It was not in the fifth act alone with its tragic mistakings that darkness worked to restrict the play's action. There was little illumination from the beginning; and when Peggy Ashcroft declared her intention to enter "a wilderness / Where I shall find nor path, nor friendly clue / To be my guide" (I.i.359–361), the meaning and horror of her commitment was defined by the vacancy with which she was surrounded. In Jean Gascon's production for the Stratford Festival in 1971, *The Duchess of Malfi* was acted on a bare stage; but the costumes—heavy, elaborate, excessive in nearly every respect—created a similar effect of oppressive constraint. As spectators, we can read the thematic significance of such restrictions on freedom as easily as we read the enforced confinement of Sartre's *No Exit*, the pressure generated within Pinter's narrow rooms, or the prisons of language and ashcans and disembodied voices that make up the dramatic worlds of Beckett.

The plays I have been discussing share another characteristic with the

41. Irving Wardle, *Times*, 4 July 1969.

contemporary drama and thus appeal in yet another way to our modern sensibility. The quality I have in mind is largely a matter of tone; it communicates itself to the spectators in a variety of ways and intensifies, to a very high degree, their experience of the play. It might do to call it uncertain equilibrium, a sense that the balance of the play and of its characters is never quite secure. In its effects, it is directly opposed to the security we enjoy in watching a play whose conventions and patterns of development are familiar and comfortable. *The Caretaker*—with its sudden and inexplicable movements from vaudeville to gratuitous threats of violence, with its extreme shifts in character behavior—exemplifies this quality in contemporary drama. In comedy, this uncertain equilibrium generated tremendous power in the Stratford Festival's *Volpone*, in which William Hutt was alternately a great comic impersonator and a dangerous and wholly amoral sexual creature and in which his relationship to Douglas Rain's Mosca was charged with energy as it ranged from the mutual delight of two accomplished actors to a seething sexual hatred between an aging nobleman and his crafty, virile servant. *The Revenger's Tragedy* and *The Changeling* have this uncertain equilibrium built into their very designs as they play desperate corruption against the most bizarre comedy. In Trevor Nunn's brilliant 1966 production of Tourneur's play (brought to London in 1969), this effect was enhanced at every point: by the masques which opened and closed the play, by a spectrum of effects which ranged "from pampered sadism and outright horror to the broad comedy of the plotting younger brothers (here played almost like the Ugly Sisters)," and by a continued emphasis on sensual indulgence (as in Vindice's encounter with a Lussurioso who "is having his all-but-naked body massaged and oiled."[42] In Luca Ronconi's production of *The Changeling*, the trick of setting out the asylum plot as the main action made the plot concerning DeFlores and Beatrice seem like a play produced by the inmates. This *Marat/Sade* technique threw into relief Middleton's precise structuring of the two plots and further illuminated the play's effect of uncertain equilibrium.

This effect was created in a most chilling fashion in the Royal Shakespeare Company's 1972 production of *The Duchess of Malfi*. Again, the play itself is built on a design of opposed attitudes with the Duchess's

---

42. *Times*, 29 November 1969; 6 October 1966.

espousal of rich life set over against the gross cynicism of Bosola and the
diseased imagination of Ferdinand. In the scene (III.2) where Cariola and
Antonio jokingly sneak away to leave the Duchess combing her hair and
prattling on about matters of no consequence, the entrance of Ferdinand
must always be an electrifying moment. In this production, that initial
shock was prolonged and made more agonizing as the Duchess responded
to her brother's presence and then firmly declared.

> 'Tis welcome.
> For know, whether I am doomed to live, or die,
> I can do both like a prince.
>   (III.ii.69–71)

Ferdinand's reply—"Die then, quickly"—was punctuated by his action of
placing the dagger in the Duchess's lap in a gesture of self-conscious
sexual brutality. In that moment, the dagger became an intentionally
gross symbol of Ferdinand's diseased lust for his sister. It was an action
that clearly appealed to the court tyrant who controls his courtiers' laughter as he controls their lives, and it highlighted a scene that defined the
continuing uncertain equilibrium of the entire production.

   I have not mentioned Shakespeare in the preceding paragraphs chiefly
because the evidence of Shakespeare's continuing importance is available
all around us. In stage productions and on film his plays are regularly
available. There are, besides, adaptations, collages (Marowitz), partial
borrowings (Stoppard), and a variety of other means by which Shakespeare
remains part of our culture. The central testimony to Shakespeare's meaning for us comes of course from stage productions of the plays. A careful
scrutiny of productions of the past thirty years might well indicate how
completely versions of Shakespeare reflect the main intellectual and critical concerns of our time, both in the plays selected for performance and in
the modes of their presentation. He is our contemporary in far richer and
more comprehensive ways than Jan Kott's narrow view of him suggests.
But his fellow dramatists, at least the greatest among them, have become
our contemporaries too.

IV

   I recognize that in claiming for our period a true understanding of the
drama of Shakespeare and his contemporaries and in asserting that there

has been no genuine Elizabethan revival until the last thirty years or so, I may appear to have been misdirected by cultural bias into a historical attitude. But a revival is not alone a matter of respect for texts, nor is it a matter of appreciating isolated passages of beautiful and moving poetry, nor is it even a matter of concern for authentic staging. All these may contribute to a revival or be a part of it: all three elements have been present in the Elizabethan Revival of our postwar years. But the indispensable center of this revival has been the deep kinship we have felt with the great playwrights of this period and with their vision of this world. It is a vision at once satiric and noble. It joins a deep need for affirmation with a profound suspicion of all institutions and all sources of value. In its presentation the most startling tensions result from the juxtaposition of characters and their values; in Shakespeare, the naïve romanticism of Troilus over against the parroted obscenities of Thersites; in Webster, Bosola's gross cynicism ("say, then, my corruption / Grew out of horsedung" [I.i.287]) over against the tragic heroism of the Duchess ("I am Duchess of Malfi still" [IV.ii.142]).

One of the most brilliant accomplishments of Thomas Pynchon in that magnificently energetic blowup called *The Crying of Lot 49* is his parody of a Jacobean revenge tragedy. Called *The Courier's Tragedy*, it features such bizarre episodes as that of a cardinal being forced to use his own toe as the host in a Mass, a goat shot from a cannon, and an ingenious assortment of entrapments and tortures. In an oblique way, Pynchon's parody may help to illustrate my point. For *The Courier's Tragedy*, through its accumulation of gratuitous horrors and manic nonsense, answers to the world of Oedipa Maas, the novel's central figure, just as the drama it parodies—the drama of Webster and Tourneur, Middleton and Ford—answers to our own.[43]

Edmund Wilson saw in *The Duchess of Malfi* and the images of the released concentration camp inmates a compelling apposition. The intervening decades have brought new evidence of man's cruelty, and they have brought as well new artistic responses to its existence. Grotesque comedy, satire, violence faced matter-of-factly but given different names—these have been the responses of such writers as Kurt Vonnegut, Jr., and Günter Grass. Some of our modern playwrights have worked toward a similar

43. I had completed this study before I saw John Boni's interesting essay, "Analogous Form: Black Comedy and Some Jacobean Plays," *WHR*, XXVIII (1974), 201–215.

vision, though without entire success. Here, on our stages, the Elizabethans have served us well. In such a revival it is probably wrong to speak of the service we have done these playwrights in bringing them into the modern theater. We have needed them, and we need them still.[44]

44. This essay was originally written for a volume dedicated to the memory of Irving Ribner. That collection will not be published, but I should like this work nevertheless to be a tribute to the memory of a generous and helpful mentor and friend.

Notes on Contributors

MAURICE CHARNEY is Professor of English at Rutgers University. His publications include *Shakespeare's Roman Plays* (1961) and "Hamlet Without Words" (1965). He is currently working on Elizabethan dramatic form.

ALAN C. DESSEN, Professor of English at the University of North Carolina, is the author of *Jonson's Moral Comedy* and *Elizabethan Drama and the Viewer's Eye* and was Guest Editor for *Renaissance Drama*, N.S. VI (1973).

MARJORIE GARBER, Associate Professor of English at Yale University, is the author of *Dream in Shakespeare: From Metaphor to Metamorphosis*, and of articles on Shakespeare, Marlowe, and Milton. She is currently at work on a study of maturation patterns in Shakespeare's plays.

R. B. GRAVES is Assistant Professor of Theater at the University of Illinois, Champaign-Urbana. He is interested in the production of Renaissance drama in the theater.

G. K. HUNTER, Professor of English at Yale University and at the University of Warwick, has edited Shakespeare's *Macbeth, King Lear*, and *All's Well* and Marston's *The Malcontent* and *Antonio and Mellida*. A collection of his essays, *Dramatic Identities and Cultural Tradition*, has just appeared.

EJNER J. JENSEN is Associate Chairman of the Department of English Language and Literature, University of Michigan. He has written essays and studies on Renaissance drama and satire and a forthcoming book on John Marston. He is at work on a study of Shakespeare's presence in modern poetry.

R. B. PARKER, Professor of English at Trinity College, University of Toronto, has published extensively on Renaissance and contemporary drama and has served as Head of the University of Toronto's Graduate Drama Centre. He has prepared editions of *A Chaste Maid in Cheapside* and *Volpone* for the Revels series of plays.

BRUCE R. SMITH, an Associate Professor of English at Georgetown University, is the author of essays on sixteenth-century productions of Roman comedy and on Queen Elizabeth's country-house entertainments which have appeared in earlier volumes of *Renaissance Drama*. As a Fellow of the American Council of Learned Societies, he is completing a book-length study of productions of Greek and Roman comedy and tragedy in Renaissance England.

FRANCES TEAGUE is an Assistant Professor at the University of Georgia. She has published several articles on Shakespeare and Jonson and is preparing an edition of nineteenth-century letters about Shakespeare study in America.

PATRICK R. WILLIAMS has held lectureships at Bowling Green State University and at The University of Michigan. He is currently an Assistant Professor of English at Marquette University in Milwaukee.